Why Hurry Through Heaven?

A Biography - Memoir of Dr. Walter P. Cottam

By
Maxine Martz

Red Butte Garden
& Arboretum
University of Utah
Salt Lake City, Utah
1999

Printed in the United States of America

Published by
RED BUTTE GARDEN
& ARBORETUM
University of Utah
Salt Lake City, Utah

Library of Congress Cataloging-in-Publication Data
Martz, Maxine, date
Why hurry through heaven? : a biography-memoir of
Dr. Walter P. Cottam / by Maxine Martz.
p. cm.
ISBN 0-87480-636-4 (pbk.)
1. Cottam, Walter Pace, 1894-1988
2. Botanists—Utah Biography.
3. Ecologists—Utah Biography.
I. Title.
QK31.C86M37 1999
580′ .92—dc21
[B]

99-30052
CIP

To Vard

"Those were the days, my friend..."

IN GRATEFUL ACKNOWLEDGMENT

With support from many individuals, Red Butte Garden and Arboretum has been honored to publish this biography on the life of Dr. Walter P. Cottam. Red Butte Garden and Arboretum wishes to offer its sincere appreciation to those who supported this important book.

Maxine Martz, writer, friend and member of the Thursday Sabbath Club, has contributed her tremendous writing talents to this book and spent countless hours assembling information and photographs of Dr. Cottam and his adventures.

Grace A. Tanner, friend of Dr. Cottam's and long-time supporter, provided a generous gift for the publication of this work. Grace also supported Doc's hybrid oak project and the publication documenting his research titled *Oak Hybridization at the University of Utah.*

Dr. Grant Cottam, son of Walter Cottam and distinguished ecologist, provided financial support for this work as well as hours of research.

Contents

Foreword

This book was a labor of love, and I thank Maxine Martz for applying her talent to bring back to life one of the most interesting and important natural scientists this country ever produced. She knew him well and admired him greatly; I, too, knew him well. He was my father. I was his oldest son and learned to love the land as much as he did. I even tried to follow in his footsteps; he and I spent many days in the mountains and deserts of Utah sampling the vegetation and discussing ecological theory. It was a great way to get an education, and in the process I learned much about vegetation science and came to admire the man who sustained and tutored me.

When Dad became an ecologist—he was awarded his Ph. D. in 1926 from the University of Chicago with Henry C. Cowles as his major professor—he was about the only person between the Sierras and the Rocky Mountains who practiced that profession. This was cowboy country and Mormon country, and the prevailing philosophy was that the land was there for the benefit of mankind, where the "benefit of mankind" was defined in terms of dollars. The Mormons were going to make the desert "blossom like a rose," while the cowboys and the sheepmen were going to extract every possible material benefit from the mountain and valley rangeland. Though most of the cowboys and sheepmen were Mormons, they did not see the contradiction between making the desert blossom and overgrazing it. They firmly believed in another favorite Mormon axiom, "the Lord will provide," and relied on heavenly assistance to protect the land from their own abuses. This attitude still prevails among many Mormons, including Reagan's former Secretary of the Interior James Watt.

Dad was born and raised in the southwest corner of Utah, an area about two thousand feet lower in elevation, much warmer, and even drier than the rest of Utah. The colony was initially established to take advantage of the mild winters there and grow grapes and sugar cane. It turned out that sugar cane wouldn't grow and the wine was terrible, but the colonists stayed, growing other crops and raising sheep and cattle. Living so close to the earth enabled Dad, a very perceptive and honest person, to see at an early age the damage that could be done by abusing the land. When he later had the opportunity to leave his position at Brigham Young University in northern Utah to study ecology under Cowles in Chicago, he took his wife and children back to homeland to live with her parents while he pursued his dream. He couldn't have picked a better place to study ecology. Cowles was an excellent teacher and a pioneer researcher who produced some of the best early research papers in this field.

When he returned to his position as the only botanist and ecologist at BYU, Dad was faced with two serious dilemmas. The first was his skepticism about the Mormon religion. Teaching in the church's university, he was so forthright that he couldn't discuss biology in his classes without expressing doubts about the Mormon dogma. The blind faith expected of Mormon professors was something Dad didn't have, and he was in hot water for his apostasy from the very beginning. The president of BYU shared some of Dad's skepticism and supported him, but in the end Dad felt he had to leave and moved to the University of Utah. This wasn't the end of his difficulties, however. When he delivered his classic public lecture *Is Utah Sahara Bound?*, it aroused considerable antagonism among the higher echelons of the Mormon Church, leading to rumors that he would lose his job at the University of Utah. When I asked him how serious this threat was, he recounted the story of the day when a group of high officials of the church solemnly marched into the president's office and stayed for a long time. The president didn't say a word to him, however, and Dad continued to voice his opinions at every opportunity. Dad's other dilemma was how to convince the public that the deterioration of the desert grasslands could well result in the ruination of the desert habitat. The church authorities, many of whom were cattlemen, did not believe that deterioration was taking place and blamed what change they couldn't overlook on unusually dry weather. Dad spent several summers working for the U. S. Forest Service; he located many permanent quadrats, which he carefully inventoried and photographed, with the intention that they be restudied periodically to document the range deterioration. He wrote numerous articles and letters to the editor of the newspaper that was not owned by the Mormon Church, the *Salt Lake Tribune*, and he achieved a large following by giving countless lectures to the general public.

Dad also made himself available to practically any group, church groups included, and usually gave at least one lecture a week. When I was a teenager it was my duty to accompany him and run the slide projector. The slides were glass plates about four times the size of the colored slides we use today. His slides were colored, too—by hand. Dad spent many hours with his water colors and his brushes painting his slides, and they were remarkably beautiful. The projector was a carbon arc machine—large, noisy, and temperamental, and very heavy for a runt like me to carry. I particularly remember one lecture given in the high school gym in a little town named Bicknell in Wayne County. It took us most of a day to drive down there. We stayed overnight and drove back the next day, stopping on the way to cut a Christmas tree, our only material reward for two days of work. I once asked Dad if he ever got paid for those lectures. His answer was, "Not a cent."

There is no way to measure the influence Dad exerted. Utah is still a desert, and much of the area that was once grassland is now desert shrubs. But there is no question Utah is in much better shape now than it would have been without his influence. I classify him with Paul B. Sears and Aldo Leopold as a leader in environmental conservation.

It is now more than thirty-five years since Dad retired. He kept very active for more than a decade afterward, working on his oak hybridization project, and would have continued to work until he died had he not been afflicted with Alzheimer's Disease, the great tragedy of his life. Dad was a vital person, living life to the hilt every minute; he enjoyed art, music, literature, and most of all the great outdoors and everything in it. He had many friends, as well as some bitter enemies, and when he could no longer remember their names or discuss their mutual interests, he was so embarrassed he didn't want to talk to any of them. His vocabulary survived even after he didn't know what the words meant, so he could put up a pretty good front, but eventually he couldn't remember anything.

It is not for me to determine which of Dad's admirable achievements marks his greatest contribution, but I think he would have been most proud of his efforts to preserve the environment. He worked especially hard at educating the public about their precious and fragile natural world. He died in 1988, the end of the Reagan era. I guess it is just as well that he didn't realize what an environmental tragedy that era and those following it have caused. All I can hope is that his teachings will eventually prevail.

If there were to be a monument to Dad, he would probably want it to be a desert grassland or a native forest with all the plants and animals living as they did before the European settlers brought their cattle and sheep to America. Dad accomplished miracles, but there are many more miracles for others to accomplish, and the number increases each year in proportion to the destruction of natural resources and the introduction into the environment of man-made toxins.

—Grant Cottam, Ph. D.

Prologue

A Chance Phone Call

Was it the Sego Lily that led me to Dr. Walter Cottam and to twelve years of an unforgettable association with a remarkable man? Or was it fate?

As a reporter for the *Deseret News* in search of a feature story, I called Dr. Cottam, University of Utah professor emeritus of botany, in July 1969, simply to find out if the Sego Lily, the state flower, was disappearing from Utah. The small white flowers were growing abundantly in the Salt Lake Valley when the pioneers arrived and the Mormons had consumed their bulbs in large quantities during the first lean years. But after more than a hundred years of development, city dwellers seldom saw the flower any more. Dr. Cottam assured me that it was still flourishing on dry hillsides and among sagebrush throughout the state.

He gave me enough information for my story. Then, as an afterthought, I asked Dr. Cottam if he knew where we might find the Brownie Ladyslipper, a small orchid said to grow in moist woods in the Lake Blanche area of Big Cottonwood Canyon. My friend Vard Jones and I had been studying, photographing, and learning the scientific names of Utah wildflowers but had been unable to find it. We needed some more specific directions than "the Lake Blanche area."

Dr. Cottam tried first to explain where to find the flower, but with my questions plainly showing my inability to grasp directions, he finally said, "I could show you better than I can tell you." That was all it took for us to schedule the three-mile hike up to Lake Blanche for the following Thursday, Vard's day off at the *Salt Lake Tribune* and my day off at the *News*.

Dr. Cottam, carrying only a pack with his camera equipment, was out of the car and on the trail almost before the car stopped, leaving Vard and me hurrying to get our packs out and catch up with him. When we mentioned taking a canteen of water, he said, "Naw, we'll be by a stream all the way."

It was a beautiful day, a magical day for us, as we hiked the trail, stopping to photograph the wildflowers, learning their scientific names and how to pronounce them. (Even when we had learned the scientific names, we found we had been pronouncing half of them wrong.) During the five-hour hike, our 75-year-old companion held us spellbound with stories of his youth, his teaching, his concern for the environment, his run-ins with irate stockmen, his previous Lake Blanche hikes, and his oak hybridization project.

On the trail up, he told us how he had taught a summer class in Spring Flowers of the Wasatch, taking the group up to Lake Blanche. It is a steep trail, and he soon saw that some of the women "past childbearing age" were lagging behind and dropping out and that the rest weren't going to make it to the top unless they sped up. So he struck out, with the hardier hikers following. Several of them reached the lake, but many of them "flopped on their backs" as soon as they got there.

When they got back down the mountain, one young fellow came up and inquired, "Dr. Cottam, do you mind if I ask you a personal question?" "No," he answered. "How old are you?" "Seventy-two." "Jesus Christ," the fellow said and walked away.

On our hike, we stopped now and then to admire the scenery—the mountains and the vista below—and Dr. Cottam said with deep feeling, "I never thought I'd be seeing all this again."

We could hear the stream gurgling away somewhere off in the distance, but never near enough to do us any good. The celery and grapes I had brought along for snacks helped, though.

When we reached the lake, Dr. Cottam was off, circling around and up into the trees, looking for the orchid before we could catch up with him. We searched and searched but found no trace of the ladyslipper. At a certain spot, Dr. Cottam said, "If I were a *Cypripedium*, this is where I would be." But he wasn't, and it wasn't. Patches of snow lingered on the ground. We decided we were two weeks too early for the flower.

We found a stream there and had a drink. Then I rested while Vard and Dr. Cottam went exploring some more. They were gone nearly two hours, and Vard said later he had helped Dr. Cottam over the stream "a hundred times," and once Cottam had spent half an hour photographing one flower.

As we ate lunch, Dr. Cottam recalled the time about three years earlier when he and his good friend Dean Brimhall had explored a canyon along the Dirty Devil River south of Hanksville in central Utah. They planned to walk along the bank and float their food and supplies on a raft, guiding it with ropes. They built the raft, composed of a big inner tube with boards under it. In the center of the tube they placed four loaves of Dr. Cottam's homemade bread, some canned food, and some dried food, all wrapped in plastic to keep them waterproof. They had timed the trip so that the water would be the right depth for guiding their craft, but the raft got stuck on a sandbar the first day out. "We knew then we had waited too long," Cottam said. But they went on, one pulling on the rope from the front and the other pushing from behind with a pole. Somewhere along the way the first day something punctured the plastic, and they found the bread floating in the inner tube, the dried food ruined, and all the labels washed off the cans. "We had surprise meals all the way," Cottam said. But they made it through in the three days they had planned. Doc was then 72 and Dean was 78. Dean, the son of the former Brigham Young University President George W. Brimhall, was a retired psychologist and teacher and an authority on Indian rock art in Utah's canyonlands. He and Walter made a pact when they started their adventure that if either one of them died on the trip, the other would just bury him and never say anything about it. "I haven't laughed so hard in years," Cottam said.

As we started back down the trail from Lake Blanche, Dr. Cottam pointed out the scratch marks made by ancient glaciers on the rocks. When we got to the car at the end of the three-hour descent, he started to thank us for a wonderful day. "But the day isn't over yet," we told him. "We have steaks to cook for dinner if you have time to join us." So at the Spruces Campground, we put the finishing touches on one of the most memorable days of our lives. When we let Dr. Cottam out at his home later, it was with the promise that he would join us whenever possible on our Thursday outings.

August found him leading us on a trip to the north slope of Mt. Nebo to see three giant quaking aspens he had discovered a few years earlier; to Albion Basin above Alta, where we hiked to Cecret Lake, botanizing all the way; and to the Uinta Mountains for an assault on Mt. Baldy. For this hike he was wearing a jaunty cap, had his ever-present camera around his neck, and was carrying a walking stick.

On the drive up the canyon to Mt. Baldy, we stopped at least half a dozen times for him to show us the trees and flowers and teach us some of their characteristics. At Lily Lake he was off like a shot to show us the peat bogs, the pond lilies blooming in profusion all over the lake, and the beautiful blue mountain gentians, which brought out the photographer in all of us. We stopped at Bald Mountain Pass, elevation 10,678 feet, for a full circle view of a vast panorama of majestic peaks, glaciated basins, canyons covered with dark evergreen forests, and glimpses of dozens of the many Uinta lakes hidden among the trees.

As we began our hike, Doc was first on the trail, sprinting up the path like a mountain goat. We were puffing along trying to catch up and looked up to see him sitting on a rock looking down at us with a little air of superiority. Every now and then Vard would say in an undertone to me, "Can't you slow that old codger down?" But if there was a flower he wanted to tell us about or test us on, he would wait for us to catch up. Near timberline we learned about the *krummholz,* short or dwarf trees that reach great heights at lower elevations but grow just a few feet high at higher elevations. They looked more like shrubs on the mountain than trees, but Cottam said that some of them might be 100 years old. Near the top he showed us some little willows growing only an inch or two high and said that they might be 50 years old. Little catkins on them were almost as large as the "trees" themselves. We cut our hike short before we reached the top because the sky looked threatening. At 11,947 feet elevation, that bare mountain is no place to be in a storm.

On a trip to South Willow Canyon near Grantsville in September, Dr. Cottam introduced us to Fernbush, a shrub with little fern-like leaves in a rosette around the stem; and to *Heuchera*, growing in crevices of the rock walls by the stream. Where the road ends in a turnaround, we hiked up a trail, Dr. Cottam giving us lessons and testing us on the trees, including the prevernal aspen growing there. They leaf out earlier in the spring than other aspen and, sometimes, if conditions are right, their leaves turn red instead of yellow in the fall. He had studied them and written an article about them for the *Naturalist* magazine.

As usual, he was ahead on the trail and, after climbing a rather steep path, we found him sitting on a rock under some trees. We took off our packs and had some potato chips and a drink. Looking off at the view, he said, "I didn't dream I would be getting out this summer on any trips like this." "Don't you have friends who like to get out?" I asked. "Yes, but they're pantywaists." Then he asked, "How did these trips with you come about, anyway?"

I reminded him of my call to ask about sego lilies and the ladyslipper that resulted in our hike to Lake Blanche. He grew pensive, then said, "I'm beginning to think of Thursday as my Sabbath."

It wasn't long after that we started calling it the Thursday Sabbath Club.

Dr. Cottam and Vard hit it off together immediately and developed a special, close relationship. Vard thought of Doc as the father he never knew, and Doc thought of him as a son. Vard was just three years old when his father was killed in a mine accident, and he grew up in a household of women, his widowed mother and four sisters. But there was nothing feminine about him. He was creative, resourceful, intelligent, and he had a fierce competitive spirit, as Doc had. An avid golfer, Vard won many trophies in both amateur and pro-am tournaments. There were few sports he hadn't tackled, all with the same intensity. And he was almost in the hustler class on the pool table. He had given up deer hunting, but was still a proficient fisherman.

As a writer and editor, Vard was knowledgeable and concerned about local, national, and world events. He could converse on almost any subject, being humorous, quick-witted, and a good storyteller. He understood the weather and geology, and, under Doc's tutelage, he was rapidly becoming an authority on wildflowers and a staunch environmentalist—in other words, a perfect leader for our Thursday outings. It helped, too, that he knew a lot about cars and could fix almost anything.

During our outings, Vard had been asking questions, gathering information and photographs, and on September 28, 1969, his story "A Man And His Mountains" appeared in the Home section of the *Salt Lake Tribune*, featuring on the cover a full color closeup photograph of Dr. Cottam examining his hybrid oak, and two full pages of text and five black-and-white photos inside.

Dr. Cottam had gone to California to house-sit for friends vacationing in Europe when the story came out, but his daughter Beatrice had sent him a copy. Vard had summarized Dr. Cottam's career as an ecologist, horticulturist, botanist, teacher, and conservationist, then noted that at 75 Cottam was still busy climbing mountains and hybridizing oak. Within days Vard received the following letter from a still eloquent Cottam:

> Dear Vard:
>
> Yesterday I received a letter from my daughter enclosing your article "A Man And His Mountains." I can't tell you how stunned I was to see myself spread over the Home cover page and over two full pages within. I am sure that many will acclaim you as a genius for making the greatest overevaluation of this generation. But I assure you that it was good for my own puny ego, and it came at a propitious time for me vacationing at beautiful Pebble Beach.
>
> I don't know why I come down here because I always feel like a pauper trying to show off wealth that I do not have. I am living here in one of the great estates along the exclusive 17-Mile Drive of the

Monterey Peninsula. The castle I am living in all alone is worth fully a quarter of a million dollars, and the man who owned it was the great cartoonist Jimmy Hatlo, author of "They'll Do It Every Time." He married my late wife's sister Eleanor. Hatlo died . . . several years ago, and Eleanor married a prominent physician here. About every two years, they make a tour of Europe, and two years ago they invited my wife and me to watch over the mansion while they were gone. Naturally, I enjoyed this paradise, but I assumed that my sojourn in it had passed away with my wife. But I was mistaken. They almost insisted that I come this year, and I have been here . . . a little more than a week.

This house looks over Carmel Bay. The ocean is little more than a hundred yards away. I can always hear the roar of the bay-imprisoned waters, and wherever I sit in this palace, each of the many spacious windows presents an outside picture perfectly framed that beckons me out-of-doors. I expected to write a paper on my new oak hybrids, but this is no place to do it—things are simply just too damned beautiful. So I have spent my time absorbing these bounteous gifts of nature, and Shelkirk-like sing from my exalted lair his lines:

"I am master of all I survey.
My rights there are none to dispute.
From land all 'round to the sea
I am Lord of the fowl and the brute."

or something like that, as I remember. I discovered after Eleanor left that she had been campaigning on my behalf among some of her wealthy and influential friends to see that I was properly entertained. One prominent landscape architect has had me to her house a couple of times, and an engineer friend of Eleanor's came and took me fifty miles upstate the other day to see a famed tuberous begonia farm. I shall never forget this sight of acres of brilliant color and every imaginable form that these remarkable flowers can take. Naturally I have been embarrassed by all the attention, but now, thanks to you, I can show them that they have not been wasting their time and money on a mere pauper but on a great man!

Since I received this flattering article, I have been thinking about our new organized Thursday Sabbath Club. You probably remember that I asked the question, "How did it happen?" Maxine said that it started when she phoned me one time about sego lilies. But I am wondering if you had this article in mind when you invited me on your weekly jaunts, and if so whether I might be utterly abandoned now that you have a story. If this could possibly be so, I shall feel very bad, for I have come to regard your Thursdays as truly delightful days of rest. The membership is just right from every point of view—transportation, the minimal crowd, and, above all, the kinship of spirit. Both of you are a comfort to me. I'll be home, I hope, in a week or so, and if the weather is no longer suitable for an excursion, perhaps we can meet at my house to review in pictures some of the splendid trips that I have enjoyed so much.

Yours,
Walter P. Cottam

On his return, fall drives took us to the West Desert, where we hunted white agate and arrowheads; along the Pony Express Trail to Topaz Mountain; to Skull Valley to visit the cemetery at the deserted town of Iosepha, where a group of Hawaiian converts to the Mormon church had settled. We took Doc to places he had never been before. He took us to places we had never been before. And together we discovered places none of us had been before.

Almost everywhere we went, he knew something of the history of the place and had some story to tell about it. Having Dr. Cottam along was like having a talking history book as well as a botany book. Well-versed in the history of Utah, he had read the journals of the early explorers—John C. Fremont, John Wesley Powell, Jedediah Smith, G. K. Gilbert, Howard Stansbury, and Capt. J. H. Simpson. From those early accounts, he learned what the vegetation had been before the Great Basin was settled and how man's presence had changed it, seldom for the better.

Old Lake Bonneville, an ancient freshwater lake that had flourished for perhaps 25,000 years during glacial times and had covered some 20,000 square miles of land in Utah, Nevada, and Idaho, fascinated Dr. Cottam. The lake had risen and fallen a number of times over the years, reaching a maximum depth of 1,000 feet at its deepest and leaving prominent bench marks on the mountainsides. Doc often said longingly that he wished he could have been here to see that ancient lake and the animals known to have lived around its shores.

He told us about an artist, L. A. Ramsey, who was painting a picture of what the lake must have looked like long ago, with the animals known to have existed at the time—hairy mammoth, musk ox, horse, deer, mountain sheep and goats. Before the painting was finished, Dr. F. J. Pack, University of Utah geologist and authority on the lake, found the skull of an ancient camel at the south end of the Salt Lake Valley. Dr. Pack wanted the camel included in the painting. "One hump or two?" the artist asked. Since he had found only the skull, Pack didn't know. So Ramsey painted the camel standing behind a bush.

Today, the Great Salt Lake, a remnant of Lake Bonneville, covers about 1,500 square miles. At one time in early pioneer days and into the 1960s, its saline content was 27 percent. But with diking of the lake for a railroad trestle and changes in the weather, salinity has varied.

Doc read more than history and science. He kept a book of poems by his bed that he read before going to sleep. He was familiar with most of the great authors and often quoted them. He was always seeking truth. Roger Bacon's "The Four Stumbling Blocks to Truth" especially impressed him:

1) The influence of fragile or unworthy authority;
2) Custom;
3) The imperfection of undisciplined senses;
4) The concealment of ignorance by ostentation of seeming wisdom.

He tacked a copy of Bacon's stumbling blocks to his den

wall at home. And once he brought a copy along on one of our trips to discuss its ideas. Much of his pondering those ideas took him back to the leadership of the Mormon Church.

On another trip he brought along an apothegm for us to consider:

> *He who knows not and knows not that he knows not is a fool; shun him.*
> *He who knows not and knows that he knows not is simple; teach him.*
> *He who knows and knows not that he knows is asleep; wake him.*
> *He who knows and knows that he knows is wise; follow him.*

We were never at a loss for lively conversation with Dr. Cottam along.

At Christmas time that year he sent me a card—a photograph he had taken of his friend Dean Brimhall at Lake Powell standing beside a huge Utah juniper tree they had discovered. On the card he wrote, "You will never know what these Thursday jaunts have done for my spirits this past summer. I have never experienced anything quite like this—two fine new friends, who in so short a time have brought such hope and zest for living."

To start off the new year of 1970, we initiated Doc into cisco fishing at Bear Lake. The Bonneville cisco, a small, silvery fish, lives only in the deep, cold waters of Bear Lake in northern Utah and southern Idaho; it comes in to the eastern shore in mid-January to spawn. If the lake is frozen, fishermen chop holes in the ice and reach in with long-handled nets to catch the fish as they swim by, usually in groups of a dozen or so. The limit then was 50 fish, but as the sport became more popular in later years, the limit was dropped to 30. If the lake is not frozen, cisco fishing can be quite a hazardous undertaking. The fishermen don waders, preferably breast high, and wade out into the icy water, trying to keep their footing on the rocks while swinging the long-handled poles to net the fish. Why this particular winter pastime has gained many advocates is unfathomable, but a piping hot chowder heated over a campfire on the beach, a little wine between fishing forays, warm clothes and good companions can make it an outing to remember. Fortunately, the cisco have the good sense to spawn for only about ten days.

After this, Dr. Cottam left us for about six weeks to take a trip to Mexico with artist Lynn Fausett and his wife, but we resumed our trips the latter part of March, traveling to Clear Lake, Black Rock, and Pahvant Butte in the Delta area, hunting for sunstones, arrowheads, and trilobites.

In good weather, we often cooked our dinner, usually steaks, over an open fire somewhere in the juniper trees. Vard and I mentioned how much we liked the junipers. Dr. Cottam said he liked them, too, but that there are times when they are an indication that things are not well on the land. Juniper roots run only 6 to 8 inches under the surface of the ground. They take up all the moisture, and any vegetation under the tree dies. He commented that he often worked with Forest Service people, who were good, common-sense men, but some of them didn't know much about the land. Once he went out in an area with one man and called attention to the junipers. "Yes, aren't they wonderful!" the fellow said. "I pointed out that in his position he should think they were terrible," Cottam said.

Later he related this incident in a talk he gave at a meeting. Much to his chagrin, that Forest Service fellow was in the audience and came up after the talk to shake Cottam's hand. "Why didn't you tell them my name?" he said. "You told them everything else."

Dr. Cottam had had operations for cataracts on both eyes in 1968 and was wearing hard contact lenses when we met him. They bothered him most of the time, but he managed to put up with them. He said he had been blind in one eye for five years before he had had the operations. He seemed to think that as long as he had one good eye, he wouldn't bother, but when the good eye started to go, he thought it was time to do something about it.

Brilliant as Dr. Cottam was, he wasn't very adept at the tedious process of cleaning and caring for contacts, especially at this time of life. He had turned 76 in March. He nearly missed a Thursday trip in April when he used a new cleaner,

Basic H, to clean his lenses and neglected to rinse one of them before inserting it into his eye. He had learned about Basic H from the Fausetts. It was said to be not a soap, not a detergent, but biodegradable and useful for washing dishes, for bathing, and for a variety of cleaning chores. On the day of his mistake, he had a hard time getting the contact out of his eye. He went to the doctor, who found that Cottam had scratched the eye in two places and had destroyed a layer of the cornea. The doctor anesthetized the eye, removed some of the dead material, and Doc could see again, but he had to be careful to keep the eye free of infection while the layer grew back again in two or three days. The doctor knew about Basic H but told Cottam "You're the first one I've known to put it in his eye."

Dr. Cottam wore his thick glasses for the trip to the Golden Spike National Monument at Promontory and to Locomotive Springs that Thursday, happy to be able to go, after having worried for two days that he might be blind. Our mentor was in good form that day, explaining the difference in the formation of the large deserts of the earth and those of our Great Basin. He also introduced us to two small early spring flowers—Storksbill (*Erodium*) in the geranium family and a tiny buttercup, *Ranunculus testiculatis.* At Locomotive Springs we hunted arrowheads, and around the water we saw a huge flock of pelicans, a Belted Kingfisher, ducks, and a Black-Crowned Night Heron. We snacked on Dr. Cottam's homemade bread and peanut brittle. He prided himself on his culinary artistry. On our next trip to Topaz Mountain, he furnished the entire dinner, starting with his homemade soup, steaks, a rice dish, an orange-marshmallow-pineapple-coconut-sour cream salad, and, of course, his homemade bread. It was delicious.

He also regaled us with stories of his growing up years in St. George. His father was a patriarch in the church at the time of the First World War, and many of the young Mormon men were coming to him for patriarchal blessings before going into the service. After one of Walter's friends had had his blessing and had left, Walter asked his father, "Well, did you tell him in the name of the Lord that he wouldn't get shot in the ass?"

Doc's eye recovered fully and he could wear his contacts again. Other trips that spring and early summer found us digging for red horn coral in Riley's Canyon; visiting Cascade Springs near Midway; getting drenched in the rain on the Stockton Bar in Tooele County looking for a rare pink *Sisyrinchium*, and finding it; locating Steershead for the first time on the Lake Blanche trail; sitting by campfires in the junipers, eating delicious meals, philosophizing, and listening entranced to more Cottam stories.

From Doc we learned the plants of the desert—sagebrush, greasewood, horsebrush, shadscale, Fourwing Saltbush, and rabbitbrush, a beautiful shrub that lines the desert roadways with golden bouquets in the fall. Also, there were winterfat, a fine nourishing forage plant, and *Kochia*, edible but offering little nutrition. Doc said the sheepherders called it fartweed because that's all the sheep got out of it. Once when he was working in the mountains, Doc had seen great fields of tall larkspur, which is poisonous to cattle. Its scientific name is *Delphinium*. Meeting an old cowhand in the area, by way of conversation Doc commented, "I guess this larkspur gives you a lot of problems." The grizzled old fellow curtly corrected the botanist, "That's not larkspur," he said. "That's *Delphinium*."

One day after spending half an hour photographing wildflowers in a beautiful meadow in the Uintas, Vard suggested that we move on. "Why hurry through heaven?" Doc replied, and we lingered while he finished making the most of the moment. But more than that, we learned a lesson, and Vard soon adopted both the philosophy and the phrase as his own.

Who was this man Cottam who had captured our hearts and minds so completely in such a short time?

Chapter 1

A Pioneer Heritage

Walter Pace Cottam was born March 3, 1894, in St. George, Utah, the seventh of ten children of Emmaline Jarvis and Thomas P. Cottam. His father was a bishop in the Church of Jesus Christ of Latter-Day Saints and Walter said he always felt that God was spying on him and the Devil was trying to catch him. His middle name came about not from any family connection but from a pact his father made with his best friend, whose last name was Pace. The two fathers vowed to name their sons after each other: One son became Walter Pace Cottam, the other Walter Cottam Pace.

Walter's paternal grandfather was Thomas Cottam of West Bradford, Yorkshire, England. The family soon moved to Waddington, where Thomas attended school and assisted his father at chair making. He married Ann Haworth January 11, 1841, and they both converted to the Mormon faith within two months. Although penniless, they determined to emigrate to Nauvoo, Illinois, where the Latter-day Saints had established a city and their headquarters. Thomas managed to raise enough money for the sea voyage and they left England on February 5, 1842, arriving in Nauvoo in April. In a history of his life written years later, he said it would be impossible to record one one-hundredth part of the poverty, sickness, and afflictions that the Saints endured before being driven from the city in 1846. Thomas's wife bore a son, John Alma, in July 1842, but her health deteriorated and she died on October 1, 1844.

For several months Walter's grandfather assisted in the exodus from Nauvoo, ferrying the brethren over the Mississippi River to Montrose, Iowa. He recalled being miraculously saved from drowning on three different occasions. Thomas then went to St. Louis, Missouri, to raise money for an outfit to enable him to emigrate to the Salt Lake Valley. There he met fellow converts George Charman and his wife Caroline, whom he had befriended in Nauvoo. When Charman became very sick, he asked Thomas to take Caroline as his wife. After Charman's death, the two were married on October 9, 1847. After several years of labor and perseverance, they acquired the means to buy a team and left St. Louis on May 8, 1852, arriving in Salt Lake City on September 15. The next year, John Alma died after a fall.

Walter's father, Thomas P. Cottam, was born September 28, 1857, in Salt Lake City and was just five years old when Church President Brigham Young called the Cottam family to go with a party of Latter-day Saints to settle St. George in southern Utah. The Cottams arrived there in December of 1862. Young had promised to pay the elder Cottam for property he owned in the Sugar House area of Salt Lake City. "He gave my grandfather a team of oxen and a wagon, and that was the payment for the property," Walter Cottam recalled. "The family has been poor ever since."

Beautiful sandstone cliffs, volcanic flows, and lava cones surround St. George, which is located in a red-rock valley at an altitude of 2,800 feet. It is blessed with mild winters but has long, hot summers with temperatures well above one hundred degrees on many days. Because of the mild climate, Brigham Young had had a white plastered one-story winter home built there to escape the cold, snowy weather in Salt Lake City. He used the home until his death in 1877.

Life was very hard for the colonists. Crops failed year after year from the onslaught of heat, wind, and sand. But the settlers persevered, eventually raising wheat, fruit and vegetable crops in the nearby Washington fields, and grapes for making wine. The idea of making wine may shock church members today because the Mormons are noted for their clean living. They shun not only alcohol, but coffee, tea, and tobacco, in compliance with their "Word of Wisdom." Another tenet of the Church was that members should "multiply and replenish the earth." Large families were expected, and the Cottams and most other residents of the settlement heeded the admonition.

As a boy in the early days of settlement, Walter's father attended school only two or three months during the winter when no farm work could be done. Schools then were held in tents, in sheds, or in any other available place. But he was a very studious child, a great reader, and he grasped every opportunity to learn. His education was acquired mostly through his own studious efforts.

Young Cottam spent most of his time doing farm work until he was 18 years old, when he apprenticed to William Burt, who was in charge of plastering the St. George Temple. After completing his apprenticeship, he and Burt went into partnership and plastered in nearly every town in southern Utah and eastern Nevada.

Walter's mother, Emmaline Jarvis, also came from a large pioneer family that had suffered many hardships before reaching the Salt Lake Valley. Her father, George Jarvis, born March 25, 1823, in Harlow, Essex, England, was a seaman most of his early life, traveling 500,000 miles on trips to Australia, Africa, Spain, Holland, China, Portugal, West Indies, Ceylon, Gibralter, Bengal, and Java. After he joined the British Navy, on the trip to the West Indies, he lost a big toe, got sick, and was blinded in one eye. Treated in Jamaica, he returned to London, where he was examined as an outpatient and given sixpence a day for life. He lost that pension, however, when he left the country.

On September 17, 1846, George Jarvis married Ann Prior, a beautiful girl of seventeen, and they went to Woolwich, where he became a shipkeeper in the British Navy, belonging to Her Majesty's Flagship for about three years. It was in Woolwich that the couple converted to the Mormon faith and were baptized on Christmas Day 1848. Ann Prior Jarvis wrote in her autobiography, "We were living on board one of Her Majesty's ships at the time." They had two children by then, George Frederick and Ann Catherine.

After this, George Jarvis worked in London for nine years; during this period three more children were born, Brigham, Amelia, and Samuel. Jarvis, having become very active in church activities, went on a voyage to China to get the funds to emigrate. Gone for a year, he had left his wife in London with five children to care for and with little money. "When he left, I was only 25, not strong-minded, not self-reliant," she wrote. But she washed for other families and lived frugally. "I passed through many trials, which, if I wrote, my children would not understand as their lot is cast in a different place."

On his return from China in 1855, the family boarded a ship carrying 800 Saints for the trip to Boston. The man who was to cook for the passengers became seasick, and Jarvis, being a seafaring man, was called on to be the cook. Ann wrote, "I thought I should have quite a treat and a pleasure trip with my husband. I do not think I exchanged a dozen words on the voyage with him. He cooked for the 800 with one assistant . . . . He would go to bed as soon as his work was done and be at his duty before six in the morning."

In Boston he worked at various jobs for three and a half years, contending with sickness and poverty. While there, Ann, ill much of the time, had two more children, Margaret and Elizabeth. The latter died of cholera when four months old. By selling everything they owned, they raised the means to travel to Florence, Nebraska, the jumping-off place for the emigration. They made arrangements to distribute their luggage among the other wagons, and the entire Jarvis family—mother, father, and six children—walked the thousand miles to Salt Lake City, arriving in 1860. A son, Heber, was born in October, six weeks after their arrival.

They lived in the Sugar House area of Salt Lake City for a year, then volunteered to join the Saints going to St. George, where they arrived December 5, 1861. This time they had a wagon and yoke of cattle for the trip to Dixie. But Ann wrote, "It was not a Promised Land to us. Christmas day we had bran for dinner. I did not have a stove to cook with, and it rained forty days and nights." Three more children arrived in the Jarvis family during those early years in spite of unspeakable poverty. Walter's mother, Emmaline, was born March 21, 1863, the first of the Jarvis children born in St. George. Victoria Josephine and

Thomas William followed, the latter being struck and killed by lightning on the Tabernacle steps when he was seven years old.

Emmaline recalled going as a child to neighbors' homes to get a start of fire for their home and of going into the fields to gather the common pigweed for the family's dinner. The children also went into the fields in the fall gleaning to earn a little money to buy Sunday clothes. Shoes were a luxury. Often the older boys would share just one pair. They would take turns going to dances, one boy going for a set or two, then returning home to let another brother use the shoes.

The Jarvis family made much of their family life. One son, George, played the flute and with the help of an accordion and fiddle, family members would sit on the porch and sing and play until far into the night.

Father Jarvis served in many capacities in the church and was in charge of all the scaffolding during the construction of the St. George Temple. He also worked on the Tabernacle. In 1902 he was ordained a Patriarch in the church. Daughter Josephine, writing about her father's life some years later, said he expressed himself as being more pleased with that calling than if a legacy of millions had been left him. "He never did crave riches, often quoting: 'Riches take unto themselves wings and fly away.' He has accumulated no wealth, yet to my mind he is rich, vastly so, in the record he has made of honesty, temperance, purity of life, and integrity in the gospel. I lived at home until my twenty-ninth year and can testify that I never knew nor heard of a dishonest act of his."

She wrote that during the last years of his life, his health was poor and his memory failed to some extent. After his wife was unable to care for him because of her own poor health, Josephine cared for him the last five months of his life. He died January 6, 1913, and his wife followed him just four days later. They had lived together more than 66 years.

Walter's mother had many boyfriends, but the one love of her life was Thomas P. Cottam. They married January 26, 1882, in the imposing white St. George Temple, which had been completed in 1877. The newlyweds moved in with Cottam's parents in the impressive two-story colonial home built by the elder Cottam on the corner of Second and Tabernacle Streets in St. George. It stood for over a century, not being torn down until

1967 to make room for the new City and County Building. The young couple lived in a part of the house until the deaths of the mother in 1889 and of the father in 1898.

Thomas P. Cottam and Emmaline Jarvis Cottam were the parents of ten children. Walter's older brothers and sisters included Emma, 1882; Thomas, 1884; Heber, 1886; Arthur, 1888; Annie, 1890; and Moroni, 1892. After Walter's birth in 1894, his brother Ivins was born in 1896, but died when about three and a half years old. Then came Clarence, 1899, and Eva, 1902.

After his father died, Thomas P. Cottam remodeled the house, which became the center of much activity and the place where Walter and his siblings grew up.

Three enormous mulberry trees partially covered the house, which was set off by a rose garden and lawn on the south and east sides and enclosed in a white picket fence. A lower porch, bordered by a white wood railing, was shaded by a thick wall of climbing english ivy. An upper porch, called "the deck," was bordered by the same white wood railing, but its floor was tin, best avoided by bare feet in the hot Dixie summer. A vegetable garden, a barn, and a vineyard of sweet green grapes lay west and north.

Inside, family living centered in the large dining room, furnished plainly with an enormous table covered with white oilcloth or set with white linen, many plain wooden chairs and linoleum. The pride and wonder of the dwelling was its south parlor, not to be entered except by invitation. Red velvet drapes kept it in a semi-twilight; dark red carpet and velvet chairs and sofa made it elegant, as did a porcelain shepherd and shepherdess on the mantle, a sparkling crystal-drop chandelier and beautiful ceiling scrolls of ornamental plastering, the product of the special skill of Walter's father. An impressive bookcase held a set of law books, four big leather-bound volumes of the *History of Utah* by Orson F. Whitney, the *Holy Scriptures*, and many other books, giving evidence of the true education of this second generation pioneer who had had only a few years' formal schooling. Many bedrooms completed the interior, along with a large bathroom boasting plumbing which included a giant-sized tub left from the remodeling of the Temple.

The Cottams always opened their large family home to

those who came to St. George to attend stake conference, the county fair, or other special events. Guests often included many high church officials. In these early days when hotels were almost unknown, the Cottams provided as many as 21 beds for guests and sometimes stabled 20 or 30 of the visitors' horses.

Walter's father continued plastering during his early married life and at various intervals afterward. In the fall of 1886, he was in charge of the ornamental plastering work in the upper part of the Manti Temple, where he labored almost six months. He had the contract for putting the first four blocks of pavement in St. George. He also did some painting. The yellow paint on his St. George home was his work, the paint colored with yellow ochre from the Washington fields.

Thomas P. Cottam did a great deal of farm work with the help of his six sons and owned a considerable amount of farm land in Washington County. Known to his children as "Pa," he was a deeply spiritual and intelligent man, with a high forehead, deep-set, pensive eyes, and strong bones. In addition to his church duties as a bishop, counselor to the stake president, patriarch, and temple president, he served as mayor several times and also as assessor. In addition, he served two terms in the Utah State Legislature and was a member of the Utah State Board of Education. Because of his intelligent, kindly and humble manner, he spent much of his time counseling people who came to him for advice on legal, religious and just personal matters.

Remembering his father many years later, Clarence said that, despite not having had any education past the sixth grade, Thomas P. Cottam was highly esteemed by almost everyone in the county and could have held almost any office that he chose to run for, and that he didn't have a descendant who was his equal in stature. Although he was not trained in the law, many people sought his legal advice. Clarence observed, "I am quite sure many people who wanted legal advice would come to him in preference to a lawyer, not only because they could get it without any cost but because they thought Father had judgment superior to that of any of the lawyers they could go to."

Honesty and integrity ran deep in the Cottam family. When Walter's grandfather was seeking means to emigrate to Utah, he borrowed five dollars from a man in New Orleans.

Years later, when his son Thomas became a bishop in St. George, he handed him five dollars and said, "The first five dollars I earned in Utah I sent back to the man in New Orleans, but it was returned 'Address Unknown.' I tried several other times without success. I do not want to go down to my grave with money that does not belong to me. As my bishop, will you take this and do with it as you see fit." Walter's brother Clarence had a similar story to tell of Thomas Cottam, their father:

> In my second year in high school, there was a terrible drouth. Only a few families had water for hay crops. The price of hay jumped from $8 to $14 to $45 a ton. Dad was one of the few fortunate ones, and we had an unusually good crop that year and barns chuck full of hay. . . . Brother Finlay, a Jack Mormon, said to him, "Brother Cottam, I would like to buy all your hay for $45 a ton." Dad looked him straight in the eye and said, "Jack, I haven't a single straw to sell to you. I will sell only to those in need and to no one for more than $16 a ton." I told Dad that I thought he should have accepted such a good offer. Dad said to me, "These are my people. What I am, they have made me. They cannot possibly afford $45 a ton. I have it figured out. I can make four or five percent interest on what I have grown at $16 a ton, and that will give me a good and fair profit for my labor.When you are a little older, son, you will accept these principles."

Compassion was another admirable trait passed on to the Cottam descendants by the two Thomas Cottams. Clarence's daughter Glenna said, "All my life I have marvelled at what a good person Uncle Walter was. He was always the one who visited widows and cheered them up and took them for rides in beautiful canyons, long after the funerals were past and forgotten and the widows very much alone. There were glimpses of his generosity and very evident views of his integrity."

Walter's mother, known as "Ma," was jolly, buxom, outgoing and outspoken, loving and hospitable. A creative artist as a cook, she loved to entertain. She accomplished a prodigious volume of housework each day. On Mondays there was the huge family laundry to be done. Each child took his turn at the handle that churned the clothes in the wringer washing machine; as soon as he became tired, another child would take his place. Of course, most women of this era scrubbed on a washboard by hand. Townspeople marveled to see her going to the temple each morning in a freshly starched white dress, a rare feat in pioneer times. A devout Mormon, she was active in the Relief Society, the women's organization of the church. She had a good alto voice and enjoyed singing duets in church with a close friend. Like other Victorian ladies, she considered that Pa should do the thinking for the family. He embarrassed her one Sunday morning when he got up to conduct Stake Conference having forgotten to remove his chore pants before putting on his Sunday pants.

The competitive spirit that surfaced in Walter may well have come from his mother. The family told the story that in her old age she began getting up earlier and earlier on Monday mornings so she could get her washing on the line before her neighboring sister-in-law could get hers out. When her rising time reached 4:00 a.m., the family insisted that she quit the game.

The three older sons, Thomas, Arthur, and Heber, called "the big boys," carried the burden of the farm activities, raising hay and other crops in the Washington fields. Moroni, Walter, and Clarence, "the little boys," had their chores as well, milking the cows, taking turns at irrigating the crops, and going to the ditch in the mornings to get the day's supply of water before the cows came up for a drink and muddied it.

But the little boys were not always very closely supervised, and Moroni, being of a peaceful nature, and Clarence, being five years younger than Walter, were often dominated by their audacious and resourceful brother. A bright-eyed, handsome little boy, Walter was a practical joker with an impish, sometimes almost diabolical, sense of humor. Children had to make their own entertainment in those days, and Walter's idea of fun was tormenting Moroni. Walter said he once overheard his father tell a neighbor, "If I don't hear Moroni yelling in the morning, I know that Walter is sick." But his father recognized Walter's quick intellect and vitality, and Walter escaped punishment for most of his pranks. However, some of his antics prompted his father to dub him "a stupid genius."

One day Moroni cut his foot quite badly with an axe. The settlers believed that urea was good for treating wounds. Walter recalled that since they didn't have any urea in St. George, they used urine. "It was my job to piss on Moroni's foot every morning," he said. "Boy, I liked that!"

Crops in the dry St. George area had to be watered by diverting water from irrigation ditches onto the farmland. In later years this could be done by turning a wheel that opened the gates of the ditches, but when Walter was a boy, the chore involved using shovels to dam up the ditch. One day when Walter and Moroni were little fellows, six and eight years old, their father sent them into the wheatfields to irrigate. When they didn't come home as soon as expected, he went looking for them. Encountering the watermaster, he said, "Have you seen my boys?" The reply was, "No, but I saw two shovels going through the wheat fields. I don't know what was carrying them."

Walter's treatment of cats sometimes brought out a mean streak in his nature. The family had two cats that got along pretty well. But one day Walter tied their tails together and hung them over the clothesline. "I never saw such a fight in my life," he said, telling the story years later. "I've felt terrible about that. . . . I only tell my closest friends. But that sure was a fight." Another time he was painting a fence when a cat walked by. He grabbed it and painted it green. The cat took off and disappeared. He thought he had killed it, but a few days later it wandered back into the yard—completely bald. Was he relieved? No. He killed the cat and buried it so no one would find out what he had done.

Saturday night was family night for the Cottams and, since the kitchen was the only room that was warm, they held the gathering there. The cook stove always got red hot. One night Walter went fortified with some cayenne pepper and sprinkled a few pinches on the stove every now and then. His father soon had to halt the meeting because everyone was coughing and choking.

Always before dinner the family would kneel down by their chairs to say the blessing. One time they had a guest for dinner, a rather odd man. But instead of kneeling down, he just sat in his chair while the family said the prayer. Right in the middle of it, the visitor said, "I'm the prettiest one of them all." His remark broke up the blessing for that day. Walter said later that he always remembered anything that broke up those rituals.

During the first early years of settlement, the pioneers did not lack in sociability and amusements, but most were of their own making—sewing bees, husking parties, quiltings—and sharing a meal after the work was done. In later years, cultural diversions had become a little more sophisticated and the town boasted a community center for plays and other productions.

When he was six years old, Walter appeared in a play about the Civil War. He was a drummer boy who got killed in the first act, so he would go to a room somewhere in the building and go to sleep on a bench for the rest of the production. An older brother also had a part in the play and always took Walter and brought him home. But one night his brother forgot him, and Walter woke up to find himself alone, locked in the dark, empty building. It was a small building made of adobe with very small, very high windows. When he found he couldn't climb out the windows, he started screaming as loud as he could. Then he heard footsteps, but fearing it might be an old, lame Indian the children used to tease, he kept quiet. After awhile he found a hat someone had left on the bench, put it under his head and went back to sleep. When he woke in the morning, he attracted the attention of a man he knew and lost no time getting out of there. On the way home, he met a kid who asked him, "You been to the community center?" "Slept there all night." "See my hat?" "Slept on it. "

During the night he had wondered why his parents didn't come to rescue him, and when he got home, he quietly sneaked up to his bedroom, which he shared with three of his brothers. There he found the answer—a cousin had decided to spend the night, and there he was in Walter's place. Pa always made the rounds at night and counted heads, but because of the right count that night, no one noticed Walter was missing. A great weight had been lifted. With a happy heart, Walter went out to the barn, got his bucket, and started milking the cows.

Funerals were another, but more solemn, occasion for people to get together. In those days the body would simply be put in a wooden coffin and lowered into the grave with leather straps. The family and friends would stay after the service while the dirt was shoveled into the grave. Unusual as it may seem, Walter always wanted to attend these events. "I never used to miss a funeral when I was a kid in St. George," he said. "I liked to hear those women holler when the clods hit the box."

Walter's pranks carried over into the classroom in the St. George school. In a science class, the teacher got out a microscope and told the students, "Now, if I had a drop of blood, we'd look at it." A fellow student was resting his hand on Walter's desk. Walter took out his pocket knife and gave the hand a jab. Then he announced to the teacher, "There's your blood." "The teacher let him look at it first and me second," Walter recalled.

Reminiscing about his father, Walter noted that Pa was quick-tempered. "One day one of our cows jumped a fence and got in the haystack. He got so mad that he picked up a two-by-four and hit this old cow on the back, and she went down like he had shot her. 'I swan!' Pa said. That's what he used to say, I swan! Pretty soon the old cow began to kick. I tell you, Pa was glad to see that. He didn't want people to think he had broken her back. He was too high in the priesthood for that."

Clarence might have been a match for Walter in will and resourcefulness except for the gap in age. Clarence remembered being enticed by Walter onto a steep section of roof and left hanging there alone, crying for hours, or so it seemed to the tiny boy. He learned to swim when Walter threw him into a deep pond and stood laughing at him. Some years later Clarence got his revenge when Walter locked him in their room. Clarence locked the door from the inside, then found a letter from a girl Walter had been seeing. Clarence read it to him through the door, putting in a few extras. Walter was so mad he ran downstairs to tell their mother. But she took Clarence's side and told Walter he was getting just what he deserved. Clarence was 18 years old when he finally got into a fist fight with his feisty brother—he hadn't dared to before.

However, the two boys were much alike in their love of nature and their quick, inquiring minds. They were always seeking answers to their questions about the climate, geography and living things they observed, including a great variety of birds. With no field guides nor anyone to teach them the names of the birds, they often invented names of their own.

Walter had become interested in the land as a boy and used to tag along after an early-day botanist, carrying his big camera and tripod. He would ask the man the names of the plants, and the man would tell him once and then have to tell him again. But when Walter asked his teacher to name all the plants they had seen that day, the teacher said impatiently, "Well, I'll tell you, but it won't do any good." He didn't know how wrong he was. He lived to learn that he had had a brilliant student on his hands, but not long enough to know of Walter's later achievements in botany, conservation, and ecology. Walter's teacher came to an untimely end: "He had all these herbs and things and thought he had the secret of life and that he would never die. But he went to Los Angeles and got run over and killed by a Model T Ford."

An incident that occurred when Walter was 13 years old made an indelible impression on him. "I was herding some cattle, most of which had their bones standing out, their hides hanging on them like clothes hung out to dry. One of them had fallen and was too weak to rise. After trying to get the animal onto its feet and being unsuccessful, I saw nothing else to do but put the animal out of its misery. I picked up a rock and struck it in the head until it was dead. I recall the range, so depleted from overgrazing from too many animals on too little land that those conditions seemed characteristic. I decided then if I ever could do anything to help change conditions such as these, I would surely do so."

Clarence also recalled, "The zoological and ecological changes in the landscape were evident to any thinking person. Walter and I nearly drove our father out of his mind with our never-ending questions as to why things in the valley were different from those at other altitudes."

By the time he was 16, Walter had become familiar with the plants, the history, the ecology, and the whims of the weather on the desert region of southwestern Utah. So when his mother told him that she and his father got down on their marrow bones and prayed that it wouldn't rain until they could get their crop of wheat harvested, Walter was appalled. He knew if it rained in St. George in August, it would be a miracle. He told his parents, "Anyone who would pray that it wouldn't rain in St. George should be horsewhipped." His father got to thinking it over and came to Walter later and said, "Son, you're right."

Young Walter Cottam spent many hours hiking in the nearby Pine Valley Mountains studying the plants and shrubs and trees, enjoying the beauties of nature and exulting in reaching the top of a mountain and gazing at the vista below. Walter did his share of work on the farm, too, rode the range and carried the hod for his father on some of his plastering jobs. One day his father asked him to help clear some meadowland of sagebrush. Walter bargained, "If you will climb the mountain with me, I will help clear the sagebrush." His father agreed, but by the time they reached the summit of the 10,000 foot peak, Pa, exhausted, just lay on his back and closed his eyes. Walter, hoping to encourage his father to look at the mountain and the view, asked, "Wasn't it worth the climb to see all this?" "Yes," his father said, "but I keep thinking of all the sagebrush we could have cleared with the same amount of energy."

Chapter 2

The BYU Years

Walter met and fell in love with black-haired, blue-eyed Effie Frei when they were both attending the St. George Stake Academy. He was 17 and she was 23. Effie was born September 27, l888, in Santa Clara, a tiny Swiss village five miles from St. George. She had been working as a school teacher, having postponed her education to help support the family while her father, Jacob Frei, went on two church missions, once to Switzerland and once to the eastern United States. Effie, of German-Swiss descent, stood 5 foot 5 inches; Walter was only slightly taller, about 5 foot 6 1/2 inches, with blue-gray eyes and of slender build, but physically very strong. Walter often walked the five miles to Santa Clara during their courting days.

They both graduated from the Academy in 1913, she as the vice president of the class and he the "commissioner of finance." Both were listed as debaters in the yearbook *The Dixie*. Under Effie's picture was the notation: "One of the most winning and cheerful girls in our Academy. Everyone loves her and she loves all. Her greatest desire is to be a mother to Walter." The comment about Walter said: "Handles the purse-strings of the Student Body. There is more greatness in him than his size would indicate. His main pleasure is to torment cats and love the Academy girls."

They married July 1, 1915, in the St. George Temple and went to live in Provo, where Walter attended Brigham Young University, receiving his A.B. degree in 1916. Marriage didn't restrain his teasing and often, in his perverse fashion, he would remind Effie of the difference in their ages. In later years, one of the children asked him why he had married an older woman, and he replied, "Because she was smart." Their first child, Celia Fae, was born October 21, 1916. Walter continued his education and in 1918 earned the first master's degree to be awarded at BYU.

During his college years, he became interested in photography and soon was taking most of the pictures for the BYU yearbooks. The editors gave him credit lines saying "Photos by Cottam." But after awhile, they found it easier to put "Photos not by Cottam" under the ones he didn't take.

His impish pranks carried over into his college days as he continued to create his own entertainment. One time, by setting up a camera with an arrangement of strings and a flash, he managed to capture a picture of a student and his girlfriend who had sought privacy in a small, dark room. The student threatened to sue. "Go ahead," Cottam taunted. "I'll furnish the proof!"

During his botany studies, Walter often went to the greenhouse to water some plants. Another student was also working there with some fertilizer he called "green manure." One day when Walter was there alone, a professor with a very precise demeanor came in and asked what "that stuff" was. Walter told him it was Tommy Martin's "green manure." "Isn't there a better name for it?" the professor asked. "Yes," Walter replied, "shit."

"I'm going to have to speak to President Brimhall about your language," the professor said sternly and left. But as he was going down the path, Walter saw him rolling in laughter.

In 1918, after making an eighty-mile round trip by bicycle from Provo to Salt Lake City for an interview, Walter began his teaching career as a science instructor at Jordan High School. According to a letter Effie wrote to her parents on August 14, 1918, she appeared less than jubilant about the move. "We are happy to be settled in our winter home even if it isn't quite as nice as the one we left in Provo." She described the various rooms in the house and talked about a neighbor with a three-year-old boy, then added, "It seems pretty hard to have to move just as one has some good friends in one place, but I'm sure the people here will be lovely." She mentioned a friend in Provo who "just loved Fae and would have tended her most of the time had we stayed in Provo, but as that was out of the question, we will have to do next best. I have felt a little blue and lonely the last two days, but as my rooms are cleaned little by little and things all in their places, I feel better. Moving was almost more than I could do just now." She was pregnant with Grant at the time. He was born August 26, 1918, twelve days later. Telling Grant of the event many years later, Cottam recalled that an older neighbor woman had come in to help right after Grant was born. "She dressed you first, then gave you a bottle. But she sucked on the nipple before she put it in your mouth," Cottam said. "I didn't expect you to be alive in the morning."

At the end of the first school year, all the Jordan High teachers had to grade themselves on their performances. Cottam gave himself a failing grade in dress but an A in everything else. When he turned in his score-card, he included the following comment:

> Dear Principal:
>
> It is with no great pleasure that I submit the accompanying score-card because I am not in the habit of blowing my own horn; but since it is obligatory that I do this, I see no reason why I should not give a blast. I can't imagine anyone with common horse sense, no matter what his profession may be, who would not declare to his employer that he is up to the standard in his business. Any self-deprecation, I imagine, he would not publish. To be frank, I do frequently call myself a "damned fool," but this kind of criticism is always done in private.
>
> I say with no reserve that I have put A effort into each and every class I have conducted this year, and I

> equally well know that some of my recitations have fallen below A grade. I am aware of some of my faults and am trying hard to rectify them, and any helpful criticisms will be gratefully received. It will come with no crash to me to learn that you and the superintendent do not agree with this not over-modest grade, which I, after much reflection, have selected; but just as soon as I am convinced that I am not an A teacher or cannot become one, I shall vacate the profession for something that I can do A work in.

The principal, A. M. Merrill, included Cottam's comments in a report he wrote describing this new method of teacher evaluation. It appeared in the *Utah Educational Review* of April 1919. Despite inducements offered him to continue teaching in the Jordan District, Cottam saw no future there, and he accepted an offer to become an assistant professor of botany at BYU.

Three more children joined the Cottam household during Walter's tenure at BYU: Beatrice, April 4, 1921; Richard Walter, October 1, 1924; and George Thomas, November 2, 1928. During the first years, the family lived in several different houses. Finally Walter and Effie decided to build a house on the last street on the east side of Provo. Across the street was a pasture, and beyond that were the foothills and then the mountains. "We lived in the shadow of 'Y' mountain, and it wasn't hard at all to get to the foothills and start to climb," Grant wrote.

The house was a brick bungalow, single-storied with a full basement and a large porch. The floor plan was simple: six rooms, two rows of three separated by a hallway. The three on the north side were bedrooms; the three on the south were parlor, living room and kitchen. Some features were innovative. Provo had a good water supply, which was carried in pipes quite far up the canyon and resulted in extremely high water pressure and very cold water. Instead of an icebox, therefore, the house had a small closet completely covered on the inside with those pipes. The clothesline was innovative, too. A wheel about a foot in diameter was rigged on the back porch, which was about ten feet above ground level, and another wheel was attached to a telephone pole on the back of the lot about a hundred feet away. The continuous clothesline ran from one wheel to the other. All Effie had to do was pin the clothes on the line, give it a little pull, and the clothes would sail across the backyard. She didn't have to move at all. If it started to rain, she could pull all the clothes in and stay dry on the porch. A coal furnace in the basement heated the house, the heat rose through an opening covered by a four-foot square grill in the floor of the living room. Standing over the grill provided more heat than anyone really wanted, but the heat didn't travel far enough to warm the bedrooms much. In the winter, pipes in the firebox of the furnace provided the family's hot water. In the summer, if they wanted hot water, they had to light a fire in a little cast iron stove next to the water tank.

All the faculty members of Brigham Young University, which was owned by the Mormon Church, were required to pay tithing. At a meeting one day, President George W. Brimhall explained to the professors that while their pay was low, the rest was being stored up in heaven for them. Cottam, in an aside to a fellow professor, commented, "I'd like to pay my tithing like that." Somehow the remark got back to President Brimhall. A short time later as Cottam was walking down the hall, he saw the president approaching. Brimhall stopped, lowered his glasses, and stared at Cottam. "I thought he was going to hit me," Cottam said. Instead, Brimhall clapped him on the shoulder and exclaimed, "That's the best thing I've heard since I've been at BYU."

During his first year of teaching at BYU, Walter considered entering the field of medicine, but President Brimhall told him he was a natural teacher and was needed in the teaching profession. Cottam, however, was determined at least to advance his own education. In a letter to his parents written in May 1920, he said,

> From all I know now, I shall very likely go to school somewhere next winter. I do not know yet just how much cash I will be able to lay aside for that purpose, but I'm going to school if I have to scrub windows for something to eat. Effie thinks that she might go home for the winter, as we have no notion how

> much it would cost were she to go with me. If I go alone, I can put up with anything, and one could not do so if there were children to care for.
>
> I hardly dare think of the cost in these times when sugar is selling at $30 a hundred, but I must go on if I am ever to be ready for something big if it should come my way. It will be a sacrifice no matter when I go, and while it might cost me a little more for breaking loose next winter, I would be one year nearer my goal. I am in hopes that I can get through school in less than three years and that I can almost pay my way after the first year. A fellow usually can if he makes good, and I am conceited enough to think that I can make it go if I have health.

In another letter to his parents in July of that year, he wrote:

> I am spending most of my time now in the mountains studying botany. I shall be obliged to teach it next winter together with high school physiology, which Professor Smart taught in the past. I want to get acquainted with nature so that I can partly fill his place. . . . My English friend, Mr. Harrison, is making the hikes with me, and we are certainly having a jolly good time. He has a fine Buick so our transportation is easily solved. We have been making our camp this last week about 8000 feet above Provo at the foot of a large snowslide, and you may be assured that the nights have been plenty cool enough with but one quilt each to keep us warm.

Walter Cottam's first real exposure to ecology came about almost by accident. He had spent the summer of 1921 at the University of Wisconsin, where he expected to continue his studies in the field of plant pathology, but on his way back to Utah by train, he used a layover of several hours to visit the University of Chicago. He had heard of Dr. Henry C. Cowles, a pioneer in the field of ecology, so he attended Cowles' first lecture of the fall term there. "I was simply spellbound listening to him," Cottam recalled. "That one hour decided my future." He was so excited about ecology that he couldn't sleep on the train that night. All the way home he wondered what he could do to get some experience with Cowles. His resourcefulness served him well. When he got back to BYU, he went to the officials and made a plea that they bring Cowles out to teach a summer class. He said, "You've never had a great man out here. The state needs it. I need it."

Cowles was invited to spend the next summer in Utah on a joint educational venture between the University of Chicago and BYU in ecological field studies. Although he had a contract to teach that summer in Chicago, Cowles replied, "I'll come." He arranged to bring his class of seventeen students with him, two men and fifteen women; they stayed for two terms of summer school. Cottam, of course, attended the sessions, traveling to all the Utah parks, the Grand Canyon, and Cedar Breaks, and then spending a week or so in the Provo area. Cottam got full credit from the University of Chicago for the two summer sessions, and the next year went back to Chicago to work on his Ph.D.

Of the quick response to his plea to bring Cowles to Utah, Cottam said, "I already knew I was going to work with him, but I didn't know it would be that soon. Cowles had a profound influence here. He was an awfully witty guy. He made such a hit at BYU that he was invited to go to the Utah State Agricultural College {now Utah State University} at Logan the next two summers, and I went up and took those classes too."

By then Cottam had changed his focus to the field of ecology, and he and Dr. Cowles had become good friends. "He took to me," Cottam said. After one of those summer sessions, a reporter asked Dr. Cowles what was the most interesting thing he had found in Utah. "Walter Cottam," Cowles declared without hesitation. Cowles' esteem for Cottam was illustrated further when he invited Cottam to come to Chicago the summer of 1930, to live in his house and teach his class at the University of Chicago while Cowles was vacationing in Europe.

Cottam's research problem for his Ph.D. thesis concerned the flora of Utah Lake, a fresh-water lake connected to the very salty Great Salt Lake by a river called the Jordan. Provo and other developments lay mostly on the east side of Utah Lake, while mostly uninhabited grazing land filled the west side.

Cottam had to make frequent trips to the lake for his research, and on one particular overnight trip, he took Fae and Grant along. He knew a man who had a chicken farm on a peninsula called Pelican Point, and his friend let Cottam use an empty chicken coop for shelter that night, although normally they just slept under the stars. It didn't rain often enough to justify even pitching a tent. But this night they were lucky to have cover.

Just as they were getting ready for bed, a thunderstorm developed. Lightning flashed; thunder boomed; and torrential rain pounded the tin roof of the chicken coop. The children, only about six and eight years old, started to cry. Failing in his attempt to comfort them, Cottam finally asked, "Do you want me to make it stop?"

"Yes! Yes!" they cried.

He pointed a finger toward the sky and commanded, "Stop!"

Incredibly, the storm stopped. Not another drop of rain fell; no lightning flashed; no thunder boomed. The children wondered at the power their father had over the heavens. Even he was amazed. Knowing about the brevity of thunderstorms, he had taken a chance, but he hadn't expected such an immediate response.

On their way home the next day, another incident occurred that must have made the children wonder again just what kind of man their father was. As they drove along the road, they saw a very impressive building in the distance. Their father identified it as a resort and said they might eat lunch there. The children rejoiced in anticipation. They had never eaten in a restaurant. As the resort loomed closer and closer, they became more excited. But then, instead of going toward the resort, the road and the car started going away from it. When they asked why they weren't going there, their father said that the resort had been built on the edge of the lake when the water was higher, but had failed when the lake went down. The building was now just an empty shell. The children ate in silence the lunch their mother had prepared the day before. Why would a man who could stop thunderstorms play such a trick on them!

Chapter 3

Chicago Sojourn and A Question of Religion

Dr. Cottam spent the fall and winter of 1925 and most of 1926 in Chicago, completing work on his doctor's degree. Effie and the children left their Provo home and spent the months of Walter's absence with her parents in Santa Clara.

His letters to her during that time were filled with protestations of love in what became a pattern during their separations. He sometimes chided her for her lack of affection, mentioned little incidents designed to make her jealous, and then when she reacted, told her how he had laughed. He said that he had only been teasing and accused her of having no sense of humor. Although he was an affectionate and demonstrative man, he couldn't resist teasing, not realizing the hurt it might inflict on a lonely heart.

In a letter addressed to "My Darling Wife" and dated September 24, 1925, he said in part:

> I almost forgot that this month you are to honor your natal day. Even now I am not sure either of the day or the year. When I was a youngster, it seemed to me

> you celebrated on the seventeenth, and when I became a little older, memory has it that you changed the day to the twenty-fifth. In regard to the year, I am more dazed than ever. At the last count I think you were thirty-two, so this year brings you just to my age, thirty-one. I have fears for you! Do you remember the old adage "once a man and twice a child"? At the rate you are going down the ladder in years, you are apt to be twice a child before you become a man. Well, anyway, if I be late or if I be early, I am glad that you were born on some day of the year, and whatever the day, I honor it. . . .I shall this day say goodbye to my mountains and take a long, last, lingering look. I think that if I am to shed a tear at parting with any of my friends here, it is sure to fall today. I know that the day will be crowded with memories of you.

Aboard the Los Angeles Limited on September 27, 1925, he wrote:

> And now I am literally flying out of the state away from you and home—from mountains, lakes, streams and people whom I love so much. It is with a sense of loneliness that I thus depart from scenes most dear to me—from love, so necessary for happiness. After all, I doubt if the goal is really worth the sacrifice! If I were assured that no ill should come in my absence and that we are really to reap the harvest of our dreams—then perhaps this forced separation would be a means to greater love and life. But who knows?
>
> I am forced to the conclusion that it is well that we do not know what the future holds for us. We have made our gamble and are now playing our game. We must hope for the best and use our best judgment to play our cards right. . . We must both place all the confidence in the world in each other and try to feel that each is doing his utmost to make our adventure a success. The one thing after health which I need most to do my best is love—and I beg you not to hold that from me.

> Well, darling, in spite of all that I am leaving behind, I am happy that I am well on my way, and I hope that the future holds for us its very best.

From somewhere in Nebraska on September 28, he confessed that he was "traveling with a heavy heart and empty purse" because on the train he found that he did not have his proper ticket and had to buy another one. He said he carried only $25 in cash, but the Union Pacific detective who was checking the tickets accepted his check. Adding more details of his embarrassment, he wrote, "I shall, of course, be glad to hear your comments. Scold or sympathize as you choose, but please keep it to yourself. I would not let the people back home know it for the world."

A downhearted Walter wrote from Hitchcock Hall at the University of Chicago on December 15 that he had flunked his French examination and would have to take it over. He said the examiner came late, tested five other students first, leaving only about five minutes for his test. The examiner had a ten o'clock class and, when the bell rang, he left. On his letter Walter drew two little before-and-after faces, the first with hair standing on end to show how scared he had been before the exam, and the second with tears falling from his eyes after the exam. "I think I should give everything of a worldly nature that I own (which is little) to have even an hour with you again. I need you badly, perhaps in hours like these more than at any other time," he wrote. "But I have not lost faith in myself, and I trust that you have not either."

On a happier note on December 23, he said he had taken two exams in other subjects and neither was difficult. "I could have done well in them without a minute's cramming. I think that I wrote almost perfect exams, and I shall indeed be surprised if I don't knock down As in both of them," he wrote. But he still worried about the French exam coming up later. "I am going to work on it quite a lot this holiday and try the exam again the very next time it is offered, and I expect to go up every following week if he flunks me again."

School was out that afternoon for the Christmas vacation, and Walter wrote that he had received Effie's Christmas box, but he wasn't going to open it until Christmas morning. "I am not going to allow myself to be deprived of all the thrills of Christmas. You can imagine me sneaking out of bed in a big, lonely hall and, like a veritable Silas Marner, caressing these prizes." He mentioned the cards and letters he had received from kind friends in Utah, then concluded: "And now, old dear, I am happy for you! I love the sentiment in each of your letters and the feeling that I always have after reading one that you love me and have faith in me. Our life when we are blessed with a new association will not always be rosy, perhaps, but I am sure there will be a better understanding and a closer companionship. I hope you feel too that I have faith in you. I love you for the mother you are, and I am absolutely convinced that no children on earth ever had a better mother than my kids have. I love you for the sweetheart you have been and promise to continue to be."

The dreaded French exam dominated his letter of January 5, 1926. "Your letter came this afternoon, and I couldn't help but smile to think that you thought of those New Years evenings too. I think we were both recalling them about the same time, for I think that I never wanted you quite so badly in my life before. Yes, I am sure that the holidays must have been a bit more pleasant for you than for me here alone with my sorrow. To think that I had to spend those days worrying over French!" He described the torture of waiting a whole hour for the examiner in the morning, only to find that the exam had been changed to the afternoon. "The suspense of waiting all day has just about ruined me, and I told Pete that I felt tonight that I had a floating ovary. But by the powers, honey, I have my French back of me forever! I hope it pleases you as much as it does me. Now you can go and phone Pa that I have my exam over and it went off well. I think that I have never felt so relieved in all my life. Now I know that I shall enjoy my work." At the bottom of the letter were sketched two faces, one with hair standing on end labeled "before the exam," the other with a big smile labeled "after the exam."

Walter's letter of January 15 indicates he had written something earlier that had stirred up some jealousy in Effie's breast and that she had reacted. In response, he wrote:

> Well I enjoyed every word, the mean ones too;

> they made me laugh more than ever. It sounded so very much like you that I am almost stricken with a fit of homesickness. Well, you old dear, I really do believe that you love me and are still capable of seeing green. I am very happy for your love, sweetheart, and I wonder if you will ever really trust me with being satisfied with it. You will never learn, will you! I believe that I could still work you up in great fashion. I had apparently more fun writing that letter to you than you had reading it. I didn't say a thing except in fun. . . . I really wish that Santa Claus would bring you once a little better sense of humor. You always take things so seriously. I said what I did about the girl to see if I could get a kick out of you, and since it worked so beautifully, I think I must tell you the whole circumstance of that wonderful evening I spoke of.

He then tells her that he did ask a girl to go to the Tivoli with him. She considered it at first, then said she had another appointment.

> So that evening that I spoke of as being hard to describe really is. School was out that day, and I simply stayed home, went to bed early and had one long evening with you, my dear. . . . So, honey, I am still virtuous; no wicked French lady has had me a single minute except in an absolute business relationship. It has now been nearly four months since I was kissed last, so you can imagine the amount of affection I could shower on you if only I had the opportunity. I don't believe you would enjoy my loving letters so well if you did not get occasionally a letter that you could easily get worked up over.

After details about going to see the opera Carmen, how much it is costing for school, how he has the children's picture on his desk and thinks of them often, he concludes:

> We shall be glad, won't we, dear, when you will not need ten days to find out that I am just joking when

I tease you. . . . Yes, I can remember when you really felt like choking me, and I dare say you will feel like it many times before death will part us. At least, I hope so. I suppose I shall never get over teasing you so long as your humor does not improve. Anyway, dear, when you feel like that again, you can just bet that deep down in my heart I think you are the finest sweetheart in the world, and I love you very, very much.

Walter's next letter later in January shows concern about his father's health, and he wonders if he should think about coming home.

I was glad to get the letter this morning and hear what you thought of Pa. You seem to notice a distinct change in him every time you see him, don't you! I got letters from Thomas and Emma yesterday. Thomas says something about Pa's color being bad—and I of course assumed that the cancer was probably destroying his liver rather rapidly. . . . Did I tell you that I wrote him quite a long letter Sunday? I found myself probably giving him the impression that I thought his case hopeless, so I got on to a decidedly lighter vein. I am wondering if he will cry or laugh over it. Probably both. . . .If Pa thinks he is going to pass on, do you think he wants me to come home? I suppose he will think it useless, and probably he is right. I think I should like to remember him as I saw him last, even though he was not very well then. Both Thomas and Arthur said it would make my heart ache to see him. You said nothing about the X-ray pictures or whether the doctor intended to operate on him in the immediate future.

Lots of love, W.

His letter of February 6 begins:

Darling: I was happy for the letters yesterday and today, for the love and sympathy they were so full of. I wrote a letter to Dr. McGregor again yesterday and asked him for a quick and frank report on the exact

> condition of Pa's health, and I expect to be put more at ease within another week or so. This tremendous worry is certainly not good for school work. . . . I don't know that I could do any good by coming home, but I do want to have the decision partly made, at least. I wonder what Pa would think about me coming home even if he felt sure that he was not long for this earth? If I thought that he wanted me to come, I should not hesitate a minute. Of course it means much to my work and my purse also to think of making such a long trip, but these are things that cannot be considered at all in a financial way. The heart alone must rule such situations.

He asks Effie to "make a fuss over the poor, old dear," and adds:

> I am convinced that frank and demonstrated affection is a great thing in this world, and I take you at your word that we are to have more of it when the opportunity presents itself again. . . . I am convinced that the one thing we must do henceforth is to see to it that the little loving things so dear to new lovers are revived. I am rebuilding my whole philosophy of home life, and when you find me under the same roof again, I am to play more than the necessary role of a fixture of the house. You are going to be confronted with a real sweetheart, a very jealous one and one who intends to keep you guessing from one weekend to the next. I shall never make the excuse again that work, either yours or mine, is a justification that we are to take each other for granted. In addition to your old role of mother and wife, you too must be the sweetheart that must be kept won. If you settle down and accept my affection like you do your meals, then by the powers, you will find me somewhere else after affection, and I grant you the same privilege.

Later on he chides her for not sending a snapshot of Dick. "A lot of good that camera has done you! I even left the films for it so that all you needed to do was press the button, and you have let five long months go by without a single snap of the kids. I am certain that the time will never come when you are really enthusiastic about any of my hobbies."

He voices concern again over his father's health in his letter of February 10 and tells Effie he discouraged his father from thinking of making a trip to the Mayo brothers.

> I believe that McGregor can do as much as anyone, and at home Pa would be around friends and loved ones. Frankly, if he is as weak and thin as everybody reports, I do not believe he would survive an operation. Does he look natural? In a way I would hate to see him. . . . I can hardly imagine how he appears now—so poor and thin and downhearted. Does he ever say anything to you about passing on?. . . My letters to Pa, I think, cease to be of any account since he is so sick. I cannot bring myself to really enjoy writing. I dare not joke with him, and I am very little good at writing obituaries.

After turning his thoughts back to Effie, he writes:

> Well, old dear, I am very proud of the things you are doing in your old home town. Aren't you really happier there as leader than you are at home in Provo? It seems to me you have stolen my fire with all the compliments you are getting. . . .I wonder if you will ever be content simply playing the role of mother and sweetheart with me. Or do you expect to make a saint of me and introduce me into society as soon as I get back! Well, don't count on too many reforms. . . . Another month and our separation will be more than half over. That sounds good, doesn't it, dear! Kiss the kids for me and accept bushels of love.

In his letter of February 15, he recalls "when I fell so hard for you as a lad of only 17 years. I shall never forget those days and the first intoxication of love." He mentions the parcels he sent with cloth to make dresses for the two little girls. "I want them to bloom out with the flowers and remember that their Dad would love to see them." Then he gives details of a party "the botany crowd" attended the night before at the home of a woman student, but comments, "I don't know whether I have ever been able to stand this night business, but I am certainly too old for it now."

Effie apparently expressed some feelings of jealousy again in her next letter, as Walter reassured her in his letter of February 21: "This much is certain—I never lost my heart or any part of it during my visits. You held that in spite of your inattention, and no one on earth can be so happy as I to hear you say that you are going to claim all of my time and every bit of my affection. I can hardly wait for the time to come when you can demonstrate it."

The last two-and-a-half handwritten pages of the letter describe a pageant, "The Miracle," which he called "the most stupendous stage production I have ever seen. The only words spoken in the entire performance were in Latin, and to think of about five-hundred women acting for nearly three hours without saying a word is indeed a miracle."

Concern about his father took up most of his letter of February 28:

> You cannot imagine how hard it is to keep my mind within sixteen hundred miles of my work. Poor old dad. I suppose he gets jawed from morning till night for not being able to brace up. It makes me entirely out of patience with the folks for thinking that Christian Science philosophy can remove a cancer. I think if I were with him, I would join him in tears rather than be unsympathetic.
>
> I think I told you about getting a short note from Dad. He mentioned at the close that he prayed the Lord would let us meet again in mortality. I thought then that he didn't expect that we actually would. Somehow I feel that he cannot possibly withstand such a slicing as will be necessary. How would you like to be so far away from home and get letters from your family that you hardly dare open? Every time I come in the hall, I look for a telegram. It is certainly not con-

ducive to good study.

The news of his father's death arrived in a telegram on March 16, 1926. He wrote to Effie:

> Dearest,
>
> Your telegram came about 4:00 p.m—two hours ago. I have been down to 63rd to send back word to mother, and I have not yet collected myself sufficiently to write an intelligible letter, so you will accept this note, I hope, with the love that is truly real but not expressible at this time, at least. I think that the telegram, after all was not so shocking and heartrending as the cards and letters that have been describing the suffering of my dear father. He no doubt was ready and willing to leave it all, and I have no fears that all is well with him. I can hardly bring myself to the realization that he has departed—and certainly his passing will require much time to heal the wounds left in our hearts. I cannot express my feelings in the least.
>
> The time may come when I shall be glad that I was spared the actual sight of his suffering, yet I wonder if I have not really suffered more here imagining it all. I feel just now utterly alone—sick at heart to think that I have not been near him during this last brief battle. I hope that you will never take upon yourself the privilege of determining finally my action in such a matter as this again. It seems to me that no one has the right to assume to see all sides of a question to such an extent that he should state so positively the only course of action. If I had been allowed any voice in the matter, I should have been home now. At least you haven't imagination enough to put yourself in my boots, and what you need is about six months away from everyone you love to give you a real sympathy. It is needless to say that I am experiencing a fit of homesickness, and after the first shock of grief is over, I shall look at this thing in a more sensible light, as you do perhaps.
>
> I shall appreciate receiving the Washington County News obituary of father, also any accounts in

the state papers. I hope that stenographic records are kept of the services so that I might read what I should have been privileged to hear. I trust that you will not read any unkindness in this letter. My heart is well nigh to the breaking point, and it is little wonder if my emotions fly away with my better judgment.

I shall try to write mother tomorrow. She is brave to suggest that she alone bear this grief. I am sure, however, that she knows she does not sorrow alone. I hope that you will offer her such comfort as I should love to do myself.

This is a queer old world. I often wonder what it is all about. There is so much hustle and bustle in it that one is not supposed to take time out to sorrow even, and perhaps it is good in the long run. If I did not have so much work here, I should die of lonesomeness. Tomorrow I am scheduled to take two two-hour final examinations. Whether I do or not is another question. Just now I would quit the whole damned business with perfect calm.

I love you, dear, and I wish that I could feel that a really deep understanding exists between us. We need it, and I am sure that a little more time with each other when we meet again under the same roof will do much to make this a reality. I am convinced that a too practical love is impractical. I am enclosing a couple of snaps taken Sunday. The camera seems to be OK. There is something wrong with the subject, and there used to be something wrong with the operator.

W.

Walter's letter of March 17 was filled with apologies and declarations of love, apparently after he had received a letter from Effie expressing fear that a gulf was growing between them:

My Darling,

The letter that came this morning written Saturday [three days before his father's death] added to my already inexpressible sorrow. It revealed clearly that the letter that came to you Friday hurt you, and for that I am sorry. I do not recall what I said, but whatever it was did mischief entirely foreign to my intentions. I could have shed more tears to have you express a thought that the kiddies bridge a gulf that would otherwise exist between us. I would be tortured beyond words if I had anything like that preying on my mind, so I want this little note to erase any such notion from your mind.

It's true that we have lovely children, and it would be foolish to argue that they do not and will not continue to add much to our happiness, but I want you to recall the time before they came into our lives. There was a beautiful love that made their mortality possible and which still exists separate and apart from them. The days before our marriage and for more than a year after, I loved you for the sweetheart you were and the wife which you became. Your life to me has been threefold—sweetheart, wife, and mother. Can't you see that it is foolish to divorce the first two and, no matter how beautiful the third, to cling to it alone? I want you to know, my darling, that the sweetheart in you has not outgrown my ideal nor has it dropped below it. I love you as passionately as ever in my life, and I am sorry beyond words if you think that without the children I would ever turn from you. You must remember that though youngsters make the bonds of a family strong, they are not always to remain youngsters, and after they have left the nest, what would we have left if we pinned our future happiness to such a tie?

We hope, of course, that the youngsters will grow up to respect us just as we want to live to be worthy of that respect, but they will not always be fed from our hands, and they will not always need us. But we shall always need each other, and you will please me greatly if you never let that thought enter your mind again. If it makes your heart light to feel that you have my love eternally secured, then enjoy the freedom that comes from it, for I shall renew my covenant to you that I made long ago that I shall never forsake the love you

> gave me nor shall I ever withdraw one single spark of mine that daily burns for you, dear.
>
> I wish you could feel so sure of my love that every liquid note from those wonderful Dixie birds would accentuate it—that it would bloom in the flowers and drift to you in their fragrance. Spring never bursts forth but that it fills my heart with new love for you and my soul with more hopes of its eternity.
>
> Enjoy the beautiful spring, and let it carry to you my love. If it makes you happy to be fat, then be fat. I want to come to you and find you well and feeling that our renewed love and better position in school and society will in time repay us for the tortured months of our separation. Above all, sweetheart, rest assured that if I scold, it is merely the bursting of a bubble and that my true love and admiration and respect for you still rest and grow on a firm foundation.
>
> Yours for keeps,
> Walter

All seemed well when Effie with the children returned to their home in Provo and found this letter from Walter, written June 2. It said in part:

> You will no doubt experience a few thrills at the sight of our home that we both love so dearly, but I hope that you find hardly a completeness until I join you three months hence. Take a glance at the old mountains for me, dear, and believe me when I say that my love for you is as solid as they.
>
> I have spent another half day on my thesis. I have been reading and not writing today. I'm working up a brief history of the botany of Utah and have been absorbed with early explorations. J.C. Fremont arrived in Utah Valley May 25, 1844, and camped there two nights. He had a very interesting and exciting journey around Oregon, California, across Nevada and finally camped on the Santa Clara Creek. He described it beautifully and, of course, visited it before any white people were there. He went up the creek to the

> Meadows and camped there two nights. His explorations are thrilling tales of adventure that make me feel like a hot-house plant. I expect to work downtown tomorrow afternoon in the library. A botany party will be held at a student's house, but I think I cannot afford a week night.

In an undated letter, probably written near the end of July or the first of August, Walter, obviously ecstatic over news that Effie will join him in Chicago for his graduation, writes:

> Now, old dear, if you get about four letters in the next four weeks, you will know that my heart is beating every beat for you and that my thoughts of love, though still strong, are necessarily few. Dr. Cowles set my exam for some day between August 8 and 12. Gosh, I have had a scared feeling all afternoon, and this means that I am going to get busy reviewing and organizing tomorrow.
>
> I shall leave the photographic work till after my examination. In four more weeks, therefore, I shall either be the happiest lover in the world or a very disappointed one. If my thesis sits well with him and if I am able to pull through the exam in good shape, then I expect to take life a good bit easier and primp and rest for you. My exam will be two weeks behind me when you come, and I hope to be all set to show you the time of your life. Don't feel bad if you are neglected for a month now, for I promise to make it all up to you afterward, especially when you get here. . . .
>
> Be sure to tell me what you think about the car. We must be ordering it if we get it through Petty. What would you say if we picked up a second-hand something here? I would hate to get a lot of trouble, but there are bargains for the guy who knows anything about them.
>
> I hope you keep the thrilling letters coming, dear. They certainly bring a lot of joy with them and make me pretty much determined that I shall do my very best to make a success of things on this end. . . . I love to

> think of the hour that I shall have you in my arms for the first time in a year. . . . You are going to find a love-starved sweetheart awaiting you.

Effie arrived in Chicago as planned and attended the graduation exercises in 1926 when Walter received his Doctor of Philosophy degree from the University of Chicago. They bought a Model T touring car and drove back home. That year Dr. Cottam was promoted to Professor of Botany at BYU.

He continued teaching at the university for five more years. But early in life he had begun questioning church doctrines and policies, and religion played a large part in his decision to leave the church-owned institution. Eventually he felt it was hypocritical to continue in his position at BYU.

When Walter returned home with his doctorate and went to visit his mother in St. George, she said, "Well, you got your Ph.D., whatever that is, but Arthur is a bishop!" Bishops in the LDS Church do not study for the ministry, but are "called" by church authorities to serve as the presiding leader of their ward, the local branch of the church. They continue in their chosen line of work, taking on the extra duties of bishop as a service to the church. Bishops serve for indefinite terms, some for several years and others for shorter terms.

Another activity of the Latter-day Saints religion is baptism for the dead. Members trace their ancestry back as far as possible to find those who did not have an opportunity to learn about Mormon beliefs. They then go through steps to qualify the ancestor and are baptized in the name of the dead person. This enables all the family members to be together in the Hereafter. Walter's mother, who had been baptized for some fifty of her ancestors, declared proudly, "And I didn't need a Ph.D. to do it!"

When Walter had lived at home, he often plagued his mother about her religious beliefs, but he admired her warm contralto voice and liked to go to church to hear her sing duets with Em Squires. He felt that it must have been from his mother that he inherited the musical talent that allowed him to play valve trombone in his brother Heber's band. At one time he also played in the BYU band under Professor Sauer: "I wasn't very good," Walter said, "but I was all he had." The German professor would get very upset and would try to bawl the band members out in English while he was thinking in German.

Because Walter had been away from home when his father died, he was given first choice of his father's things. To the surprise of other family members, he chose the family Bible. Although he eventually left the fold, he was never excommunicated and he remained on the church rolls. All other members of his family were devout Mormons, including his younger brother Clarence, who also had an impressive career.

Clarence joined the research staff of the U.S. Biological Survey in Washington, D.C., as a junior biologist in 1929. By late 1944, he had advanced to Chief of Wildlife Research of the enlarged Fish and Wildlife Service. Two years later he was named Assistant Director. In 1954 he left his government career to become Dean of the College of Biology and Agriculture at BYU. After a year there, he organized and became the first director of the Welder Wildlife Refuge in Sinton, Texas. BYU honored him with the Distinguished Alumni Award in 1964 and in 1971 presented him with the James E. Talmage Scientific Achievement Award in recognition of his lifetime work of distinguished service.

Discussions of religion between the two brothers often became so heated that Clarence finally declared he would no longer talk to Walter about it at all. Howard Cottam, a son of their brother Heber, sat in on some of those discussions. Recalling the experience years later, he wrote, "These two articulate intellectuals exerted a pervasive, if subtle, influence on my personal philosophy, Walter as an agnostic and Clarence as a devout Mormon who brilliantly rationalized incongruities of science and religion. I was privy to many of their conversations. Dad didn't say much, but his diffidence was evident in his preference for fishing trips on Sunday, in which I often joined him. . . . My ambition was to become a scientist like my two Who's Who uncles, Walter and Clarence." Two decades later, Howard, who had become ambassador to Kuwait, was listed in *Who's Who in America* and four years later in *Who's Who in the World.*

Of his brother Heber, Walter said, "Heb was smarter than any of us and, although he was ten years older than I, I made him my idol. He could have been a famous man." Heber went on an LDS mission to Switzerland, but developed lung trouble and returned to the United States to complete his mission in Minneapolis, Minnesota. Family members said he was not critical or outwardly bitter because of the circumstances of his mission. Yet he rarely attended church. He built a home in Provo, but during the depression he had to take a job in southern Utah. As he drove home during a February snowstorm, his auto skidded off the road and overturned. He suffered neurological injuries and died June 27, 1932. He was forty-six.

Earlier in his teaching career, when his salary was meager, Walter received a letter from his father saying that he had seen by church records that Walter was not paying his tithing. When Walter got his next $300 check, he sent $30 to his father with a note: "Here is the tithing. Now my conscience is clear, but my ass is bare."

An incident that made him question some LDS policies had occurred when he was courting Effie: she had asked him to go to church with her. In those days, if anyone sinned, he had to stand up in church meeting and tell all the details of his transgression and ask for forgiveness. At the meeting, a young man stood up and confessed that his girlfriend was pregnant. She then had to stand up with him and recount what had happened. When Walter returned home, he told his father that if anyone ever told him to get up and confess like that, he would tell him to go to hell. His father, who was then a counselor to the stake president, said, "So would I!" and promised to see that the practice of public confession was stopped.

Walter never did believe his father to be fanatically religious. In fact, he believed that his father sometimes sided with him or at least was not really disturbed by Walter's beliefs. He said, "My father would have been more upset that Clarence was a Republican than that I was not religious."

During his studies at the University of Chicago, Walter and his friend Pete Hayward loved to philosophize on life. In a letter to Effie dated December 23, 1925, Walter outlined his reply to a question Pete had posed: "Supposing you were convinced beyond all shadow of a doubt that there is no life or consciousness after death. Would that realization affect your moral standards?" "I answered him that I would be no less moral, but probably no more moral either, for I am not as moral now as I should like to be. I explained to him that my present actions are in no sense traceable to my old conception of the fear of God. No Hell, I continued, could be worse than the knowledge that I had deliberately subscribed to the unhappiness of any other human. This is my philosophy of life, in fact, my religion. I shall never have occasion, I think, to fear God so long as I know I have been square to my fellow man."

While she was in Santa Clara with her parents during Walter's stay in Chicago, Effie wrote to him about a sermon she had heard. In reply, he wrote: "You used to enjoy that sort yourself, and so did I. I wonder if we were not just as happy believing all that nonsense as we are now doubting it. How true it is 'where ignorance is bliss, 'tis folly to be wise.' Yet I can no longer tolerate the old point of view, and I am glad that you cannot either."

In 1937, Pete, writing under the pen name Peter Eliot, wrote this poem and sent Walter a copy.

A Sonnet

And we, like birds, do also beat our wings
Against the walls of our restricted clime;
We eat and play and do the futile things
That seem so all-important at the time;
We rail aloud at fate and strive to win
The highest perch atop the world of men;
We taste of love and hate and joy and sin
And then forget . . . and do it o'er again.
And does a Seeing Eye that we evade
Observe our deeds, our sleep, the way we gauge
Each day, the friends or enemies we've made?
Could there be One outside our worldly cage
Who really cares the way we come and go?
I cannot tell, but how I'd like to know!

Later in life, Cottam's idols were the great naturalists John Muir and John Burroughs, and he came to subscribe to Burrough's philosophy of Pantheism—that whatever it was that brought about the universe and everything in it and brought man to his state of awareness was god enough for him, and he didn't believe in a personal god. Cottam often quoted Burroughs' creed:

> *I am persuaded that a man without religion falls short of the proper human ideal.*
>
> *Religion is a spiritual flowering, and the man who has it not is like a plant that never blooms.*
>
> *Amid the decay of creeds, love of Nature has a high religious value.*
>
> *This has saved many persons in this world,*
> *Saved them from mammon-worship, and from the frivolity and insincerity of the crowd.*
> *It has made their lives placid and sweet.*
>
> *Nature is their church, and the rocks*
> *and hills are the altars.*
>
> *The creed is written in the leaves of the trees,*
> *in the flowers of the field,*
> *and in the sands of the shore.*
>
> *There are no heretics in Nature's church.*
> *All are communicants, all are believers.*
>
> *Communion service is at all hours, and the bread and the wine are from the heart and marrow of Mother Earth.*
>
> *Natural Religion is now and here and everywhere.*
>
> *The crickets chirp it, and the birds sing it;*
> *the breezes chant it, the thunder proclaims it,*
> *the streams murmur it.*
>
> *Its incense arises from the plowed field and is borne*
> *on the morning breeze; it is in the forest breath,*
> *and in the spray of the wave.*

The frosts write it in exquisite characters, the dews impearl it, and the rainbow plants it on the cloud.

Although Walter never got into any professional trouble expressing his honest views at BYU, he did receive some criticism. Once a woman said to him, "I never expected to hear such remarks at BYU." He replied, "I'm sorry, but that's what I believe." And someone else told him he was an evil influence. He also heard that Vasco M. Tanner, a zoologist, said of him, "Cottam is a hybrid artist and botanist, and like most hybrids, he isn't very good at either."

Shortly after Franklin Harris replaced Brimhall as president of the university, Cottam, on meeting him, said, "You probably haven't heard much about me." "I've heard more about you than you know," Harris replied. When Cottam went to President Harris to discuss leaving BYU, he told the president that he felt like a hypocrite remaining there because he didn't believe many of the church teachings. Harris indicated he harbored similar doubts, "But I can't say the things you do."

Cottam said the only reason he was a member of the church was that he was born into it and that if he had his choice, he would probably be a Unitarian. In addition, he said that he could never get the testimony everyone said he should have if he were to continue to teach at BYU.

Even though he left to accept a position as professor of botany at the University of Utah, he recalled later, "Those were great days at BYU."

CHAPTER 4

NEW DOORS OPEN

The move to Salt Lake City and the University of Utah in 1931 opened numerous doors for Dr. Cottam's many talents. Over the years before color film, he had photographed more than three thousand wildflowers on 3 1/4 by 4 1/4 inch glass slides, which he had meticulously colored by hand, spending more than half an hour on each slide. In Salt Lake City and throughout the state, he gave hundreds of illustrated lectures—to garden clubs, to religious and civic groups, and to scientific organizations. He also helped establish the Salt Lake City Shade Tree Commission and served on it for 25 years.

And he planted trees. Hundreds of trees. Thousands of trees. Dr. Cottam's fascination with trees lasted throughout his life. In his forays into the out-of-doors, he was always looking for the largest, the tallest, the most beautiful, the most unusual trees. He photographed them, measured them, made scientific studies of them, wrote articles on his findings about them, and eventually hybridized them.

Early in his career as a botany professor at the University of Utah, he asked President George Thomas for a place on campus where he could plant various kinds of trees. They selected a little ravine, which the president promised would never be changed in any way. And President Thomas kept his word, later resisting a request when the library was being built to fill in the area by then known as "Cottam's Gulch." The gulch remains today an oasis of beauty on the lower campus.

Dr. Cottam had a story to tell about almost every tree in the gulch, from hauling the Fremont Cottonwood up from Santa Clara on the running board of his Model T to planting a six-inch seedling in 1936 that now towers as the magnificent Sequoia Redwood on the bank of the gulch. The tree that makes a picturesque arch over a bench in the bottom of the grove is a Peachleaf Willow, native to Utah and the north-central United States. A stump at the base of the tree was left after someone cut down the willow's twin when Dr. Cottam wasn't around. Otherwise, the twin would be forming an arch in the opposite direction. The senior class of 1947 officially bestowed the name "Cottam's Gulch" on the area. An item in the *Utah Chronicle*, the student newspaper, noted: "Dr. Cottam is more proud having the 'gulch' named after him than he would be having a structure of any sort built in his name, probably because it is a living thing that grows every day."

But his tree planting didn't stop at the gulch. Over the years more than 5,500 trees, including three hundred different species, grew to shade and grace the university grounds. In 1961 Cottam and Helen Wells realized their dream when the Utah Legislature designated the entire campus a State Arboretum. Dr. Cottam couldn't claim all the trees, but his score ran into the thousands.

He taught autumn classes on trees for many years, one designed specifically for students of architecture and another for the general public with the main emphasis on shade trees of the city. He justly received the Certificate of Merit from the National Shade Tree Commission in 1959. He expressed his deep feeling for trees in an Arbor Day speech he gave in 1961 at the university: "The admiration and the reverence of man for trees seem to have been born of the race. For sustenance and shelter, man, through all time, has been dependent on the forests and their products. For spiritual rejuvenescence, man, since history's dawn, has sought solace and strength in the groves that were God's first temples."

Dr. Cottam pursued small injustices with the same fervor as the larger goals he championed, and adversaries sometimes bore the brunt of his caustic wit. When he began teaching at the university, Ralph Chamberlain headed the biology department, and Kim Newby had a key to the stockroom. Cottam could get supplies only when he could find Newby. This arrangement didn't sit well with Cottam. He finally told Newby, "Only three people can get into this stockroom, you and Chamberlain, and Jesus Christ!" "Newby went straight to Chamberlain and told him what I had said," Cottam recalled. A short time later, Chamberlain approached Cottam, handed him a key, and said, "Here. Now four people can get in, Newby, Chamberlain, Jesus Christ, and Cottam."

On another occasion, Cottam went to see President Thomas on some matter. He found the president beside himself because another professor had just been in to see him and had asked for a raise because he had so many children. "How many children do you have?" he asked Cottam. "Five," Cottam replied, "and if I had another one, I'd have to kill it." The president's irritation dissolved in a burst of laughter.

One of the advantages of being a professor is the tradition of the sabbatical leave. After seven years at the University of Utah, Dr. Cottam arranged to take off the spring and summer quarters of 1938 to pursue his own interests, mainly collecting plant specimens for the university herbarium. He used this six months to make a grand tour of North America, and he took the whole family with him—seven people in a 1935 two-door Chevrolet. They camped all the way, all sleeping in an ordinary nine-by-nine-foot umbrella tent.

Grant, who was 19 years old then and did much of the driving, recalled that the tent and the camping gear were carried in a one-wheel trailer, six feet long and four feet wide, attached to the back bumper at two places. A small rubber-tired wheel was attached to the body of the trailer, much like the casters on a piece of furniture. "When the car turned a corner, the trailer became essentially part of the car," Grant recalled. "There was no way it could bend independently, but because the wheel did move like a caster, the whole apparatus could turn a corner without having the trailer wheel skid sideways.

However, it did mean that the single wheel of the trailer ran down the middle of the road, half way between the tire tracks of the two rear wheels." The roads often were filled with potholes in those days, and the standard way to avoid running into them was to straddle them. But the Cottams' ingenious travel arrangement put the trailer wheel, only a foot in diameter, directly into the path of the potholes.

The trip began at the end of March, the day after a six-inch snowfall in Salt Lake City. But they headed south to the warm weather of St. George and a short visit with relatives before moving on to the North Rim of the Grand Canyon. Just before reaching Jacob Lake, a small resort some 40 miles from the rim of the canyon, Grant saw a large pothole in the road, and his automatic reaction to straddle it put the trailer wheel right in the middle of the crater. The trailer bounced in the air, then hit the ground and rolled along on a blown-out tire. They didn't have a spare. The closest tire of that size was in Salt Lake City, 400 miles away.

"We pulled off the road, unhitched the trailer, and Dad drove to Jacob Lake, made a phone call to Salt Lake, and came back to announce that a tire would be on its way on the next Greyhound bus and would reach us the following afternoon," Grant recalled. "We pitched our tent, built a fire, ate a good supper and went to bed. That night a foot of snow fell. We had to get up several times to knock the snow off the tent, and next morning we lighted our camp stove and ate, huddled in the tent."

They stayed in the tent until that afternoon, when the bus came with the tire, and they were on their way again. That night they camped at Lee's Ferry on the Colorado River, some 7,000 feet lower in altitude and a whole lot warmer. The respite didn't last long, however. The next night they were back up on the Colorado plateau and cold again. But instead of snow, they had a violent wind storm. Grant recalls:

> Dad loved the mountains and liked nothing better than to camp out in the wilds without any facilities at all. Mother, on the other hand, firmly believed that the toilet seat was the most comfortable seat in the house, and she complained when we were at a campground

> with limited toilet facilities—and in those days no campground we ever encountered had facilities which met her standards. Dad much preferred to avoid campgrounds and pitch his tent out in the desert or in the mountains. That is what we did the night of the great wind. In the absence of any facilities at all, mother took a glass milk bottle to bed with her. She was used to chamber pots in her youth, and this was the closest she could come to that ancient facility. The wind was fierce, and it was cold. The tent bent and moaned and creaked most of the night, and finally the tent pole just broke, and the tent fell down on top of us. None of us moved. We just lay there and shivered all the rest of the night. At least the flapping and creaking of the tent stopped, and we all slept a little. . . . The morning was calm and peaceful, and one by one we extracted ourselves from within that pile of canvas and faced the cold but rapidly warming air. Mother was the last to come out, and in her hand she held the bottle, half full. Dad was absolutely amazed. No one except mother knew when or how she accomplished this remarkable feat, and she wasn't talking. Dad wrote a little story about this achievement, and I imagine he read it to all their friends. It was his type of humor, and apparently mine as well.

Grant concluded: "The next night found us in a really good campground outside Tucson, Arizona. There were sunlight and warmth and pretty good toilet facilities. We spent several days there recovering from that hectic beginning of our trip. The rest of the trip had its share of joys and miseries, but nothing ever managed to top those first few days."

Dr. Cottam also kept a journal of the trip, begun on March 22, 1938. The Cottams stopped in St. George to attend a birthday party for Walter's mother. "To prove her youth, Ma attempted in one breath to extinguish the seventy-five candles, and she nearly did it," he wrote. "Grandma Frei provided beds for all of us."

The next morning Cecil Frei, Effie's youngest brother, suggested that there were onions to plant—just a few—a mere 8,000. "All the males labored until past 3:00 p.m. helping Grandpa and Cecil plant this trifling number of breath-knockers. And we enjoyed the return to the farm—the odors of the barnyard, the old-fashioned privy, the songs of Dixie birds and the constant noises of the farm." In the afternoon, they went for a ride up the Santa Clara Creek and visited the town cemetery, where Walter said, "I expressed again my wish to sleep on this sandy bluff. The scientist in me doubts the value of such a wish and the utter folly and futility of any care of these bones when life has flown, but 'To die, to sleep; to sleep: perchance to dream' in such an artistic spot, with beauty fresh and lovely in all directions would be worth the chance."

After two more days of visiting, they left the morning of March 26 for Zion Canyon, where they did some hiking, then continued on, intending to camp that night at Lee's Ferry. But, as in Grant's account, as they neared Jacob Lake, there was "a report similar to a shotgun discharge," and they discovered the flat tire on the trailer.

The calamity would have evoked cursing and kicking in most men, but not in Walter Cottam. In his journal, he wrote:

> There was nothing to do in the absence of a spare but pull off the road and camp. The setting was ideal, and we could not have found a more lovely spot had we been seeking one. The deep snowbanks surrounding our unexpected campsite added a cooling atmosphere to our home, but our spirits were far from being chilled. . . . Night found us hugging a big bonfire. Dark clouds now filled the sky so that no stars shone. Flickering flashes of lightning and rumbling thunder soon gave way to blinding flashes and to thunder claps that left little doubt of an approaching storm. We took to cover and to bed and listened with considerable joy to the pelting hail which soon changed to snow. . . . Slumber overtook us. I was awakened hours later by the sound of sliding avalanches down the tent sides. Being leader of the party and sensing the danger of a cave-in, I found myself very apt at commanding Grant to knock off the snow from all sides of the tent. I hard-

> ly dared to leave my bed for fear that Effie should chill. The wind was strong and raw, and its chill breath soon found its way into our beds. I ordered Grant to make a fire, which he did with considerably more grumbling than an obedient son should, and the fire he created was certainly not worth the effort of my command.

The journal indicates that he, Grant, and George tried to drive to Jacob Lake the next morning to meet the bus, but the car stalled in deep snow on the road. With considerable effort, they turned the car around and drove back to camp to await the bus. It arrived about 11:00 a. m. with the tire, and the Cottam party was on its way again shortly after noon. Periods of having to extricate the caravan from sand and mud slowed progress, but they reached Lee's Ferry on the Colorado River in time for "a splendid meal" before time to go to bed. "While no one seemed to be sweaty, this night was extremely comfortable compared with the wintry blast that had greeted us at Kaibab. We slept late."

The journal continues:

> The morning of March 28 on the Colorado at Lee's Ferry will not soon be forgotten. Clouds hung like smoke from a thousand fires of heaven over the peaks of the Vermillion Cliffs. They rose and fell like scenes from a huge tableau. The cliffs, wet from rain, shown brilliantly with the splashes of momentary sunshine. Rapidly moving clouds exposed a sky of deep cerulean. Hills on all sides, practically barren of vegetation, displayed the paintbox of ages petrified in stone.

After breakfast and spit baths taken in shallow pools, they spent the forenoon at Lee's Ferry, had a hasty lunch and moved on. "We decided to pitch tent somewhere on a protected spot of desert east of the Kaibab Plateau. Again Pa erred! We camped in a wash near the approach to the plateau, where a high wind was starting to blow. . . . The tent groaned and swayed under a sixty-to-eighty mile gale." Cottam piled into bed with Dick, who had developed a fever, but soon the worst began to happen. "Our tent pole began to bend in the middle, and like a liner at sea, crippled by ghastly tragedy, it began to settle fast. Ma matched forces against the hurricane and held the crumbling pole, but soon, as with most weighty problems, decided to let the matter drop, and down went the tent.

"Mama Bear in the dark with the blown-down tent flapping in the cold gale cried, 'Papa Bear, has the cub much fever?' Papa Bear growled, 'Not enough temperature to help out a damned bit.'"

Daughter Beatrice, recalling the trip in a tribute to her father some years later, wrote: "The family trip had begun in a setting of snow, grit and chilling wind, but the sun of the Arizona cactus country brightened Cottam hearts and dispositions. Today those five kids would say, 'Thanks, Dad!'"

They left Salt Lake in March, went south to Mexico City, east to Florida, up the coast all the way to the Gaspe Peninsula, then came home by way of Niagara Falls. The trip had taken them 18,000 miles and cost $2,000.

Chapter 5

Memories of Family Life

No one should have expected Walter Cottam, a 21-year-old bridegroom who became a 22-year-old father, to give up playing tricks on people when he got married and had a family. In reality, Walter gained five new victims. The timidity and fearfulness that all of his children displayed at times may have been the price they paid for his strange playfulness. And no one should have expected a young man who loved to climb mountains to fail to introduce his children to the out-of-doors. The five Cottam children never experienced an amusement park until they were grown, but they had slept on the ground in rattlesnake country, crawled up the rock faces of most of Utah's mountains, and slid down snowbanks as soon as they could climb.

Fae, the oldest child, the artist among them, felt close to her father, possibly his favorite. She said, "I felt secure in my father's love because he took me everywhere. Dad let me hold the stuffed birds at the university and watch the dancing girls at the ladies gym. He taught me to hike and took dozens of pictures of me. When Grant was older, we both went with him to track meets and football games, never realizing we were being tended. When I started my formal schooling at the BYU training school, my father supervised my reading every night. I went through all the children's books at the public library before I was nine. After that I concentrated on learning to turn cartwheels, to stand on my head, and to climb trees."

But Fae, like her siblings, had moments of fear and apprehension. When she was just a little girl, she went along with her father and a group of his students on a hike in Rock Canyon near Provo. At the top they came to a snowfield where they were to slide down. "Dad wanted me to demonstrate, and I went to the edge fully expecting to please him. But when I looked down, I realized I needed a minute to get up my courage. Impatient, he gave me a push, and I went hurtling down head over heels." Hearing that story some years later, he told a different version. He said he took her on his lap and they slid down the snowy slope together. Fae blames that experience for her never learning to ski with her athletic family.

When Fae was just learning to talk, her father used her to play a trick on Effie, whose maiden name was Frei. Cottam showed Fae a picture of a man with a monkey, pointed to the monkey and said, "That's Grandpa Frei." He kept working with her until she could repeat the phrase. Then when Effie came into the room, he pointed to the monkey, said, "Who's that?" and Fae chirped, "That's Grandpa Frei!"

Early in his career, Dr. Cottam had considered becoming a doctor, as had many of his friends. It was natural, therefore, that he assist in the births of all of his children except Fae. All were born at home, and he photographed each new arrival. Years after they were all married and had children of their own, he came across a negative in a yellow envelope with the notation: *Miss ? Cottam, age two hours, born April 4, 1921, 6:15 a.m.* The picture was of daughter Beatrice, the middle child. Toward the end of his life, he sent her the negative and described the events of her birth: "I called Dr. Carroll about three a.m. We had a nurse engaged, but she did not arrive for a couple of days. . . . Mrs. Smart asked me to call her when the show began, but Carroll said, 'Hell, let's make this a stag affair, and even if it's a girl, she will not object.' You did not. May I remind you that you were my darling then and have been ever since. The older you have become, the more I have adored you for your great intellect and for your uncommon good sense."

When Grant was three or four years old, Cottam found him next door walking on some beams over the basement of a house under construction. He brought Grant home and told him that if he did it again, he would get a whipping. Next day Cottam found Grant over there again, so he got a switch and whipped him, giving him a little switch now and then as they walked home. Grant didn't flinch or utter a sound, and his father finally burst out laughing. Grant, in a fury, turned on him, flailing and kicking, and blurted, "You've got a right to whip me, but you don't have any right to laugh at me."

While on a family Easter outing, Cottam, sitting on a hill holding six-month-old Dick, suddenly rolled the baby, wrapped in a blanket, down the long hill to a horrified Effie. And when Dick was two or three years old, the Cottam family went on a fishing trip on the Provo River with Cottam's brother Heber and Heber's family. Grant and Dick were wading in the river. Dick was contentedly playing in a shallow part of the stream when his father began urging him to go into the deeper water. When Dick held back, Walter and Grant picked him up and threw him into the deep water. Dick didn't make a sound, just fought his way onto a rock and let out a blat that could be heard a mile upstream. But the boulder was slippery, and Dick fell back into the water. Cottam was bent double laughing when Effie burst upon him with a big stick and beat him over the back as Aunt Edith shouted, "Give it to him! Give it to him!"

One of Dr. Cottam's tricks was getting in the car and starting to pull away before the children had time to get in. They had to move fast when they heard the engine start. One time on an outing in Millcreek Canyon, Dick saw a car he thought was theirs and thinking he had been left behind, started running after it. He chased it all the way to the mouth of the canyon. The family spent the rest of the Sunday afternoon hunting Dick, getting more and more frantic. It was after dark when they finally found him. "And," Bea said, "Dad was so relieved to see Dick that he whipped him." Dick remembered that licking as the worst he ever got.

Although Grant was the favored son, he also received the most lickings. Once after Grant had broken a neighbor's garage window with a rock hurled from a stationary flipper he had designed, he received such a licking that Bea remembers cowering behind her mother's skirts, wondering why her mother didn't do something to stop the punishment. Grant's memory of the incident is of no real pain. But he does recall that the fears that he would do something to arouse his father's anger or not do something he should do were always with him: "I never got the garden hoed to suit him. He was always mad about the weeds." Grant said later, "I was the oldest boy and, in retrospect, I believe Dad expected much more of me than he should have. Certainly, he expected much more of me than I delivered."

Bea recalled that her father sulked: "When he did, I always suspected a lovers' tiff between my parents. Sometimes Dad wouldn't speak to anyone for days. The house would be a tomb." But she remembered getting only one spanking herself. "The family had a fine chicken dinner one Sunday. Afterwards, Dad sent me to the corner store for ice cream. When I returned, he, in his teasing way, dished out ice cream to everyone but me. I threw a hairbrush at him. That's when I got that one spanking."

All of the children but Fae remember being afraid of their father at times, recognizing a dark side of him that his students and colleagues seldom saw. "He was always nicer to other people than he was to us. He was very polite and accommodating to others," Bea recalled. "But with us he was a hard taskmaster, expecting perfection. He had little patience with wrongdoing of any kind."

Like most children of that era, the Cottam kids were terrified of the dentist. In the Cottam household, the dentist was their father, who would come at them with big pliers to pull their baby teeth—and do so with relish. Then, laughing, he would show them the fruits of his efforts. Once, using a string to pull Fae's tooth, he afterward handed her a horse tooth he had already tied to another string.

This versatile father also acted as the family barber. And he managed to nick an ear with almost every haircut.

Walter loved professional fights and sports contests of all kinds. He would shout and laugh whenever he watched or listened to such events. Once when he was roaring his team on in the living room, Effie in the kitchen commented, "If anything happened to Dad, I'd miss his hearty laugh." It was natural, therefore, that he foster competition among the children, staging fights between Fae and Grant. Fae recalls her private system for winning: "I would put one leg behind Grant's knee, and he would go down like a rock. Dad would always cheer for me and say I should have been the boy. Once I used that same technique on a blond, blue-eyed girl in my grade school class after she got me in trouble with the principal. After school, I not only dropped her to the ground, but I rubbed her long, shiny hair in the mud. Dad loved it and gleefully told the story over and over."

He promoted foot races between Bea and Grant. Her father had entered Bea in a baby-crawling race when she was just turning one. But Uncle Heber had taught her to walk the day before, so she got up and walked across the finish line. Bea was two and a half years younger than Grant, but tall for her age. She was a fast runner and usually beat him. "I regarded those events as unfair," she said, "but I always tried to win."

Cottam tried to make a boxer of Dick, buying him gloves and matching him against the children of Walter's cousin Joe Jarvis, who often came to visit. Dick so feared boxing his better-trained second cousins that once when he was having a bath as the Jarvises arrived, he climbed out the bathroom window naked to escape a match with Boyer Jarvis. It was a cold evening, and he was nowhere to be found. And he didn't show up until the visitors had left.

Walter also pitted himself against Grant in fierce horseshoe pitching battles. And later, when the children were grown and various members of the family would play bridge, the house would ring with gloating laughter whenever Walter won. "Dad was the worst winner in the world," Grant wrote. "He gloated; he tried to make you look foolish; he laughed; he got very good at dodging decks of cards and chess sets, a reaction he often got from Mother, which so convulsed him with laughter that he became absolutely helpless."

When Grant was only six years old, he greatly impressed his teacher when she asked the students to tell what they had done over the weekend. Grant said he had been out with his father looking for wildflowers. "And what did you find?" she asked. "Quite a few flowers," Grant replied, "but mostly *Erythronium grandiflorum parviflorum.*"

This ultimate competition, the spring wildflower hunts, continued over the years and inspired an essay Dick wrote in 1942 for his freshman English class, an essay that appeared in the University of Utah literary magazine, *The Pen*:

COLLECTING TIME

> Everyone knows and everyone remembers a feeling that's common property in spring, a feeling of powerful composition, that of starting to live all over again. Even the most unimaginative bohunk, far from being immune to this all-engulfing spirit, invariably finds himself in a foreign and unbelievably light state of mind.
>
> This season of new life with its breaking through of the first spring flowers has a special significance for our family since it unfailingly predicts the beginning of collecting time. Collecting time is a tradition that my father very conveniently manufactured in order to procure the flowers that are necessary for his classes. Every Sunday in the spring is devoted to the big hunt.
>
> Each moment of the trip to the hunting grounds is utilized by this scheming father in raising enough enthusiasm for the hunt so that he will have no trouble in meeting his pedagogical requirements. His offers of a dime for the first three *Fritillaria*, a nickel for the first three Dogtooth Violets, and fifteen cents for the largest number of Spring Beauties, together with his betting that none of us will find anything, goad us with greed and excitement and insure his class sufficient flowers to dissect. There is no age limit to the excitement: it belongs as much to my older brother and two older sisters as to my younger brother and me.
>
> At the first stopping place, the car is completely emptied of hunters before it has reached a full stop. Away we go running over hills and gullies to investigate around every scraggy oak and all along each stream bank until we make a find. We now become as

> silent as the empty hills until each flower is uprooted and the omnipresent chance of other hunters sharing our booty is removed. Then off again. Our competition knows no fatigue, and though our flesh and clothing are torn in the mad rush through barren brush and sharp rocks, we feel no pain. To return empty-handed and to have the cruel name "Blindeye" thrown at us by an unappreciative father haunts us to action. Besides, the thrill of discovering a bed of paying plants is ample reward for any sacrifice.
>
> Of course, I always considered myself inferior to the others and constantly informed the carload that the competition was unfair. Age with its natural supply of knowledge of the flora favored one sister, and thoroughness was the middle name of the second. My older brother's advantage was his speed, while the younger brother's youth drew forth the full sympathy of his mother and father and with it all their resources for finding hidden plants. So there I was, slow and dumb. However, in my desperate plight, I discovered a potent weapon. It was to listen from a strategically hidden position to my father's instructions to my little brother, then dash wildly to the place he had indicated and seize the prize before my little brother had time to get there. By means of this animal cunning, I held my own and received the most money as often as any, and my claims were voiced the loudest of all.
>
> Our tradition has left a permanent mark on each of us—an unspoken love for the damp, dark soil, for the barren but spring-conscious trees, for the windswept hillsides with their retiring snowdrifts—for the whole revitalized world.

Dr. Cottam also tried to interest his children in political events. He subscribed to *Time* magazine for many years, always reading it from cover to cover the day it arrived. Bea remembers his getting the family up before dawn in 1928 to go to the Provo train station to see presidential candidate Al Smith. A few years later he took the family to the capitol building in Salt Lake City to see Franklin D. Roosevelt.

"Walter Cottam was a handsome, charismatic youth with many talents and interests. He had a fine creative mind and was often so engrossed in his thoughts," Fae recalled, "that he was unaware of the activity around him. He covered his timidity and insecurity with a glib tongue, a biting wit, and great charm. Instinctively he must have realized that he needed a practical, confident wife who could manage his career as well as bear his children. Effie was a perfect choice."

Dr. Cottam took all the children along on many outings, but he took Fae and Grant more often than the others, leaving Bea, Dick and George home with their mother. In fact, the three younger children thought of themselves as "Mama's kids." Effie, a warm, caring woman, had great empathy and great social intelligence. She loved going to plays and to other social events. She belonged to two bridge groups and held offices in various women's organizations. While Dr. Cottam was at ease in the classroom, giving his lectures and showing his slides before hundreds of diverse groups, he didn't care for going out socially, even though when he did, he usually starred.

Grant said, "One of my most vivid memories as a boy was of the times I was permitted to push the slides at Dad's talks. In those days the projector was a carbon arc affair, and the slides were big ones, all colored by hand. I recall that when Kodachromes first came on the market, I was convinced they could never equal in fidelity and beauty Dad's hand-colored slides."

On a trip to Yellowstone when the family had camped in Logan Canyon, Fae and Grant came back from a hike claiming to have seen a rattlesnake. Their father didn't believe it could be a rattlesnake and told Fae to go get it and bring it back to him. She went, but soon returned saying, "I'm not going to pick up that snake." Cottam investigated, found the rattlesnake and killed it. He brought its carcass back to camp and told the children that when a rattlesnake died, its mate would come looking for it. That night the girls made their bed on the ground with some apprehension. They didn't often use tents. Soon after going to sleep with visions of that rattlesnake coming to look for its mate, they woke up screaming—and found their father pulling a rope across their bed.

During his BYU years Dr. Cottam spent several summers teaching at Aspen Grove, a church-owned facility at the foot of Mt. Timpanogas, a majestic 11,750 foot mountain, graced with snowfields, waterfalls, glacier lakes, and teeming with wildflowers in the summer months. For more than 50 years, BYU sponsored an annual hike on the mountain in July, attracting up to 4,000 participants. Dr. Cottam made this twelve-mile-long round trip for many years, leading many of the hikes himself. The annual event was discontinued in the 1970s because of serious ecological damage to the trail.

The Cottam family stayed in a cabin at the grove, and it was there that the youngest son, George, was stricken. "After brightening our lives with his intelligence and charm for nearly four years, George contracted spinal meningitis and suffered brain damage," Fae recalled. George also was left poorly coordinated and subject to seizures. George's illness was a devastating blow. But the Cottams kept him at home and, through the efforts of his devoted mother and visiting teachers, he learned to read and write a little. In his adult years he was able to hold a job doing maintenance work at Liberty Park in Salt Lake City. But he was smart enough to know that he wasn't like his brothers and sisters, who were brilliant.

Seeming to have little compassion for imperfection, Dr. Cottam said more than once that it would have been better if George had died when he was stricken. But Walter felt a responsibility to take care of his son. Even in later years after Effie had died and Walter remarried, it was with the understanding that George would always have a home with them.

One time Doc took George with him on a trip up into the mountains to do some work for the Forest Service. As the light faded and it was time to go home, Cottam found that there was no gas in the car. Since they were fourteen miles from the nearest town, he opted to wait for daylight before deciding what course to take. The next morning they started out on foot to do a transect. As they were walking through the dense forest, they saw a small bottle by a tree and found it was filled with gasoline. George was elated. "Ah hah," he said, "I prayed half the night that we would find some gasoline!" "Well, for hell's sake," his father said, "Why didn't you pray for a quart? This won't do us any good at all." But by adding all the gas from their lanterns, it was enough to get them to a place on the mountain where they could coast the rest of the way down.

After the Cottam family had moved to Salt Lake and George was in his teens, he kept begging his father to let him drive the car. Cottam didn't think George capable of driving on the streets, but one night when Fae, Bea, Effie, and Doc were playing a heavy game of bridge, he told George to go drive the car from the driveway into the garage.

"Suddenly I heard a noise like a thousand nails being torn loose," he said. Realizing immediately what had happened, he ran out and found George had gone clear through the garage, through a wire fence and ended up against a tree in a neighbor's yard. George was still sitting in the car and the neighbor, Mrs. Jump, was out on the lawn in her nightgown "almost in hysterics." The roof of the garage lay on top of the car. "I couldn't stop laughing," Cottam said. "The next morning I photographed the destruction. I show it every now and then. Can you imagine a thousand nails coming out all at once?"

He found that George had just put the car in low gear and plowed ahead. George never asked to drive again.

Fae, Grant, Bea, and Dick all got their bachelor's degrees at the University of Utah and all but Dick took classes from their father. Bea said that when she took a class from him, he always graded her paper first and was very critical of any mistakes she made. But she finished college with all As and she, Fae, and Dick made Phi Beta Kappa.

Despite the memories of sometimes fearing their father, memories of the happy times growing up with him far overshadowed memories of the bad. "Most of my time with him was exciting—he was not capable of being bored," Grant recalled. "He was charming and vivacious, an excellent raconteur, a highly intelligent man with a great love of beauty—female beauty, art, music, mountains, deserts, flowers, trees. And he was the most honest man I ever knew."

Dr. Cottam, a stickler for morality, didn't use his influence to help his children get work. "He was bound to his strict moral code. If we got a job, we had to get it on our own," Bea said. She remembered how kind he could be. "He did such tender things," she said, remembering the time he came into her room carrying a bunch of wildflowers he had climbed the foothills to pick early one morning when she was in the hospital. And when she got a low score on an IQ test in grade school and her classmates were taunting her about it, her father, putting his arm around her, said, "I don't care what you got. I know you're smart."

Reminiscing with his 83-year-old father many years later, Grant said, "One of my greatest memories is of you arguing with the ward teachers. I don't think you convinced them, but you convinced me." "It's too bad you had to be in an environment like that," his father replied. "I guess I made an atheist of you." "No, Newell did that," Grant said. "In response to some comment the teachers had made about Heavenly Father, Newell said, 'Oh, Heavenly Father's big toe.' And the thought of Heavenly Father's having a big toe made an unbeliever of me."

Newell was Newell R. Frei, Effie's brother, who had lived with the Cottams when Dr. Cottam was teaching at BYU. He had stopped in Provo on his way to Washington, D.C., to attend George Washington University Law School. He had only enough money to get to his destination, and Walter suggested that he attend BYU for a year to get a better background before making a final decision on his future. He accepted the advice, and Walter and Effie provided him with board and bed. Some years later he wrote:

> From that day on, like a homing pigeon, I landed on Walter's and Effie's doorstep whenever it was at all possible. Some of the very happiest moments of my life were spent with the Cottams. The warm greeting from my sister Effie left no doubt that I was welcome. Walter's handshake together with his always cheerful salutation made me feel that I was home indeed. I was always welcomed with enthusiasm; I always left with reluctance.
>
> An important part of my education was acquired there. The lively exchange of ideas and the friendly arguments served as an intellectual whetstone for my mind. Here, for the first time, I saw youngsters stand

toe to toe with their parents in an ideological exchange and not have parental authority or "rank" brought to bear. In this home there was complete freedom of the mind to seek out the truth, to look at all questions objectively and without prejudice. It was a privilege just to be there in that intellectual climate with those two wise parents and their brilliant youngsters.

The home Walter and Effie made was a place where true Christianity was really lived. Being a good neighbor was the only kind of life that meant anything to them. Walter's one consuming interest was the preservation of the land and its resources. Effie shared this interest. They believed that the good of all the people is the only worthwhile goal for the genuine believer in Christian ethics. It was Walter's life—not money, not power, not glory—just service.

These two pioneered a new kind of life together, a life unencumbered by fear of the trappings of formalized creeds. They have earned an immortality that will cheer the hearts and enliven the minds of their children, their family, their friends, their neighbors, and will burn bright and clear as long as the land they loved shall remain green.

Chapter 6

Letters from England

Fae, Grant, and Bea had married and left home when the United States became involved in World War II. Grant and Charles Olson, Fae's husband, served in the Pacific Theater as captains in the Field Artillery, U.S. Army. They had both been in the Reserve Officer Training Corps at the University of Utah. Grant won the Silver Star for gallantry in action during the battle for Attu. Bea's husband, Bill Fowler, served in the European theater as a staff sergeant in a Railway Battalion, U. S. Army. Dick Cottam joined the U. S. Navy but did not see action.

When their husbands went overseas, Fae, with two small children, and Bea returned to 1114 McClelland Street to live with their parents until their men came home. Despite their concerns for their sons and sons-in-law, Walter and Effie were happy to have their daughters home and the laughter of little children in the house again.

When the war in Europe ended in April 1945, the U.S. Army set up Shrivenham American University in Shrivenham, England, to provide an educational program for servicemen waiting to be shipped home. It was designed to offer college courses to the soldiers and to help with their transition back to civilian life. Because officials wanted programs to be accredited, they mounted an intense campaign to recruit qualified instructors from both military and civilian life.

Dr. Cottam was among those chosen to teach at Shrivenham, and he joined "a rare group of 170 men" to board the Queen Elizabeth on July 4, 1945, for the ocean voyage to Europe. This exciting new adventure produced another stream of eloquent letters to Effie. He wrote at the outset, "I am in big company, and just why I was selected as the only civilian botanist from the entire nation to come to Shrivenham is perhaps more of a mystery to me than it is to you."

Writing seemed to come naturally to Walter Cottam, especially in his letters to Effie. Thoughts came flowing out onto paper, open and honest, sometimes beautifully descriptive, sometimes philosophical, frequently frankly down-to-earth, and often ardent. At 51, he still craved more words of affection from Effie in her letters and the promise of more closeness when they would be together again.

After getting settled in his room on the campus—a large estate, complete with an old stone manor house erected in 1487—Dr. Cottam attended faculty meetings, began outlining his courses, started preparing a key to the trees on the campus, and sorted out some three hundred or so of his slides that had arrived in his footlocker scattered about but undamaged. Characteristically enthusiastic, he quickly made friends with his fellow professors. His frequent companions on bike rides and hikes in the woods were Dean Anderson, a fellow Mormon, and Major Charles Deevers, an old friend who had got his Ph.D. in botany from the University of Chicago in 1936.

"We are very close to a dense woods. Some lovely thrush gives us a morning and evening solo," Cottam wrote. "I think he must be the famous nightingale. I am quite certain he is a thrush, for I saw him tonight. The only thing that could possibly make his song sweeter would be to have you here with me." He went on a trip to see the trees with a forester from Amhurst who would be teaching forestry, "and to my surprise and his also, I knew twice or more as many as he did. He thinks that I am a real dendrologist. . . . I don't know why I have such an inferiority complex because I find that I am much wiser on the flora here than either of the other two botanists. I shall be happy when we are settled down to the teaching job."

Dr. Cottam's thirst for knowledge, not only about the flora of the country but about the English people themselves, led to many interesting encounters. On a bike ride, he and Dean met a woman who knew the plants and who took the men home for tea and cakes. "She was in moderate means and thought it unfortunate that there had been a change of government. She expressed great fears about the food situation. She seemed very proud and expressed a determination never to go on the dole. I feel quite certain that the old people of England, around here at least, are very conservative and opposed to the Labor Government. On the other hand, the young fellows still in the army are practically all just as far to the left. England is in for a change, mark my words."

He visited an English pub, had a stein of beer, and "enjoyed a chat with the people that swarm to these places of intimate social relationships. . . . The people here are very friendly, but one has to speak first," he wrote to Effie.

He loved the English countryside and took frequent bike trips to nearby villages with Dean or Major Deevers. "The only straight road I have seen is an old Roman road built in 55 A.D. and very much in use still. The English are gradually placing some curves even in it. The little villages are enhanced by the beautifully curved, narrow streets. . . . Everyone rides bikes here, including old, fat women. The girls go riding along in the wind with their skirts flying up. Sometimes you see a husky mother riding along on a bike with a youngster tied securely in a wicker basket fastened over the back wheel."

Despite his busy schedule, he found time to write long, descriptive, affectionate letters to Effie almost every night. Although he had the capacity to enjoy nearly all aspects of his new life, he did have a few complaints, the greatest being the damp, gloomy weather and lack of sunshine that hampered his photography. "To see great patches of blue is a rarity. I am beginning to understand why primitive man sometimes worshiped the sun." Other complaints included the lack of any heat in his room, a hard bed, the Army red tape and waste, and the abysmal postal service that left him without letters for days at a time.

But these momentary distractions didn't prevent him from

making the most of every available opportunity. The campus was close to dense woods and, when the sun cooperated, he would go there to photograph the trees and flowers and to work on his key. "Several of the profs have trailed me around getting acquainted with the flora here. Many are interested," he wrote. When he completed his key, a hundred copies were printed, but the demand forced a reprint of another hundred. Then the Forestry department asked for still another hundred copies. A short time later an interview with Cottam about the trees appeared in the school paper. "My key has made quite a hit on campus," he told Effie.

Continuing the letter, he said, "I ate part of a can of peanuts last night and left the remainder on my table with a little note in German addressed to our German POW, telling him he could have it. I presume I misspelled most of the words, but tonight I found he took the nuts and left me a nice bouquet of flowers."

Weekends were free for the men. "I have had a great day—a trip to Oxford, magnificent with its many colleges and beautiful old buildings. I photographed one built in the eleventh century. Several of them were designed by Christopher Wren. We were ushered into the central library, where we were obliged to sign a large register and read an oath swearing that we would remove no books, deface none and never smoke in the building. I consider these rules worth adopting in America, where vandalism is not rare." Cottam bought some books on British flora there. And he and two other professors took a cab and drove around seeing all of the college campuses.

A trip to London later was "two days I shall never forget," and his visit to the Kew Botanical Gardens, "275 acres of glorious trees, and greenhouses as long as a Salt Lake City block was the greatest botanical thrill of my life. There are more than two hundred species of oak here!" Later, the men walked around seeing the great landmarks, such as Buckingham Palace, No. 10 Downing Street, Westminster Abbey, and Big Ben. In the afternoon a visit to an English vaudeville with skits, musical numbers, and considerable nudity "didn't excite me in the least, and I genuinely regretted the two hours spent there when I consider what I might have seen that was really worthwhile. Dean rather insisted on going. He is much like a good many other

Mormons I know who live rather strictly by the written and spoken formulas of virtue, but whose minds are likely to stray beyond the bounds of purity. . . . The next day we visited the old town of London. Here is the scene of great destruction by German bombs. Many churches were blasted and blown to bits, including the Church of St. Giles, which Milton attended and in which Cromwell was married. But nature is quick to act—in the basements of wrecked edifices, ferns and flowering plants are growing in profusion. In the weeks I have spent in Shrivenham, I had acquired a feeling of pity for the German POWs, but now when I see what these barbarians have done to London, this sort of feeling pretty well vanishes."

After three weeks of no letters from home, several finally arrived along with a surprise visit from Bill Fowler, Bea's husband. "I felt that I was a bit goofy—was seeing ghosts. He looked so damned good to me that I felt like kissing him." Bill had a week's leave and they spent it together, talking about home and family, going on bike rides, going to the country fair held at the manor house, and walking about the campus "picking up the loose threads of a year's separation." Cottam added, "I wish he were going to attend the school. It seems so good to have a member of the family here."

The university opened August 1 with a great ceremony, about 3600 boys (Cottam's term for soldiers) standing at attention. Classes began on August 2. Cottam's botany class had an enrollment of ten, his advanced ecology class four. He reported later that the boys were enthusiastic about their work. By midterm he said, "The boys are anxious to go home, but most are doing extremely good work. . . . I spent two hours with my 8:00 a.m. lab class in which I demonstrated the relationship between photosynthesis and respiration. Major Deavers brought his class down for the demonstration."

Cottam took his students on many field trips and showed them his slides. By the end of the term, one student told Cottam that he had learned more in his class than in the other two he was taking put together. Another boy said he had decided to major in botany and wanted to come to Utah and study with him. "Naturally, I am quite flattered," he wrote. "Almost every boy has spoken to me some very kind and flattering words."

Continuing threads through all of his letters to Effie were

thoughts of home, declarations of love, and a wish for more letters openly displaying affection. "If I had the speed of a radio wave, you would find me at your side very often. Be assured, though, my thoughts are with you always at evening, and I go to sleep thinking of you and home—our fine girls, George, and the lovely grandkids. How great is the memory of all of you."

From his letter of August 8: "I have admired other women and naturally have developed a close friendship with some of them. But of all the women I have ever met, I still would choose you if I had it to do over again for this life and for any other that we have been told awaits us. Eternity would never be long for me with you, but it would be a dreadfully dreary road without you. I am convinced that a congenial sex relation is absolutely essential to a happy, full married life." Cottam hated parties:

> I still can't quite understand why you need me at parties. You know I never like them, but you admit that you love to go when I am home to go with you. . . . This about proves my point that I am a mere object of display, a husband to parade around. I wish desperately to be with you, but a good bit of the homesickness vanishes when you remind me that when I get back, I shall be hounded again about these damned parties. When I see couples all dolled up for this sort of thing, I don't get a bit homesick, but if I see them taking a private stroll along some beautiful, peaceful nook in the woods, then I do get lonely.

Effie apparently expressed a desire to collaborate with him on some of his work in one of her letters. His reply was somewhat less than tactful: "I agree with you that now the family is raised, we would be brought closer together if you did take more interest in my work, and we could do much together. But you must know that technical information lies behind my botanical interest. Last year when you were so disgruntled in the field, I swore that I never would take you out again for such work. Do you really think that you could acquire a real technical interest in the subject?"

It isn't surprising that in a later letter he had to apologize for some things he had written that offended her. Whether it was the comment on working together that hurt her or something else wasn't clear: "I am terribly sorry and truly ashamed for the unhappiness I have caused you, and here again is reason for being entirely frank with each other. I know that I have dwelled considerably on this subject that has proved to be so distasteful to you, and I assure you that I should have written differently long ago had I been told off in such frank terms sooner. I feel thoroughly squelched. . . . Will you please do me one favor—burn all of these offending letters and try to forget them."

On the subject of frankness, he wrote a little later: "I spout off what I think, then forget it. You hold back your thoughts until the rising tide forces an explosion, and then one never knows if you got everything off your chest. You certainly have discovered a swell way to cure homesickness."

Still later he wrote: "I am sorry that you are not enjoying my letters. I always try to write good ones, but evidently I do not succeed. The next time you get a letter that you really like, I suggest you send it back as a model."

Writing to his daughter Fae in September, he said her letter was the most satisfactory note he ever received from anyone: "The descriptions of my babies were music to my lonely soul. Of course, I miss all of you. But there is nothing so sweet, so genuinely honest and frank as the love and companionship of children."

A letter laboriously written by George to his father prompted a kindly reply, praising George for having worked and earned some money and offering to give him a dollar for every dollar he earned from someone outside the family. He went on describing in great detail an owl with a broken wing found on an English estate he was visiting. He even drew a sketch of the owl with a face "like a full moon."

After news of the atomic bomb and prospects of the war with Japan ending soon, Walter wrote Effie: "Before this letter reaches you, my guess is that we shall have celebrated VJ day. The thought of it overwhelms me. This will mean that our boys will be home perhaps before I shall—and how wonderful it will be to go to bed sans the horror of these past years that the morrow might bring us dreadful and tragic news."

Rejoicing over the end of war on August 15 also brought speculation about the future of the school. But classes and activities continued as scheduled.

As part of an Army program for the professors to get acquainted with English home life and to be ambassadors of goodwill, Cottam spent a weekend in late August in the country at an English manor: "As you may guess from my letters," he told Effie, "I do not need this experience in order to become a genuine Anglophile. I am thoroughly in love with the people and with this country. If only I had your gift for conversation and friendliness, I would anticipate this experience with considerably more enthusiasm." Cottam's companion on the weekend visit was a Dr. Nielander. Their hostesses were Lady Grogan and Lady Noble. Cottam described Lady Grogan as owner of the manor, about 75, and crippled, "a tall queenly looking lady. She is gray and the proud possessor of a beautiful moustache and a fair beard. Yet she is very feminine in her appearance, and there is dignity and royalty in every word and act. Lady Grogan is a very dear friend of old Queen Mary and, during the London blitz, the old queen lived for some time at this manor house with Lady Grogan."

They were shown through the garden and 600-year-old house. "It would take that long to get all the art treasures and antiques of china and metal and wood that adorn it." They had tea and dinner, with Lady Grogan "wearing an evening gown that trailed yards behind her. I was scared stiff, knowing the state of my table manners." They talked until 11 p.m., "when we were in perfect Lady fashion ushered to bed. A short door opened into my bedroom, and above the door was a sign 'Watch your head'. One wonders if it was built for some royal dwarf."

He described autumn in England as having little color: "Things just get tired of living over here and without a sob, slip silently away. I guess people do that too. . . . It's sort of depressing, not cold enough to swear or do something about it, but never warm enough to be comfortable."

Trips to Stratford-on-Avon and to Scotland soon dispelled these gloomy thoughts. Of the Shakespeare plays, he saw *Much Ado About Nothing* and *Henry VIII*:

> I venture to think that in another three hundred years people will still be crowding their way to see the

> products of Shakespeare's pen, for he did indeed search men's souls. . . . How little man has changed in three hundred years! I presume that the most constant phenomena in a dynamic nature are the emotions of man—jealousy, rage, fear, sorrow, and joy are remarkably as Shakespeare recorded them. . . . Never have I been so thrilled in my life and never did I believe before that Shakespeare's blank verse could be rendered in such a fashion as to sound like ordinary conversation.

Some150 professors boarded buses for a five-day trip to Scotland the last week in September. Cottam, as usual, made the most of every hour. They arrived when the royal family were in residence at the palace for three days. While waiting in the crowd of thousands for the king, queen, and two princesses to drive by, Cottam struck up a conversation with a young Scottish woman who was answering the Americans' questions. After the royalty had passed, he said he found her trudging along by his side, pointing out interesting spots along the "Royal Mile." Soon his three companions disappeared and "I found myself alone with a very marvelous guide to whom I shall ever be greatly indebted for a wonderful visit to Edinburgh."

She walked up to the palace with him, where he got a few pictures. Then she told him about a songfest on the palace grounds that night that he shouldn't miss because there he would be able to get a good view of the royal family and learn something of their Scottish folk songs. She offered to meet him later and take him there, then said she hoped he wouldn't think she was unladylike. She was living with her widowed mother while her husband was with the forces in Belgium. "Well, what would you have done?" Cottam wrote. "She seemed so darned nice and so genuine that I accepted her offer."

Tens of thousands of people crowded the palace grounds, and the festivities equaled their promise. "My guide then walked me half way around Edinburgh, back up the 'Royal Mile,' past the university, clear around the castle. With my new shoes pinching my poor feet, I nearly died, yet this Scotch lass pulled me along and refused the street car. She was a most interesting and intelligent woman. It was nearly midnight before we reached her home." He declined an offer to come in for tea, but the next afternoon he had tea at her home with her and her mother and then took them to the movie *Thunderhead,* which had been filmed at Cedar Breaks in Utah. The following day he met her again, and they spent the day alternately riding the double-decker bus and walking all over Edinburgh once more.

"I enjoyed this girl very much," he wrote. "In her genuine friendliness she reminded me much of you. While she is not beautiful, she is rather pretty with large blue eyes and an extremely happy personality. She showed me the picture of her husband, to whom she is greatly devoted. . . . This was the first time since I left you that I had conversed with a woman for any length of time, and it seemed wonderful to have a woman's arm in mine! She says that she will send you some little gift from Scotland."

His thoughts turned again to religion when he wrote on October 17,

> Your account of church was interesting. I suppose if it were not for my constant evil influence, you would reform rather quickly and soon have your garments back on and your heart turned fully toward the Lord. You are, I think, by nature deeply religious. I think that I am also, but not at all in a sectarian way. I doubt if I shall ever be able to accept the dogma of a given creed. Yet there are those with a lot more brains than I have who have done so. I suppose time will tell eventually. I hope, though, that if you are in the habit of going to church, you will not discontinue when I return.

Attending a lecture on "Science and Religion"—a subject that often occupied Cottam's thoughts and on which he had done much reading—brought some criticism of the ideas of the speaker, a man who taught theology at Oxford. Cottam wrote:

> He made the surprising statement that the conflicts of the past were due mainly to the arrogance of the religionist and his refusal to accept the truths of sci-

> ence. Now he says the boot is on the other foot and that the conflict now is mainly due to the ungodliness of the scientist. What I think he failed most to point out was that scientists are themselves human beings, subject to the same emotions as nonscientific people and that religious concepts lie beyond the pale of science. He asserted that the methods of science do not necessarily contribute to morality, and in this I violently disagree. The methods of science require first of all the application of the simple virtue of honesty, and honesty, I claim, is one of the weakest threads in the fabric of present-day civilization.

Cottam's letter of October 18 disclosed the shocking news that the Army had canceled all teaching contracts as of September 23 and that all faculty would have to sign new ones to receive further pay or would be brought home. "If you would like to see an irate bunch of professors, you should be on the campus here just now," he wrote. "This order is just another step to get everyone so damned mad that no one will wish to stay beyond this term, which closes December 1."

Earlier in the month he had been invited to give a lecture on the flora of the Rocky Mountains to a large civic organization in Swindon, his first lecture off campus. "Word is getting around about the beauty of my slides," he said. Though he had happily anticipated the lecture, he thought he would have to cancel it when he learned that the auditorium had direct current, which his projector could not use. The physics department came to the rescue, however, fixing up a simple device to adapt the machine to work on direct current. Dean Anderson went along to change the slides while Cottam talked for an hour to an audience of 300 people. Walter found the group "the most appreciative I have ever talked to. When I would say something that they liked particularly, a large chorus of 'Hear! Hear!' would ring out. I tell you it was altogether a thrilling affair."

As he was leaving the hall, a man approached and said, "Well, one thing I have learned tonight is that there are fine people in Utah besides Mormons." "Both of us are Mormons," Cottam replied. "And that knocked him for a row."

In another letter Cottam mentioned the cigarettes he had

sent Effie before he knew it was illegal to do so. "It thrills me somehow to keep you just a wee bit wicked," he said. In his absence, Effie would go down to his den in the basement and have a cigarette. Her daughters didn't dream their mother smoked until Fae went downstairs one day and found out her secret.

Complaints about the erratic mail service continued to fill his letters, and he often scolded Effie for not writing often enough, for not commenting on things he had written about. Despondent when he received no mail—and he often noted how many letters his friends got while he got none—he became equally ecstatic when Effie's letters did arrive. After receiving three on October 24, he wrote: "I found myself trembling like a school boy when I began to open them." Still, as he read them, he complained that she didn't give details of a party she attended, that she didn't comment on his Scotland letter, and that she didn't report on the success or failure of pictures he had sent home to be developed.

At a meeting October 26, the general read a memorandum from headquarters stating that all contracts made with civilian instructors would be honored to the letter. "During next week we must sign for one of three options open to us: 1. To return home and cancel our contracts after the closing date of December 5. 2. To return home after the termination of seven months. 3. To sign for one year's work over here. If I hear nothing from you by the time I must sign, I suppose I shall decide to stay for the seven months—or until February 1." He said the entire faculty had suffered a drop in morale over the change in plans, and they felt that their services were no longer needed. He agreed and said, "I would be happy to come home after this term. I have seen enough of the scourges of war already, and I have little desire to be pushed around for a couple of months on the continent, but I suppose I can take it." He added, "It seems definite that I shan't be seeing you until the first of March and perhaps not until next summer."

One of Effie's letters ended with the hope that he would not cease loving her. He wrote:

> Of this you certainly need have no fears. From the hour I met you, I have loved you, and if there is a con-

> sciousness beyond the grave, I know that I shall go on loving you desperately throughout eternity. If I didn't love you so, I would not feel the anguish of spirit that I feel when I receive a letter of rebuke from you. (I am of course admitting that this rebuke was justified.) No, darling, you need have no fears. When I was a youth of sixteen, I regarded you as the perfect embodiment of all the virtues of womanhood. I called you then my 'Isolde.' Do you remember? After thirty-five years of loving you, I should have the maturity of judgment to know that these youthful impressions were founded on facts of character as true and fine as life itself. I have never loved another; I shall never love another; and I cannot even imagine an existence without you. Keep well, my sweetheart. We shall have a happy reunion. And if I have my way, I shall never be separated from you again.
>
> Yours eternally, W

In a later letter he commented on her remembrance of a deer hunt they had gone on together. "It is fine to hear that you really have pleasant recollections of our summers in the forests. At the time I felt that you had much to disturb you, and I really expected that last summer to be the end of your trips with me. Maybe you will actually wish to try going again. But don't you really think your life would have been much more to your nature if you had married a man in another profession, one who was more inclined to like social functions!"

On November 1, he wrote that his classes were doing well generally; only one boy was failing, and most of them were in the A and B range. "My ecology class is the best I have ever had. I have one boy here that I should like to take back to Utah. He has discovered two errors in my tree list. I think he is the best student I have seen in a long while."

In another letter he commented on her carelessly written letters and on several events that had postponed her letter writing—an opportunity to go to a show and Bea's getting sick.

> This letter made me mad, and you should have known it would. I have always resented your parties

> interfering with your household concerns and duties. A letter written thus on the run reminds me of an old woman knitting—something that can be done while you are listening to or seeing something more interesting, If you sluff me any more because of social reasons, I hope you will not bother to tell me about it. . . . I think it a fine thing for you to be so busily engaged in family duties and outside chores that you must still neglect me when I should, at six thousand miles away, require so little of your time. One thing is certain, I do not even wish to return home until I know that you are going to have a little more leisure than you apparently had last winter. I hope you won't be mad or hurt at this. My concern as well as yours should be for a more congenial life together. We are at an age, I think, when we should expect that family duties should permit a little more time together than we have experienced. This isn't a good letter, I know, but you touched on a sensitive issue with me in the letter that came today.

He castigated the army again, citing the "tyranny of rank" of a colonel getting a new man a room with heat while a gray-haired man on the faculty had been trying since arrival to get changed from his cold room. "This whole damned army is a disgraceful, undemocratic product of our democracy. Whenever or wherever I have a chance to strike at this organization, I shall do so. I would have been in the cold yet if our department head, Coulter, and division head, Whitaker, had not appealed to Colonel Harding."

The lack of letters for a few days prompted the comment: "The days are long and dreary when no word comes from you." Then he asked Effie if he should take out $10,000 term insurance for the continent trip, as some of the men were doing. "$10,000 would come in handy if I don't return." He added that he expected to go over on the continent when this term ended, but did not relish seeing the destruction and the suffering rampant over there.

Later he complained that the company in London that had developed his photos had scratched his Kodachrome films "something terrible. While I was right good and mad, I wrote the Kodak company and griped plenty about it." Three of the scratched slides were of the grave of Effie's 21-year-old nephew, Keith Hafen, who had died in an air raid over Europe.

Walter finally received three letters from Effie, "all good letters," but they failed to cheer him up much, as he had a bad headache and was worried about the future. "I think I have never been so low. With school over in three weeks and no knowledge whatever about my future activity, I had a rare fit of homesickness. I wrote a long letter last night but concluded this morning that it portrayed too much my ugly mood, so I have not sent it, thereby wasting an airmail envelope and an hour's time."

In a later letter he observed that she seemed to have a great regard for a certain couple that he too thought were fine people.

> However, as I look back on our lives, you have always adopted some couple like this as the embodiment of your ideals in marriage, and I warn you not to expect to mold me in Eden's cast. I think that this idealism of yours often backfires. I have my own personality and, as desirable as it might be to make me after the pattern of another, I fear you will never succeed. I expect to change about as much as I expect you to change. In fact, I want you about as I have always known you. The improvements I wish in you are in degree and not in kind. I am and always have been and perhaps always will be a person of strong emotions. I would like to run on an even keel as Eden does, but I think I never will. I hope, however, to be a much better husband, more considerate, more affectionate, if you want me to be, and more sociable. The latter, I fear, will be the hardest to do. I find myself over here prone to crawl into a shell even more than I did at home. I get no fun out of wild parties; I enjoy myself more alone with my thoughts of you and home. It is really a pitiable condition to be in, for small matters are prone to be projected into mountains. This virtue of your personality to enjoy yourself thoroughly in the presence of most people is one I would give anything

to possess.

In this letter, he also noted that the army had decided to reinstate their contracts. "The Brass Hats found that they had a wildcat by the tail, so reneged," he wrote. Rumors about what was going to happen abounded. "All these rumors are terribly hard on my nerves."

Later he wrote: "Can you imagine magnolias blooming in England on the tenth of November? This is a strange country." When the sun was out, he managed to get two shots of one bloom, one for Dr. Ward Evans, professor emeritus of chemistry at Northwestern University and head of the chemistry department at Shrivenham. "He is a great lover of flowers, and when he saw this magnolia, he went into ecstasy over it and told me he would pay any price for a picture of it. I enjoy him almost more than I enjoy any man over here. He has a great enthusiasm; he is a scholar; he is friendly and very helpful to the students and brutally frank with everybody. He seems to have taken a liking to me too and keeps inviting me over to his room."

He told Effie he had received his October pay and intended to send her a check for $100, which he wanted her to use for Christmas and some nice clothes. "When I come home, I want you to be dolled up to the point of perfection that any of your close friends exhibit. You have gone too many of your years without sufficient and appropriate clothes, and now that we are beginning to have a little more cash for ourselves, let's use it. You needn't worry we shall. I have a lot of thrilling trips planned for the future, and some of them I want to have alone with you."

After spending the morning of November 11, a Sunday, seeing Dean off, Cottam found himself alone with his thoughts of longing to be an artist. "In a way it's hell to have been born with something of the soul of an artist, but shorn of the necessary skill to express adequately my feelings, either through the medium of pen or of brush. Because of public opinion, I do not try to give expression to these moods through the medium of the camera. I could easily be misunderstood."

What prompted this wish was his being out with his camera and seeing the "marvelous trees, their delicate, pastel leaves now almost gone and the indescribable beauty of their limbs. They remind me now of beautiful girls almost completely disrobed. As I photographed them today, I wished that I could have a few girl models underneath the trees, dancing in the checkered shade with just their delicate silk panties on—to match the mood of the trees."

But he had no need of pen or brush to draw a word picture of his surroundings.

> My new home faces a dense woodland, and my room is in front, not fifty feet from the edge of what appears to be and is the forest primeval. Darkness is fast obscuring the individual trees, and the sounds of night are beginning to filter through my window. Crows are cawing loudly to each other, and pairs of them continue to flap their wings violently through the dusk as if they are afraid of the approaching night. The nightingale is beginning to flood the mist with his rapturous, clear tones that make each bird sound like a choir. The owl, too, must punctuate these mysterious sounds of the night with his forlorn 'Hoo! Hoo!' Each night as I close my eyes in sleep, the forest sings out of the darkness, and as sure as the morning begins to stand 'tiptoe' above the forest, a cock pheasant yells his rasping call just outside my window. If I had my shotgun here, we could have pheasant for breakfast almost every morning. These are the sounds and moods of solitude in which I write most of my letters to you. Can you wonder then that they are emotional, sometimes deep in despair, sometimes lofty and aesthetic, but always genuinely lonely for the companionship that you alone can give.

Commenting on the actions of some men to seek female companionship while away from their wives, he wrote,

> I think that if I had not been so conditioned against such behavior in my youth, I would not let my fires die out completely over here. It is silly biologically to do so, and you can find any number of books that

> warn of the physiological dangers of enforced continence. . . . The regrettable thing, it seems to me, is rather that our evolved morality is content to sacrifice the physical man for a doubtful spiritual one. I am persuaded that many homes are needlessly wrecked by an outmoded and biologically unwarranted code of morality. And I am not preaching the doctrine of promiscuity either. It is certainly interesting how these old profs are coming out into the open with their paramours.

The arrival of three letters raised his spirits to the level of telling her to "shake a leg and have a hell of a good time."

> I can't understand why you do not wish to accept these invitations to go out to such functions as the Utah Academy. In fact, I think that in my absence it would have been proper for you to have represented me there. . . . I think your attitude about going out where men are present is positively silly and very much unlike you. What has happened to you since I left? Surely the nonsense I wrote in my letters long ago has not made you a man-hater! This new attitude displeases me very much, and I certainly am far from being complimented over it. I can tell you this much, I am so damned hungry for a woman's companionship that it would be dangerous for me to meet someone that I like very much. You, on the other hand, don't care to associate with any man. I am not sure that you can interpret this behavior as evidence of an abiding and burning love for me. It might mean that you are so damned fed up with me that no man looks good to you.

Delighted to learn that Grant was back on American soil, he told Effie not to expect too much of Grant's time. "You have spent your life worrying about and slaving for your kids, and I have often complained about it," he wrote. "I have no doubt that he will be genuinely happy to see you, but mark my words, you will see very little of him. Diana will attend to that, and I hope that you will not grieve a lot about it."

On a trip to London, Cottam and a companion, Dr. Rudolph Kempton of Vassar, went out one night "to do a bit of research to determine what effect the winter climate had on London prostitutes," as Kempton put it. Cottam wrote that they walked around Piccadilly Circus and up some side streets and saw "swarms of these women." None approached Cottam, but a couple did Kempton. The next night, however, when Cottam went alone to see a play, "four girls offered to take me home with them, and I was not out looking for them either." He described it as "a disgusting experience" and said that they would have to pay him to go out with them. "I cannot imagine the act of love shorn of affection, so I suppose I shall keep my virginity until I see you."

He divided his time one afternoon between the National Museum of Art and the Royal Academy of Art. "What a feast," he wrote. "I was very much impressed by how many treasures are there." Another day he spent visiting the town where his Grandmother Jarvis had lived as a girl. He found the old church she had mentioned in her autobiography and also a plaque that had impressed her as a child and which depicted a fish swallowing a ring. He photographed the plaque and also the old church, which had been wrecked by the bombing.

The next day he arose early and took a subway to Liverpool station on the east side of London and entrained for Harlow, a little town of 2,500 some 25 miles northeast of London. "Around the town are lovely fields and rolling hills." Grandpa Jarvis' mother died in Harlow in 1875. "She was a midwife and the obituary notice told of her useful life. I heard of three families with the Jarvis name, but none were relatives. One old lady, though, remembered my great-grandmother."

At this time he wondered what his prospects at the university would be when he returned, as well as what his remaining months with the army would involve. "I shall be happy if I find that my assignments are useful and not like sublime WPA jobs. I know that I shall see and learn much. All I want from you now are cheerful letters and the feeling that you are happy as I am over my decision."

Commenting on "a wonderful letter" he had received from his son Dick, he wrote: "He described the place well and as usual injected his political philosophy. He is not happy over his position or about his immediate superior officers. Dick is a proud youngster. He will go places yet, I have not the slightest doubt, and we shall see to it that he does not lack the opportunity."

He had been feasting on some pine nuts Effie had sent him, but decided to save some. "I am taking away so much treasure from England that I simply must leave something, and I have a hunch that these nuts would thrive on the Chalk Downs. I am therefore going to write Kew Gardens tomorrow to offer them the nuts if they will experiment with their culture. You can imagine that this is a real sacrifice, for you know how I love to eat them. This act should be evidence enough that I still possess some sense of generosity."

On Thursday, November 22, he slept late; went for a vigorous bike ride; returned for a good Thanksgiving dinner, which included a package of candy-coated chocolates and a fine cigar; went to the 2:00 p.m. show; then went for a walk in the foggy late afternoon and enjoyed the fat cigar. He recalled how he used to smoke cigars as he and Effie returned home from an Ogden Extension Division class he taught. "I so rarely smoke cigars that they invariably recall for me hours with you—and they always make me feel a bit wicked."

Since he hadn't heard whether Grant and Charlie had returned home, he complained again about the slow and irregular mail service. He wrote that he presumed that when Charlie returned, he and Fae would soon be leaving on a planned trip "and you will be tied down rather closely with the children. I hope Fae realizes the many favors due you daily and especially for this proposed trip. When it comes your turn to take a vacation, I can imagine that there will be no one available to care for George and that you will not feel free to leave him. He will have to be on his own sometime, and I think that you had better begin to train him for these eventualities."

On November 25 he reported that his flu shot had apparently caused a light case of the flu, but he called it good insurance if and when he finally landed on the continent:

> I wish I could give you a change of address, but I cannot. No one has the least idea when we will leave here or where we will go. I doubt if the army has any

clear plans except that the post here must be vacated by January 1. One speculation is that we will be sent to London or Southampton for a couple of weeks. I would like that because there are many more things to see there. . . .

This uncertainty used to bother me a lot, as my letters no doubt reflected, but now I have become amazingly serene about the future, and I feel content to be tossed about like a cork on a troubled sea and just drift. I refuse to get excited about rumors any more, and I shall bide my time until that happy day for my return rolls around.

If he should return early in February, he fancied a leisurely trip to Dixie:

I can think of nothing that would please me more than to hike with you in the Dixie sunshine over the landscape of our youth. This would be a vacation, to me at least, entirely ideal. Do you recall the day when we hiked up the creek as far as the Indian farm? As I sort out the treasured memory shots of our yesterdays, this afternoon stands out as one of the most satisfactory experiences of our courtship period. I recall now how passionately I loved you and what a temptation it was to indulge in familiarities that we considered then most wicked. But thanks to you, we resisted these natural impulses of the flesh, and I can't recall if we stole even a kiss that glorious afternoon. More than thirty years have sneaked by since then, and I suppose if we were to repeat that jaunt, we should be conscious most of aching joints and tired muscles. But it is something to know now after all these years that our affections that burned then with the passion of youth glow still, even if they have mellowed with age. Memory and imagination are wonderful qualities of the mind. I recall these passionate hours with you with a vividness and satisfaction that seems to grow stronger with the years, and now when we are so far removed from each other, I can imagine nothing so thrilling as an attempt to repeat them. I think of you now it seems still with the passion of youth—yet with vastly broadened horizons. It is wonderful to contemplate our association of the future, dedicated to a greater leisure and to an understanding of each other that the obligations of a family have so long denied us. I have no great ambitions, I suppose, but any future will be entirely satisfactory if we can live in such a fashion that we genuinely regret the passing of a day. I am convinced that more intensified living can alone compensate for the loneliness of these months of separation.

Yours with great love.

After meeting with University President Cowles, Effie sent Walter a telegram saying his salary was assured for the spring quarter. Walter wrote: "I certainly will be glad to get that letter telling of your visit with Cowles. It's a pity that I have been obliged to wait so long for every word regarding my future over here."

"The rumor today is that we will be in Paris by December 15. I wish I could tell you where to write me there."

Chapter 7

Letters from Germany

Christmas Eve found Cottam not only in Germany, but in a hospital in Frankfurt suffering from aches, fever, and bronchitis brought on by the rigors of the trip by bus, boat, train, and truck from England to France to Germany. He told of the ordeal in his letters to Effie.

"The trip down to Southampton was without incident, but it was with mixed emotions that I found myself on my way out of England. I was happy to be on my last lap home, but sad to leave the peaceful countryside to which I had become so greatly attached." It rained all the way to the camp, and the men had to wait for an hour until they were issued three blankets.

> We took to our crude huts with their cruder beds of straw-filled sacks tied up like Bull Durham tobacco sacks and only about half long enough. I had dressed in my best, with the newly pressed short coat, but before I retired, it was soaked. My shoes were covered with mud as were also my pants. We were informed that we must be up ready for breakfast at 3:30 a.m. A Catholic priest who slept next to me made the hut vibrate with his snoring, and I doubt if I slept fifteen

> minutes before we were ordered up. The whole camp was a mess, muck knee-deep, and the loose pavement cement blocks giving enough under each step to squirt a good stream of water first up one pant leg and then the other.

After breakfast, they stood in line for two hours in the pouring rain and chill waiting to board buses. "Some GI wag yelled out, 'Better get these old men out of this hot sun,' which livened up the spirits of the crowd, who commenced to sing Christmas carols until the buses arrived." At the dock they waited in line another hour to board the cold, drafty boat, only to be turned back by stormy weather, high winds and waves too high for a safe crossing. They boarded the same boat the next day and had a pleasant crossing, entering the harbor of Le Havre about sunset. Here they boarded huge open-air trucks and waited another hour before leaving for an ancient French fort, where they were billeted.

> Our bays have domed ceilings, and there are fifty of us in each bay. We were issued five blankets, and our beds are much better than at Southampton. I slept well last night, but of course was awakened several times by men who had to go out in the night for personal reasons, most of them muttering unholy phrases and stumbling. . . . And with fifty men in one room there are many diverse noises that float over the unventilated air. I was sort of happy that I had temporarily lost the sense of smell. There were the usual snorings that sounded like a frog pond with all the frogs a little out of par so far as harmony was concerned. And the farts were as diverse as the snoring and definitely more sonorous. In fact, one of the birds with an especially tight sphincter frequently traversed the aisle up and down in a most amazing manner. Others without the knack of this guy were content with a boring monotone. You can guess that the rations for the day had been mostly beans.

They were told that they would be leaving at 11:00 p.m.

but would not be stopping long in Paris. "This night riding in cold conveyances is tough on old men, but I am glad for the experience. If I survive it, it will be fun to look back on."

During the afternoon, Cottam went downtown and found Le Havre, once a town of 175,000, now a junk heap. "The Yank airmen certainly made a complete job of destruction there as in all the towns I have seen so far in Germany," he wrote from his hospital bed in Frankfurt.

In Le Havre the men waited in the usual line for an hour and a half before boarding their special train to Paris that night. "Just why special trains have to be run in the night is a mystery we poor pedagogues will never understand." He didn't have enough clothing to keep warm in the unheated train and chilled and shivered until they reached Paris at daybreak. They were bused to another station, where they were to leave for Frankfurt at 11:30 a.m. on another train. He and three fellow professors went into town for a few hours, returning at the appointed hour, "only to discover that the Brass Hats had figured out that by waiting until evening, they could get a special with sleepers for them."

> So, of course, we stayed over and were supposed to leave at 4:30 p.m. By this time, since I had developed a couple of degrees of fever, the boys took me over to the Red Cross, which furnished me a bed for the afternoon. I am sold on this organization and shall support it in the future even more than I have the past few years. . . . Well, at 4:30 p.m. we lined up as usual and were still in line at 7:00 p.m., and I felt so damned sick I wanted to die. I certainly dreaded the night again on a cold train, but we hadn't gone far before this fear was entirely dissipated. In fact, we were parboiled all the way to Frankfurt. There seemed to be no possible way to govern the temperature. We took off our coats and opened the windows, which action, of course, produced cross currents of cold air that did no one any good.

They arrived in Frankfurt at 8:30 a.m. Because of all the senseless destruction everywhere, the entire trip had been a depressing sight. Trucks took them to headquarters, where Walter at 1:30 p.m. finally decided to go to the dispensary. "I was soon loaded into a Red Cross wagon, and here I am spending my Christmas Eve and possibly the next few days in the hospital. Don't be alarmed. I would not have had to come if the damned army had provided billets for us. I felt, however, that there was no sense being a pedagogical martyr, so I came to get a little rest and attention. Two of the boys who had come up to see me said they looked for me first in the psychopathic ward. They had heard me cussing these senseless Brass Hats yesterday."

Cottam had a good night's rest and his temperature was nearly normal, but because he had a touch of bronchitis, the doctor ordered him to stay in the hospital another day or so. He found the hospital, which had been built for the Luftwaffe, wonderful. A group of German children even sang yuletide carols for them, one song in English.

"Naturally I shall be following you closely tonight and tomorrow in the activities of Christmas. Who would ever have dreamed a year ago that we would be celebrating this Christmas so far apart and under such variable circumstances. I shall take comfort in the long, continuous line of happy Christmases I have known with you."

For Christmas Walter had arranged to have a local florist deliver to Effie a bouquet of seven red roses with this message:

> Merry Christmas, Effie, Darling,
>
> My love comes to you this Christmas day, 1945, in the form, odor and color of red roses. If Santa has filled his order well, they will number seven to symbolize our family. The most beautiful of the lot, the one with petals opened, flawless in form, fragrance and features is you. The other opened bloom, perhaps not so perfect, but reflecting somewhat the beauty of the rest is I. The five buds are the kids, the finest kids parents ever had.
>
> I hope these flowers will symbolize my affection, for roses are to me the queens of Nature's floral creation. Their color breathes warmth and passion. Their odor is seductively divine. Their form and texture

> always command the eye even in age. Such is my love for you, born when our life was in the bud, nurtured through 30 years of wedded success and failure and tempered with five good children.
>
> Though a quarter of the globe separates us this hour, I am with you in spirit, enjoying the merriment of children's voices, the unwrapping of packages, the odor of roasting turkey, and the comradeship of a family in love.
>
> Walter

From his hospital bed on December 27 he described his Christmas day. "There was much going on, the ward full of patients and visitors. The Red Cross women (bless them) determined not to let us get homesick. One Red Cross lady had invited some of the patients to a dance the previous night. I asked her what about pants, and she remarked very casually, 'Think nothing of it; no one will be in pants.' I assume that I really missed a show by not going, but even this semi-nudist affair did not draw me away from my bed." He continued:

> Christmas really passed quite pleasantly. Santa Claus came early in the morning with a Red Cross package for each of us. It is surprising how much a small thing like that can do to lift the morale. In the package were cards, a tiny book of short stories, a small address book, a package of gum, two packages of candy, two packs of cigarettes, a pocket comb, and a tobacco pouch. So you see I was quite well provided for. And the dinner was wonderful. . . . I read the short stories and also a tale by H. G. Wells. Most of the day I just lay here and let the Christmas memories of my yesteryears chase each other through my mind in no seeming order. And of course I followed you hourly throughout the festivities, from the late afternoon shopping to the midnight ritual of arranging the presents, to your bed and the usual 6:00 a.m. Christmas arising. I was sure that George would not let you sleep longer than that. Then at about 9:00 a.m. (5:00 p.m. here) I supposed that Joe Neff brought the family my gift of

flowers. I hope that he did a good job and that you were both surprised and pleased with the gift. It was something new for me, but in my absence, I thought it would be most appropriate.

When Cottam was released from the hospital that afternoon, no vehicle was available to take him to his billet. He boarded a bus and told the driver where he wanted to get off, but the driver let him out a mile from his destination. He wandered around for a while, then asked directions of four German boys, who volunteered to show him the way. "They carried my handbag of slides etc, for which I was very grateful. Luckily, I had four bars of candy to give the youngsters, and they seemed happy."

His friends had taken his baggage to his room, made his bed, and were waiting for him. His letter written to Effie that evening said, "I have just returned from dinner. The casino where we eat is a swell affair—with a fine ten-piece orchestra of Germans to play classical music while we dine. The hall is about as large as the Hotel Utah dining room, where we used to go. Nice Polish girls wait on the tables. These girls are all young—twenty-five or under—and are said to be some of the workers the Germans brought in. "

Cottam complained that it had been raining the past twenty-four hours with no more than an hour's sunshine since he had arrived. "Not even knowing where the sun is has confused my sense of directions, and I feel very uncomfortable. . . . I wish I could have your calmness of spirit in this respect. But my keen sense of direction does stand me in hand in the mountains, at least."

He described the terrible conditions in Frankfurt. "Nothing I have seen yet compares with the city in utter destruction of the homes. You will see block after block of ruined structures, with parts of walls standing and a glimmer of light showing beneath the rubble. There are families still living in the basements like rats. The whole mess makes me sick. . . . Yet the boys who fought their way here whom I have talked to, and there were several in my room, including a Catholic priest, have neither compassion nor sympathy for these people. Man's inhumanity to man is about the most certain characteristic of the human race in general."

On the morning of December 30, writing from his bed because his little room had no heat, he described a trip to Heidelberg, the oldest university town in Germany. With 20 other men from the camp, he visited the ancient Heidelberg castle and toured the university campus and the town. "The most pleasant experience came to me when two sweet little German girls, Ruth, six, and Henneka, four, sidled up to me and mutely inquired for confection. I had slipped a package of gum into my pocket, and I had also a bar of candy. These I divided with the little girls, and each took my arm for most of the tour of the castle. They chatted in German all the way."

The group returned at 6:30 p.m. to dinner at their clubhouse. "The food is excellently prepared. Breakfast costs twenty-five cents, lunch thirty-five cents and supper forty cents. We eat to wonderful classical music and are served by nice-looking girls. Our meals here are easily equal to $1.50 meals at the Hotel Utah. I should get fat."

He bemoaned the lack of sunshine and said that if it were decent weather, he would photograph "some of the interesting and horrible features of Frankfurt."

"It will probably be late in the week before I am assigned definite duty. There seems to be no plan as yet, and I am convinced that the army finds us a problem. The fears I had in Shrivenham about useful work here were justified."

In another letter that evening, he told of walking through the town of Hoechst, a suburb of Frankfurt, where they were billeted. Again he took candy along to give the children. "I am partial to the little girls," he wrote. "Two I saw carrying their dolls, and one cute little thing was crying, and I heard her say in German that she was cold. This candy and a stick of gum cheered her a lot. Children seem to be the only happy people in Germany. The grownups along the street meet one variously—most seem to have a rather vacant stare and seem not to see an American at all. Others greet me with 'Guten Morgen,' and I find that all of them would speak if spoken to first."

He went back to camp for lunch, did some washing, and wrote letters to Bill and Dick, then set out for town again with more candy. "I have been saving my rations for weeks with this in mind," he said. He offered one little tot a candy bar, but his mother, several yards behind him, came up and said, "Nein, nein, danke," and Cottam took the candy back. A German who saw the incident asked if he understood German. When Cottam said a little, "the fellow proceeded to talk to me as though I were an old hand. I understood only a little of what he said, but enough to figure out that the woman was a Nazi of high rank and that it certainly wasn't 'schön' for her to act the way she did." The fellow told Walter how many battles he had fought in and how Germany's sad plight was due to these Nazis. He expressed the hope that Germany could now become a real democracy like America. "I asked if he had children, and when he answered, 'Ja, Ja,' I gave him the bar, and he was grateful for it. So you see all kinds of people here—but the kids really eat my heart out. I think I would give away my pants if I stayed around here long."

Complaining of the inactivity, he wrote, "It has been nearly a month now that I have done nothing, and you can well imagine that this sort of life is not meant for me. I find the other men feeling the same way . Many of them have changed their minds about staying. The waste of manpower at this headquarters is nothing short of wicked. It's not only our group but hundreds of others in various organizations who are doing nothing while the people back home are footing the bill."

He said that he planned to ask to be sent home by the first of February. "This should land me home by February 15. We shall then have a couple of weeks to play before I start my school work at the U. I am, of course, glad to see Germany, but it is a highly immoral way to see it, at government expense with no justification. The office here was totally unprepared for us, yet that damned fool of a colonel who brought us over did not let us see Paris, and we traveled clear across France in the dark. If you can beat this for utter stupidity, I would like to hear it. This army of ours, without question, is the most stupid, wasteful, inefficient organization in the government."

He planned to send her a telegram to wish her Happy New Year and to let her know that he was well before she received the letters telling of his illness. "It is almost six months since I left you, and long enough to convince me that the major part of my existence is bound up in my life with you. I think of you during every conscious moment when I am not engaged in work."

He described the hike that he and Sig Olson had made along the Main River all the way to Frankfurt, seven miles from their camp. He had taken scenic shots of the river and of the destruction in Frankfurt. "It simply passes the imagination—block after block of magnificent municipal structures and lovely hotels in complete ruin, with twenty feet or more of debris piled on the ground floor where many thousands of people are said still to be buried. The railroad station there used to be one of the finest in Europe. The walls are still standing, but not a glass remains in the windows. Piles of rubble twenty to thirty feet high line the streets for blocks."

On their hike back, they came to an army camp about a mile out of Frankfurt, where they stopped and asked for food. Dinner had been served, but the sergeant took them to the officers' private mess and cooked them some spam and eggs.

> The real treat, though, was a lovely Russian girl who served us. It was worth fourteen miles of hiking to see this beautiful creature, and I am tempted to do it again. She is dark with strong facial features, snappy eyes, white teeth, and a smile that will linger long in memory. It is a compliment to me that I should even have noticed her face, for that lovely head adorned a body of delicate grace that seemed almost ethereal. She appeared to be an unworldly creation, a wild thing of some fabled forest. I began to comment to Sig about the grace of our waitress when she remarked, "Better be careful, for I understand every word you say, though I don't speak English well." I am convinced that if some Hollywood shark should see her, she would soon land in America, where she very much wants to go. She was captured by the Germans early in the Russian campaign and imported to Germany, where she spent two years in a concentration camp and two in a labor camp. She refused to return to Russia and says there is little difference between Bolsheviks and Nazis. Her parents were killed, and she has no other relatives. She appears to be about twenty years old.

Later in the letter he wrote, "Let us hope that the New Year is the dawn of a happier world in general. The world undoubtedly stands at a crossroads. Either we as nations learn to live in peace or take the other road to complete annihilation. The destruction wrought here is but a hint of the destructive power of nuclear energy. It is time for New Year's resolutions among nations!"

He said he hesitated to make resolutions himself "because my erring flesh rarely keeps them. But I have missed you so much these past six months that I think you shall never again hear an unkind word from me." He added that it had been a whole month since he had heard from her. But because of the move from Shrivenham to Germany and his not knowing where to have her send letters, he had not expected any and did not blame her.

Another all-day hike took him and Sig to the little alpine village of Königstein, where they had dinner at the 87th Hospital Headquarters, located in a former millionaire's lodge. They explored a castle built in 1100 and hiked through a heavily wooded forest on the hills by the castle. "I certainly dragged some tired legs home, but I am confident that the outdoor exercise is what I need to tone up my body."

On January 2 the professors met with representatives of the army command to discuss the type of lectures that might appeal to the soldiers. Cottam's friend Sig Olson, who was quite a famous guide and sportsman as well as dean of a college in northern Wisconsin, suggested that he and Cottam present a program together on "America Out of Doors." Sig would speak first on hunting, fishing, natural history, followed by Cottam showing his slides of the deserts and mountains of the West. Cottam liked the idea. "If we can make this thing click, we should have a very good time together," he wrote. "This month's idleness has just about got me down. . . . I do miss you so much. I would be happy forever with you alone. The more people I meet, the more really fine friends I make, the more I am convinced that you possess fewer faults and more virtues than any other human being. Believe me, whatever success or failure I meet, it is with you I wish to share it."

On January 5, Cottam gave a lecture on his own to a group of thirty patients in the Red Cross room at the 97th Hospital. "Despite the poor conditions under which I was forced to operate, the boys and a few girls seemed to enjoy it very much. The Red Cross woman had explained to me beforehand that these patients were very restless, that half of them would probably walk out on me and that I should not notice if they did. Not one left the room, and I think I could have held them even longer."

He noted that the previous day he had gone with a group to Frankfurt to listen to a panel discussion by four of the professors on "Can Germany Be Controlled." The audience was made up of about 300 paratroopers. In an open discussion after the formal presentation, one soldier advocated the extermination of the entire German population and another suggested more punishment. "These kids, I suppose, are so used to the sight of destruction of the German cities that they seem not to regard it as punishment."

Cottam said that the authorities had decided that he, Kempton, and Olson should make up a panel on sex education and that he was to be the chairman. "I don't relish either the position or the subject," he said. "Kempton is a physiologist and gave some very good lectures on the subject at Shrivenham. It appears that early next week we will be sent out from here for a week's lecture tour, then return for a few days. Before I leave for the trip, I expect to file my request to leave for home by February 1 and certainly not later than February 15."

His next letter described a trip to Wiesbaden, a place once of great beauty and fabulous wealth, now lying in ruins. "The British did this job, and there are two current rumors as to why they did it. The city had no military value, and the one theory is that the R.A.F. bombed it by mistake, but another is that the raid was a reprisal for the bombing of Bath, England. Whatever the explanation, the sad fact remains that they made a very thorough job of their mission. It is almost incredible that such destruction could be wrought in a single half hour of a single night. You can imagine the general attitude of the people if you think of Salt Lake City ruined and finally occupied by Japanese and Germans, the local people furnishing the waiters and musicians, and the townspeople going hungry."

He saw hundreds of children skating on ponds at many city parks, "destruction rampant on every side. The hope of Germany certainly rests with these kids, and their future depends on the type of education they receive. It is my opinion that these occupation years can be only negative, a time when peace can be forced until this generation of children take over. I do not believe that we should attempt an Americanization of Germany. I don't believe such an attempt would work. The future is a gamble. If the destruction here can serve as an object lesson of the results of aggression, good should come of it. If, on the other hand, these kids grow up in a spirit of hatred and revenge, only continual occupation can prevent another world tragedy."

He described a beautiful Russian church in Wiesbaden that had a mural with the All Seeing Eye in the center. "I had not seen that symbol since I was a child in St. George." But the loveliest church he saw in Germany, also in Wiesbaden, "is of red brick and bears a striking resemblance to the Salt Lake Temple. I'll bet that the motif of our 'peculiar' architecture came from here."

Cottam and Sig Olson gave their "Outdoors" lecture on January 7 at the Palm Garden Red Cross uptown in Frankfurt in a largely undamaged building formerly owned by a baron. But the building was headquarters for the entire Information and Education program, "and the GIs simply have more entertainment than they need." Only 20 people showed up at the lecture. "Sig was so mad that he refused to start the meeting, so I introduced myself and showed my slides. The crowd was so enthusiastic that Sig gave his speech at the close."

Cottam said that another lecture he was to give on his own later in the week and the trip of the panel discussion group would help him decide whether to stay on for another month.

> If I find my services no more needed out in the sticks than they are here, I shall ask to be sent home as soon as possible. It's bad enough to be drawing pay for doing nothing, but worse to be wasting time. Most of the men have done absolutely nothing for more than a month now, and they all feel pretty low about the situation. I think the entire I. and E. program should be discontinued. It's the most flagrant misuse of tax money and the most wicked waste of manpower I have ever seen anywhere. And most officers in the army here are doing no more than we are. Don't think that I am

> homesick and building up excuses. Actually, I am having a very good time. I am well and seeing much. It's just that I have a conscience. If I find that there is need for my services out in the command areas, I shall be happy to stay as long as possible and still be at the U for Spring Quarter.

In a later letter, Cottam described another trip to Wiesbaden with Kempton, Johnson, and Olson where Olson "put up a tall tale to the motor pool officials, who furnished us with a command car and German driver for a trip along the Rhine river to the Grand Canyon of the Rhine, where the famous Lorelei is located."

> In the deep canyon, whose walls tower perhaps a thousand feet above the river, our German driver turned off on a steep mountain road that led directly on top of the Lorelei. There the terrain is flat, and nice buildings adorn the spot. After enjoying the view for about half an hour, we visited the building used as a guest house and occupied by a German family. They were very gracious, and the good-looking Frau soon brought us barley coffee. She was a talented musician, a beautiful singer. She played the piano and we all gathered around and sang German songs. She gave us each a glass of hot wine before we left. . . . The Germans refused money, but we left them fifteen marks and a few candy bars and cigarettes, for which they were thankful. They seemed to enjoy us as much as we did them, and I couldn't help reflect how generally friendly mankind is if only the politicians would pursue peace.

A blizzard was raging when they went outside, making the 30-mile ride back to Wiesbaden in the open car biting cold. But the storm abated before they arrived home about 7:00 p.m. Cottam reported the day the most satisfying he had spent on the continent. "Every day it seems that I have become a little more proficient as a first-class racketeer. I have seen much here and enjoyed the experience, but it has really been hard on my conscience. Ten thousand others are doing no more here than I am, but still I cannot justify the waste."

When the panel on sex education finally performed before an audience of 400 men from the 405th Airborne regiment, Cottam served as its critic. "The danger of a subject like this, before men whose sexual standards of morality are a bit warped, lies in the tendency to flippancy, and this is my greatest criticism," he wrote.

Cottam remarked on the great number of Poles in Germany who refused to be repatriated because of the Russians occupying their homeland. "Yet the Poles here have an understandable hatred for the Germans too." Paratroopers at the lecture told the professors that a few nights earlier some Poles broke into German homes in Frankfurt and killed every soul. The women and children had been shot through their heads and the men had their skulls battered in. "The soldiers reported the atrocity as though it were nothing unusual, and the Stars and Stripes today has an article claiming that such atrocities are common throughout Germany. The hatred is universal and widespread. These slave laborers brought into Germany by the Nazis a few years ago are indeed proving to be a Frankenstein that threatens the peace of mind and the physical security of their former conquerors. Such are the products of war. Rather than curing an evil, war engenders a hate that is almost certain to plant the seeds for a new and better war."

On January 20, he told Effie of a second trip to Königstein with Kempton and Olson to visit the old castle there. They encountered some German young people who were kidding and laughing.

> How very like a similar age group of youngsters at home they were. The basic emotions of mankind are the same. If these kids had the environment that ours have, they would doubtlessly mature into just as good citizens. I am convinced that mankind fights his fellow not because of basic differences, but because of differences in education and experience. Civilization, I am sure, is a thin, artificial veneer that covers man the animal in a social way. Crack this veneer, and the savagery of mankind expresses itself. Break it, and a whole peo-

> ple who produced the divine art of Wagner, Schiller, Göethe and Strauss stoop to the savagery of Buchenwald and Dachau. Remove this veneer, and peaceful boys like our Grant soon take delight in shooting the Japanese. In fact, our boys over here, many of them, commit atrocities equal to those of the Germans.
>
> A captain of the air troops the other night recounted how his group were instructed to take no prisoners. When two German youths came out of their foxhole with their hands above their heads to surrender, they were promptly seized by our boys, who straightaway cut their throats. He also told how an old German man and his wife came bicycling down a road after the battle was over. One of our boys shot the old man through the head and laughed boisterously at the manner in which he fell from his bike.
>
> I believe that as human beings we are basically no different from these people and that it is conceivable that a majority of Americans could one day vote into power a government that would lead us into a similar calamity. The trouble with the Nazi gang was that they edged their way into power, and when they had it firmly in their grasp, they went mad, and there was little the people could do about it. It took outside help to free them as well as to protect us. I suppose that by nature I am a softhearted sentimentalist.

After visiting Königstein, Cottam and his friends hiked through a forest, coming to a beautiful estate where they conversed with a German couple who owned the property. A large mansion, once their home, which they called "the castle," had been taken over by the American army. The couple lived in a small outbuilding. The officers in the castle were still asleep, but a maid there prepared food for the unexpected visitors. Inside they found elegant tapestries hung on the walls, a great array of fine paintings, the entire building projecting an atmosphere of great wealth.

"This was another fine day," Cottam wrote. "The walk through the woods back home was very pleasant, but long. We came to a crossroad where a great number of German guns and especially vehicles of various sorts lay in ruins. One sees sights like this everywhere. A convoy was no doubt attacked here, and the whole outfit destroyed. Bullet holes made the charred frames look like sieves."

The hikers commented that they themselves would be perfect targets for the supposed underground youth organizations. "Doubtlessly we could be disposed of without a trace. But I rarely feel that there is anything to fear over here, and I have no evidence of sniping, although we hear occasionally of cases."

Walter was elated when six letters from Effie arrived on January 21, along with a photograph he had requested earlier. "You have no idea what an uplift these letters have given me. I have worried about you. I thought perhaps you were more ill than you had reported to me. I have had nightmares. Now I am buoyant!"

Of the photograph, he said, "It's the loveliest sight I have had since I left you. I can hardly take my eyes off it, and I shall carry it to bed with me." But photographer that he was, he couldn't resist critiquing a little. "The picture is really nice, but if you had given just a slight relaxation of the mouth so that the corners turned up instead of down, it would have been excellent."

He suggested that she might meet him in Chicago after he received his discharge papers in New York. Then they could travel to Madison to visit with Grant and come home together. He asked her to think it over and have her mind made up by the time he called her from New York. "If you do not come to meet me, I shall spend only a day with Grant, then hurry home to you."

He said he hoped the complete responsibility of the children while Fae and Charlie went on a trip did not tire her too much. "I know how much these girls at home have taxed your strength. What I have resented most is that they have robbed me of much of the time that I felt you should have devoted to me. But these war years have been difficult for them too. I am thankful that the boys have returned safe in body. And I hope that all of us can resume more nearly normal lives."

He wasn't sure when he would get his orders to leave, but had been told it might be within the week. "The whole thing is demoralizing," he wrote. "The trouble is that we are forced to do nothing. If I could get out to see the country, I would be happy—but just to sit and read anything that might be available in the office all day has got me down." He closed, saying, "When I see you next, I want at least three days without another soul to intrude on our privacy."

His letter the following day said that he had been on a three-hour hike and that he would continue to get as complete an impression of the country as he could from his own resources of hiking and bumming rides. He said her picture was his inspiration but that she was very inconsiderate not to have sent it earlier.

"When you get to feeling better, I shall insist on a really fine portrait. I think that you are in a beautiful age. There is so much character expressed in your face. I see sadness there—mostly, I think, the consequence of the tragedy of our last born. There's serenity, reflecting the noble spirit that bears up under deep sorrow. There's friendliness and compassion, for you have made a life's work of both. There's love, for you are the essence of it. There is the sweetest face I know, and it is wonderful to have something that intensifies my mental image of you. I feel a calmness and serene satisfaction that I have not felt for months."

Before Walter finished the letter, he discovered that his orders had come and that he was to leave the next day. He said that he was all packed and hoped to get his papers cleared in time to leave with two other men who were going.

> I dread to travel alone. But if I miss the train tomorrow night, I should catch up with the others at Le Havre. When I started this note, I had no idea that it would be my last. I am glad that my correspondence with you ended in a love letter. It is a strange benediction, and if by chance the rolling deep should swallow me on my way home, this spontaneous expression of love and appreciation will register the love that lies always in my heart. In some of my letters, the love may have seemed hidden, but I declare to you an eternity of affection. I'll be seeing you soon.
>
> Your sweetheart always,
> Walter

One final letter, written from London January 29, 1946, was a virtual travelogue. "Before receiving my orders, I had given the German Hausmutter some washing to do for me. I wrote her a note in very unorthodox German explaining my sudden departure. At noon, I found her frantically trying to dry my clothes that she had put to soak the night before. But the dear, old soul had them ready for me at 3:00 p.m., when the truck was scheduled to call.

"At the station, we found about 500 others waiting for the train to Paris, and we all feared that there would be no reservations for us. But they were there, and what a thrill it was to discover that our reservations were for first class berths."

They arrived in Paris at 8:30 a.m. One of his traveling companions, who had left his footlocker in England, needed to go to London to reclaim it and Cottam wanted to check on a lost box. "The officials accepted this excuse and amended our Frankfurt orders to Le Havre, instead giving us a two-day stopover in Paris with orders to go to London via Dieppe."

They made the most of their time in Paris, one morning taking an organized Red Cross tour to the Louvre, the Place de Concorde, the Arc de Triomphe, Napoleon's tomb, and the Notre Dame Cathedral. That afternoon, Cottam went alone to the Louvre again, but got lost on the subway and had only an hour and a half in the museum. "I was so intrigued by the exhibitions of sculpture that I had only a few minutes with the paintings and did not have time to locate the Mona Lisa. The thrill of seeing the Venus de Milo and the Winged Victory was unforgettable." They also went to see the Paris Follies at the Casino de Paris. "It proved to be a naked but clever and extremely beautiful affair. The French live in a world of art, and even this show was much more lovely than it was vulgar."

That evening Walter met Howard Cottam, his brother Heber's son, who was food economist at the American Embassy. They went to Howard's apartment to have dinner with his wife Kay and their daughter Meredith. "It was a grand experience to kiss a woman again and to hold a child in my arms. Kay looks well, and Meredith is quite a lady. She is rapidly learning to speak French."

Cottam and his friends boarded the train to Dieppe at 10:00 a.m. the next morning, caught a boat at 4:00 p.m. for a rough crossing of the channel, arrived at the port of New Haven at 7:30 p.m. and reached London by 10:00 p.m.

"Sunday we spent a fine afternoon at the zoo. Monday we devoted largely to business matters, trying to get our orders changed to allow us to sail from Southampton rather than Le Havre. Tomorrow we shall learn our fate. This morning we visited Buckingham Palace and saw the ceremony of the daily change of the guards. Afterward, we spent an hour in the National Museum of Art. This afternoon I have been washing, and tonight I came home after dinner to nurse a fresh cold. I shall wire as soon as I know my sailing date."

With no more letters to Effie, Walter did not record the remainder of the trip home. She did not go to Chicago to meet him, and their private lives became private once again. Whether he received the love and affection he craved so during his absence remains their secret.

Back at the university Cottam soon resumed his many former activities—teaching, lecturing, doing research, and writing papers, planting trees and urging the creation of a state arboretum. In 1948 he was named head of the department of botany at the university, a position he held until 1959.

The other men in the Cottam family also picked up the threads of civilian life when they returned home. Grant earned his Ph.D. in Wisconsin, taking some classes from Aldo Leopold, noted naturalist and author of the classic *A Sand County Almanac*. On one test paper, Grant received an A++ and the notation by Leopold "I couldn't say it better myself." After getting his doctorate, Grant landed a job as an assistant professor of botany at the University of Hawaii. When he received an offer the next year from the University of Wisconsin, he returned to the snow and the cold and spent the rest of his professional life there, serving two terms as head of the botany department. He retired in January, 1987. He and his wife, Diana McQuarrie, had two sons and three daughters: Cynthia, Richard McQuarrie, Daniel Grant, Margaret Effie, and Liatris.

Richard Walter Cottam, Dick, received his Ph.D. in political science at Harvard, spent one year on a Fulbright scholarship in Iran before he went to work for the State Department and spent two years with the U.S. Embassy there. He then became a professor of political science at the University of Pittsburgh, from which he retired in 1990. He interviewed the Ayatollah in Paris shortly before Khomeini returned to Iran to take over the country when the Shah was deposed. He is a top Iran specialist and was consulted frequently by the U. S. government during the Iranian Crisis. Dick has written four books, one of them with his daughter Martha, who is also a political scientist. He and his wife, Patricia Louise Ferrell, had two sons and two daughters: Russell Walter, Martha Louise, Douglas Ferrell, and Carolyn Saroya.

Fae and her husband, Charles Olson, who was the nude model for her life class in the art department at the University of Utah, spent five and a half years in the army. Fae wrote, "Charlie and I lived in many places during our army years, but the area that won our hearts was the Pacific Northwest. Before we were married, Charlie often talked of building his own house. He meant literally, with his own hands. His letters contained plans and ideas, sometimes conceived in a foxhole, which should have told me he was serious." They moved to Gresham, Oregon, where he became head of the mathematics department at the district's new high school, served as the ski coach for the district, earned a master's degree and built his dream home in their six acres of woods. They had four boys and one girl: Charles Kent, Christine, Eric Walter, Gregg Andrew, and Nils Alan.

Beatrice and her husband, William L. Fowler, remained in Salt Lake City, where Bill earned his Ph.D. in music composition at the University of Utah and eventually became a professor of music there. They moved to Lakewood, Colorado, in 1974, where Bill was a professor of music at the University of Colorado at Denver until he retired in 1988. Bea taught English at Granite and Cottonwood High Schools in Salt Lake County. In Colorado, Bill and Bea started their own publishing company, Fowler Music Enterprises, for which Bill has written many music instruction books. And they have produced several CDs featuring their five musician sons: Bruce Lambourne, Steven Cottam, Thomas William, Walter Ernest, and Edward Grant.

CHAPTER 8

THE CONSERVATIONIST

Dr. Cottam said he never had had much direction in his work. "Cowles was the father of ecology in America, so you can see how close I was to the beginning of this. I could see that ecologists had to get some way of measuring these things. Many of my papers were quantitative." As a young man in St. George, he saw the U.S. Forest Service begin to manage the Pine Valley Mountain range. And he listened with some bitterness to the older and more respected cowhands scornfully deride the young college students as they counted and measured blades of grass in their protected plots. "I was witnessing unawares the very beginnings of a research program for range and watershed problems, the knowledge from which, so laboriously gained, would in my lifetime help save the stockman from utter economic collapse and would prevent the humid mountain uplands from discharging their frequent floods on helpless communities," he wrote.

One of Dr. Cottam's early research projects, a study in 1929 of the Mountain Meadows area 50 miles west of Cedar City, Utah, demonstrated how the area had deteriorated in just 20 years from an area rich in lush vegetation with numerous fresh water springs to an area of desolation. Cottam directly attributed the change to man's introducing herds of sheep and cattle in numbers too great for the range to sustain. The tremendous overuse, followed by torrential rains, resulted in floods that cut huge gullies and arroyos in the area, causing the loss of plant litter, of the plants themselves, and of the soil. Dr. Cottam's article on his study titled "Man As a Biotic Factor—As Illustrated by Recent Floristic and Physiographic Changes At the Mountain Meadows, Washington County, Utah" was published in *Ecology* in October 1929 and cited in the bibliography of Juanita Brooks' book *The Mountain Meadows Massacre.*

As Dr. Cottam's skills in research and field work became recognized, the Forest Service engaged him as an associate forest ecologist during the summer months through part of the 1930s and 1940s. In 1933 he led a survey of vegetation on the Great Basin Desert Experimental Range in Pine Valley near Milford, Utah. Early in the 1930s, tremendous dust storms were occurring in the Great Basin because of overgrazing followed by a period of drought. The study sought to determine the amount of range land necessary to support a single head of cattle. Vegetational types were studied and enclosures were set up to allow rehabilitation of the plant cover. The study concluded that to graze a single head of cattle required one square mile and that stockmen should graze the area always keeping in mind the carrying capacity of the range.

During the summers of 1937 and 1938, Cottam headed the Forest Service Western Range Survey, Region IV. This survey, together with many others in the Intermountain Region, showed evidence of gross deterioration of plant cover and a large loss of forage values. Because of these findings, Cottam and others made an intensive study on two adjacent valleys near Milford representing distinctly different degrees of grazing use. The results showed that the more palatable grasses and shrubs tended to die out because of heavy grazing and were replaced by forage of low palatability. Dr. Cottam, George Stewart, and Selar S. Hutchings described their research on the project in a publication titled *Influence of Unrestricted Grazing on Northern Salt Desert Plant Associations in Western Utah,* published in 1940.

Dr. Cottam also did a study comparing the vegetation in two adjacent canyons east of Salt Lake City: Emigration

Canyon, which had been heavily grazed since 1847, and Red Butte Canyon, which had been closed to grazing. Conclusions of the study showed that only 42 percent as much forage was produced in Emigration Canyon as in Red Butte Canyon, but that before cattle and sheep grazing, Emigration probably had vegetation equal to or surpassing that in Red Butte. Evidence also showed that ten native grasses found in Red Butte were not found in Emigration, showing the danger of extermination of highly palatable species through grazing abuse and their replacement by unpalatable shrubs. The study concluded that sheet erosion was general in Emigration and that advanced gully erosion was common along the sheep trail. The results of the research, titled "A Comparative Study of the Vegetation of Grazed and Ungrazed Canyons of The Wasatch Range" by Dr. Cottam with Frederick Evans, was published in *Ecology* in 1945.

Dr. Cottam had the greatest respect for the Forest Service and the work being done on problems of land management. He was especially fond of three men he worked with in the service, George Stewart, Lincoln Ellison, and Reed Bailey. When Stewart died of a sudden heart attack, Cottam's eulogy at the funeral so impressed Ellison that he wrote a letter expressing his feelings and asked for a copy of the remarks.

> Dear Walter:
>
> What you said this afternoon at George Stewart's funeral was the finest statement for such an occasion that I have ever heard. It was creative, a sincere philosophy ably expressed. I should like to borrow it, if I might, to make a copy.
>
> Speakers with your candor and your courage are needed to break funerals away from the gibberish and meaningless sentimentalities to which we are now enslaved, toward a ceremony of honorable dignity for the participants and honest respect for the departed. I was impressed, and I know others were too, by the simple yet eloquent way you brought out what most of us wonder about when we face up, in fear and awe, to the mystery of death. The awe we feel—as you said in better words—is a good thing for us, the living, to experi-

> ence in its true dimensions. What a pity to have it diminished at such a solemn time as it is by most funeral orations!
>
> But not by yours. No man could ask for a more eloquent tribute in his memory than so sincere a statement. As I listened to the line "An honest man is the noblest work of God," it took on new and deeper meaning for me. The writer of that line didn't know anything about the religion and ethics of science, but Walter Cottam does and practices them in his daily life and thought.

Ironically, less than six months later Walter Cottam expressed many of the same thoughts in a eulogy for Lincoln Ellison, who died in an avalanche on March 9, 1958:

> It is futile, I know, to speculate on those last few moments of life spent on that surging avalanche. . . . Some have conjectured unspeakable fear for the rider. But knowing Lincoln Ellison as the naturalist he was, I choose not to believe this. Rather, if he had lived through this last ride, I think that he would have described it more in the language of John Muir, who survived a similar flight down the steep slopes of the Yosemite. "The start was so sudden and the end came so soon that I had little time to think of the danger that attends this sort of travel, though, at such times one thinks fast. . . . This flight in what might be called a milky way of snow-stars was the most spiritual and exhilarating of all the modes of motion I have ever experienced."
>
> Thus it was that Lincoln died—gloriously and adventurously—as he had lived. John Muir and Lincoln Ellison, I believe, were kindred spirits. In life both soared so far above the mediocrity of the crowd that few of us can claim the capacity, let alone the right, to judge them. We might as well seek to discover why the break of dawn triggers the robin into rapturous peals of song as to try to fathom that inner impulse of the soul that drove these rare spiritual men forth into the tem-

ples of Nature to learn from her and to enjoy her every mood while most of us placidly accept the comforts of home.

He said that Lincoln lived the religion of the naturalist. "He has gone from us but he can never die. No man could associate with him without incorporating into his own ideals and actions at least some of the dignity and human worth that Lincoln continually radiated. And the goodness of this fine gentleman will be reradiated through the lives of us who were made better by his presence through time without end. This is the kind of immortality—this is the type of salvation—that has a genuine basis of fact."

Dr. Cottam called Ellison's untimely passing "a downright tragedy for the entire state of Utah. Ill can we spare a man of his knowledge, his integrity, and his courage at a time when the biological resources of this land are so imperiled by a few powerful men who seem to place self above the common good, expediency above lasting security for our people, and opinions above knowledge."

A few days after the services, Dr. Cottam received a letter from Lincoln's wife, Laurel, saying, "Thank you for having the trained mind and soul to write so beautifully the words that made Lincoln's mother accept this blow. On the way home from the funeral, she said, 'Is it snowing or blowing up there?' and then, 'I wondered if I would hate the mountains, but I don't now. The words of those three fine men were a healing to me.' Later she said, 'I don't feel any more that it was a tragedy or an accident. I see in it great beauty.'"

The next year Dr. Cottam was the main speaker at an event honoring Reed Bailey on his retirement. Before the speech he told the sponsors, "By golly, I've talked at two of these guys' funerals, and now this speech that I'm going to give for Reed Bailey has got to do him." In telling the story, Cottam added, "By hell, he died the next year and they didn't dare ask me to speak because I had already praised him." Bailey drowned in Pineview Reservoir.

Dr. Cottam's insatiable desire to know the "why" and the "how" of natural occurrences and his early research projects served him well as a basis for his work in conservation. Preservation of the environment became a more important force in his career as time went on. He felt strongly that people needed to know about the natural environment, and he did everything he could to educate them through his many slide shows and lectures and dozens of papers presented at scientific meetings.

"You've got to have people care about these things for any impetus to do anything," he said. He captured the widest attention by far with the Eleventh Annual Reynolds Lecture that he delivered at the University of Utah in 1947. In a few months the entire state would be staging a great celebration commemorating the one-hundredth anniversary of the entrance of the Mormon pioneers into the Salt Lake Valley on July 24, 1847. In pageants, songs, speeches and parades, Utahns would be praising the efforts of those hardy pioneers, their forefathers, who made the desert "blossom like the rose." On February 19, 1947, Dr. Cottam, a botany professor of unimpressive stature but a determined thrust of the jaw, stepped on the stage at Kingsbury Hall and in a speech titled *Is Utah Sahara Bound?* told his audience that rather than making the desert blossom like the rose, they were about to ruin it. It wasn't a message the people wanted to hear in this centennial year. But knowing he could substantiate every claim he made, he pointed out the severe damage being done to the state's ranges and watersheds by gross overgrazing of sheep and cattle and called for action to stem the devastation.

"We have witnessed the denudation of our mountain slopes through fire, poisonous gases and unregulated grazing and then, like whimpering children, have bewailed the cruel, devastating floods that have followed these abuses," he declared. "It seems incredible that a full half-century of intermittent but devastating floods has not taught an intelligent people the obvious relationships between vegetation, soil, and water." The floods that descended on helpless towns along the Wasatch Front were caused by denuded conditions on the watersheds and could not be dismissed as "acts of God," he said. He cited the tremendous upsurge in sheep population in Utah during the 1880s and 1890s and its effect on the mountain ranges. "From the populated valleys far in the distance, the numerous herds of sheep could be detected by clouds of dust created by many hoofs. It is little wonder, then, that the early 1900s saw the beginning pay-offs for this extravagant exploitation of the vegetational resource," he said.

Dr. Cottam emphasized that the future of the state would always depend on the proper management of the renewable resources that spring from the soil. "Although national forests in Utah were established half a century earlier, with regulations imposed on livestock use, overall gains in watershed conservation were not substantial," he said. "Soil losses still continue, the little revegetation of denuded areas leaves much to be desired, and the need for further livestock reduction on most ranges is still with us. And worse, the original idea of water conservation as a basis for forest management seems to have been lost in the popular demand for big game and livestock production."

He said public education was the only answer to bring about change and that conservation education "should permeate every course in every grade from kindergarten through college." To this end he recommended specialized college courses in all phases of conservation for students going into the teaching profession. He said there was a general public need for information about Utah plant resources, the history of their use, the consequences of mismanagement on plant succession, on the soil, on floods and on water deficiencies, and the relationship of those losses to society in general. "The answers to these questions of resource waste can come only from an enlightened and aroused voting public," Dr. Cottam declared. He said the major purpose of his lecture was "to arouse the public consciousness to the fact that serious range and watershed problems do exist, that they are definitely our concern, and that we can do something about them."

Before giving the lecture, Dr. Cottam talked the matter over with his wife, knowing he might be putting his career on the line with his outspoken pronouncements. He also showed the talk to University President A. Ray Olpin, who had misgivings about the subject, particularly because the legislature was in session. But with assurances that Cottam could back up every statement, Olpin approved the lecture and ordered 2,000 copies of it printed instead of the usual 500.

But on the night of the lecture, it was announced that there had been a delay in printing the talk and that copies would be available later. Dr. Cottam, who already had a printed copy, was disturbed by the announcement, but being concerned with presenting his talk, he didn't make a point of it. Copies of *Is Utah Sahara Bound?* weren't distributed until a month later—after the legislature had adjourned.

The lecture aroused a storm of controversy and the enmity of some of the most powerful men in the state. Many of them were stockmen who also held high positions in the LDS Church. There was some pressure to remove him from his position at the university, but Olpin told the protesters Cottam was too valuable a man and he wouldn't dismiss him. That he kept his job was a tribute to the high regard in which he was held by the general public and by university officials. The lecture did not ennoble him to the livestock men of the West, but it did much to awaken the public to the land resource problems and to the need for conservation.

However, change came slowly. On April 18, 1948, the *Salt Lake Tribune* carried a bland editorial entitled "Neither Storms nor Drouths Molest nor Make Afraid" that, commenting on the storms, floods, and tidal waves afflicting other areas of the nation, proclaimed Utah to be uniquely spared. "Utah will continue to produce grain, sugar beets and fruit of many kinds without much risk or legislative protection. On a thousand hills are flocks of sheep and herds of cattle . . . the state embraces many fertile and productive valleys." This complacent pronouncement was too much for Walter Cottam, who fired the following letter to the editor: "Anyone who is basically informed about the present conditions of land resources of Utah is forced to wonder if some modern Rip Van Winkle, completely oblivious to events and conditions that place our so-called 'peaceful valleys' at the mercy of a ravaged and defiled Nature, has recently invaded the *Tribune* offices." He then enumerated the calamities that proved Utah not the Shangri-La the *Tribune* had pictured it: dust storms of 1934, starvation of sheep and cattle, floods in Box Elder and Davis counties, thousands of cubic yards of top soil from the slopes of Little Mountain already at the bottom of Mountain Dell Reservoir, and the sheep trail, with its loose manure, passing literally in front of this major water supply. And he concluded: "This editorial, I believe, is unfortunate and performs a genuine disservice to the people of Utah, not only because it is lacking in basic truth, but because of the false security it engenders in an uninformed public."

A later editorial in the *Tribune* branded Dr. Cottam a "Puppet of Pessimism."

An even more daring encounter occurred in 1957 when J. Reuben Clark, second counselor to the president of the Mormon Church and also a prominent cattleman, attacked the Forest Service for cutting the number of livestock permitted to graze on the national forests in Utah. Clark delivered the emotion-packed speech at a convention of the Utah Cattlemen's Association in Salt Lake City. Again Dr. Cottam reacted with a letter to the *Tribune* editor: "By far the most inflammatory and undisciplined address delivered at this convention was that of J. Reuben Clark Jr. . . .Despite the fact that Mr. Clark made it clear in his opening remarks that he was speaking as a 'cowman' and assumed 'full and complete responsibility' for what he said, the probability remains that people so long conditioned to his spiritual leadership and generally uninformed, also, on the complex scientific aspects of land management are likely indisposed if not unprepared to give this address the degree of objective scrutiny that it certainly deserves."

Rumors followed that the president of the university received from delegations of stockmen renewed requests for Dr. Cottam's dismissal. The messages Dr. Cottam received had a different tone:

> Anyone who has the courage to take on an ecclesiastical demagogue of the stature of J. Reuben Clark is either senile or recklessly foolhardy or tremendously courageous. . . . We need more men like you in this world, and I hope you live forever.
>
> Newell Frei, January 1958

> Your statement of the need for expert judgment and public welfare as criteria for administration of watershed usage is magnificent—clear, temperate,

informed, wise. Such debate is essential to democratic processes.

Local citizen

The people of this state often get so confused concerning the nature and pertinence of their directives from authorities that it requires the outspoken comment of less gullible specialists to help keep thinking straight.

Citizen

I admire the way you have defined the problem despite the certainty of kick-backs from the stockmen. If there were only a few more people with the courage to stick their necks out, conservation would move a good deal more rapidly.

William Vogt, author of *Road to Survival*

Of his brother's strong stance, Clarence Cottam said: "He created a healthy situation with his delivery of the Reynolds Lecture. He stirred up a hornet's nest both at the university and in other circles in Utah. He cannot be accused of waiting to see which way the wind blows before he forms an opinion. He does what he believes to be right no matter how much criticism comes from it. He is one of a breed of men who, when their information is backed up by scientifically drawn conclusions, do not back down or change their minds on the basis of pressures which may be brought to bear."

A professional colleague at the university, Dr. Angus M. Woodbury, observed: "He has probably done more than anyone in Utah in bringing attention to the problems of conserving our renewable resources in the West—for more than twenty-five years he has labored, argued, and written on the importance of conservation. Unlike many other scientists content to study and report, he followed up his scientific findings into their social implications and attempted to arouse the public to the danger and consequences of vegetation despoliation. This gave him local, state, national and international recognition."

Unlike some scientists who are content to search for the

Truth but not proclaim it publicly, Cottam felt it was his duty to speak out about the abuses of the land. And speak out he did—in his writings, lectures, teaching, prayers, and conversations: "There is, in my opinion, no more justification for a 'public be damned' attitude for those of us who could well dedicate our efforts to conserve a resource than there is for those who would selfishly despoil it. In the field of public education, we should find opportunities to attain more quickly the goal of our research and certainly to attain new horizons in the service of mankind. . . . Surely if men who created the atom bomb consider it their moral duty to warn society against its use, can the ecologist or range manager logically shun his responsibility to warn society against the evil exploitation of the soil resource?" he said in an article in the *Journal of Range Management,* January 1951.

Because of the public interest generated by his original Reynolds Lecture in 1947, Dr. Cottam was asked in l958 to review the picture he had presented eleven years earlier. He delivered the follow-up speech *Is Utah Sahara Bound?—an Eleventh Year Retrospective, an Eleventh Hour Warning* on April 17, 1958. The outlook remained grim. Cottam took to task Congress and the State of Utah, its universities, stockmen, boards of education, and other leading institutions for the somber picture of the Utah water conservation program. "I wish that it were possible for my talk to exhibit more optimism than it did eleven years ago, but unhappily this is not the case. For not only do we commit the same transgressions against the land as we did then, but there are some hundred thousand more souls to spread their sins over the landscape."

Among the items he termed against the public good, he mentioned "a powerful clique of forest users—the stockmen—who place an annual flow of bills in the congressional hopper to prevent the Forest Service from making reductions in the number of livestock grazing on certain portions of the national forests. . . . The people of the Intermountain West have been propagandized by a campaign designed to make this area a baronage of a minute but powerful clique whose actions suggest that the cow is the most sacred creature in it." He said they had used untruths and half-truths to convince the public that they were the victims of a senseless and growing bureaucracy "manned by a few unscrupulous and fanatical conservationists. . . . Our cherished land, for all its lavish endowments in renewable natural resources, cannot long endure the degrading assaults of men who place self-aggrandizement above the public good. . . . If the streams discharge their floods, where can man retreat; if they fail in their life-giving water, where can he quench his thirst?"

Commenting on a Utah Senate bill under consideration in 1958, Dr. Cottam made this statement: "Four decades of careful observation and research on the wild lands of Utah and on certain areas of Arizona and Nevada contiguous to our state have convinced me that the most sacred obligation of each and every generation of mankind is a proper stewardship of the resources of earth that sustain us and which we must inevitably relinquish to an ever expanding progeny. No generation has a right to be judged with honor which passes on to its children a land made poorer through use or which denies to future Americans the opportunity for that spiritual fulfillment that an undefiled wilderness affords."

Cottam often pointed out that the most important use of watershed lands in Utah and all semiarid mountainous regions is to provide water. "Every other use such as grazing, lumbering, recreation, or wildlife preservation must forever be subservient to supplying water. To maintain grazing on these lands at the peril of the water resource merely because ownership derived from a misguided national policy of land disposal or because of priority of use is to deny the basic principle of democracy which seeks to guarantee to the greatest number of people the greatest good from the resources of the land."

He emphasized: "Our law is a fanatic regard for prior right, not total human rights. Each generation should review and decide the best use of our resources. Prior use does not necessarily determine proper use, especially if those in control of prior right are in the minority."

A continuing thread through Dr. Cottam's writings, lectures, and conversations over the years was the fear of a burgeoning population that would overwhelm natural resources. He said, "Balancing total populations with the physical resources is a biological necessity for a progressive and healthful economic and social future. We've got more people now than we can take care of."

Headlines, editorials, and news stories in Utah and throughout the country today echo this thought. Because of population growth, millions of visitors overrun parks, rivers, lakes, mountains, and trails, inviting more and more restrictions and the need for more facilities. New and noisy recreational vehicles—snowmobiles, jet skis, all-terrain vehicles, mountain bikes—invade previously pristine areas, disturbing wildlife, creating pollution, and damaging the soil and vegetation. Many years ago Dr. Cottam thought recreation guilty of the same problems that overgrazing had caused 30 years earlier. "We've got to quit having kids," he said. "You can't talk about having kids without expecting to need facilities, and we're supersaturated now." In 1970 he became incensed over an LDS Church editorial that said it was ridiculous to worry about over-population since the Lord wouldn't have put us here and then not provide for us.

Dr. Cottam's reputation as a conservationist and environmentalist continued well into his retirement years. In 1972, a representative of Utah Congressman Sherman P. Lloyd called on him to ask if he would serve on a committee to advise Lloyd on the environment. Cottam said he thought Lloyd needed advice but pointed out that he was a Democrat while Lloyd was a Republican. Later, however, Lloyd himself called, and Cottam agreed to serve on the committee. Shortly thereafter, Cottam and his wife left on an extended trip. When he returned home on October 26, he was shocked to find in the October 15 issue of the *Salt Lake Tribune* a paid political ad listing his name as endorsing the environmental record of Sherman P. Lloyd and recommending Lloyd's re-election.

Again Cottam fired off a letter to the editor of the *Tribune* detailing exactly how it came about that he had agreed to serve on an advisory committee for Mr. Lloyd because he thought Lloyd needed advice. "No meetings of this committee were held before I left September 15," he wrote. "I contributed no money or advice. I granted no permission for the use of my name supporting Mr. Lloyd's record or his reelection. I understand that Mrs. Caine, listed as secretary of the committee, tried to locate me to get such permission. I received no call from her myself. . . . Mr. Lloyd's environmental record is well documented by Common Cause, The Sierra Club, and various publications. In no way do I want my professional standing as an ecologist to be associated with that record. Perhaps I was politically naive when I assumed he really wanted advice, not endorsement." Many Democrats urged Dr. Cottam to make more of the incident, but he said he felt he had knocked Lloyd down and didn't want to kick him. It was enough. Lloyd lost his bid for reelection.

While Dr. Cottam seemed to be waging battles with the *Salt Lake Tribune* over its views on the environment in the days of his Reynolds Lecture, he later won a lifelong friend and champion in Ernest H. Linford, editorial writer and columnist for the paper. Even after Linford left the *Tribune* and went to the University of Wyoming, he continued to write a weekly environmental column for the Salt Lake paper. Many of his columns concerned Dr. Cottam's projects and accomplishments, and Linford depended on him to verify their accuracy. He wrote: "Walter was my best and most helpful friend, and the more so because he was a specialist in plant life and so willing to share his knowledge. He kept me on the straight and narrow in my conservation writings. And how he would chew me out if I made a blooper in spite of his watchful eyes. . . . Walter's Reynolds Lecture in 1947, 'Is Utah Sahara Bound?', remains the number one classic of its kind and started off the movement which saved much of Utah from becoming the desert he warned against. I still depend on much of his writing for facts and inspiration."

Dr. Cottam firmly believed that man is not inherently materialistic and that beauty is vital to the good life. He wrote:

> Each generation of mankind must ultimately stand at the tribunal of history and its basic morality be judged by its stewardship of the land. Dust bowls, floods, silted streams, plundered forests, impoverished ranges, depleted soils, wasted minerals, and squandered gas and oil are disturbing signs of unwise resource use that threaten the foundations of democracy and of world peace.

In the proper management of the land resource lies the temporal and spiritual health of this generation and of generations yet unborn. . . . When we see man annihilating time and space with his gadgets of communication or unlocking the very secrets of matter, we must agree with Shakespeare that this intellectual biped is god-like in apprehension, but when we witness with what reckless abandon he dissipates the resources of earth that support him, we can only marvel at his paradoxical stupidity. . . . Better living does not necessarily imply the progressive accumulation of material wealth either for the individual or for society collectively. It does imply the sacred right of every child to the basic necessities of life—food, raiment, and shelter—and an opportunity to experience that spiritual fulfillment that comes from intimate contact with an unspoiled and undefiled nature.

Chapter 9

The Oak Project

A 1954 discovery by Rudy Drobnick, a graduate student in the botany department, resulted in a project that kept Dr. Cottam occupied throughout the rest of his years at the university and during most of his retirement years. One day in May, Rudy came to Dr. Cottam with some specimens of an unusual oak he had found while hiking in the Oquirrh Mountains, 20 miles west of Salt Lake City. On examining this clump of oak on the slopes of Harker's Canyon, Drobnick had found that the small green leaves were leathery in texture and sharply toothed in comparison with the large, relatively thin and roundly lobed leaves of the common Gambel oak.

Dr. Cottam was equally excited when he saw the oak specimens. Believing the oak to be a hybrid, they sent the specimens to Dr. Cornelius H. Muller of the University of California at Santa Barbara for confirmation. Dr. Muller quickly identified them as a hybrid cross between the widely distributed Gambel oak and Utah's only live oak, *Quercus turbinella*, common now only in the warm Dixie area of Utah where Dr. Cottam had grown up. Cottam and Drobnick then sent the specimens to Dr. John M. Tucker, professor of botany at the University of California, Davis, who confirmed that they were indeed hybrids.

Drobnick immediately decided to make the hybrid oaks the focus of his master's thesis. He needed first to determine when and how these two oak species had managed to get together and whether there were more such hybrids in the area. His investigation showed more clumps of the hybrid oak occurring sporadically in a pathway from the Pine Valley Mountains in Dixie northward along both sides of the Oquirrh Range, along the Traverse Range and north along the Wasatch Range as far as Ogden. In the Pine Valley Mountains, Drobnick located numerous hybrid oaks where both parents currently exist.

The presence of all these hybrid clones distributed in this way could mean only that in very recent geological times, perhaps 7,000 to 7,500 years ago, the live oak of southwestern Utah had migrated northward along the base of the mountain chains for approximately 250 miles and consorted freely with the Gambel oak during a warmer and presumably drier climate than the current one. The researchers concluded that when the climate changed to the present colder one, the live oak, unadapted to the more rigorous winters, succumbed to the cold but left behind the hybrids, blessed with an infusion of cold-resistant genes to combat the colder climate successfully.

Cottam said that this pathway of hybrid clumps supported the supposition long held by biologists that this low mountain chain was an important migratory lane for many species of plants and animals of both the Wasatch and Oquirrh mountains. The hot, dry period during which the oak successfully migrated from its present position in southern Utah northward 250 miles into the Great Basin lasted 3,500 years, ending approximately 4,000 years ago.

After successfully raising several young trees from acorns gathered from some of the self-pollinating hybrid oaks, Drobnick and Cottam began their experiments with controlled pollination. Their first attempt at artificial hybridization occurred in the spring of 1961, with pollen from the live oak of southern Utah transferred to a vigorous burr oak (*Quercus macrocarpa*) growing on the university campus. They planted four successful hybrids of this cross on the campus.

In 1962, they accomplished the first cross, using the live oak as the female parent and the Gambel oak as the male parent. A reciprocal cross using Gambel as the female and the live oak as the male succeeded in 1964. The leaves of these reciprocal crosses matched very well those of the natural hybrids, both showing an amazing variety of leaf forms.

The researchers saw a great opportunity to produce superior creations of oak trees through hybridization. They expanded their efforts to include various other species of oak and in 1965 they began receiving pollen from other parts of the country.

Since oak trees produce both male and female flowers on the same branchlet, the process of hybridization is complicated. The staminate (male) flowers, borne on catkins, must be removed from the branch at just the right time before the pollen is shed. The female flowers are extremely small, about the size of a pin head, but since they are generally bright red at maturity, they are fairly easy to see. After careful emasculation, the entire branchlet is enclosed in a large waxed paper sack and the ends of the sack tightly sealed with tape to prevent the entrance of foreign pollen. If the desired pollen is available at the time of emasculation, a handful of the mature catkins can be inserted into the sack before it is taped. If it is not available, the pollen can be inserted later because the female flowers remain receptive for two weeks or more. Since oak pollen remains virile for longer periods than do the female flowers, it is possible to hybridize species with different flowering periods.

After the male catkins are inserted, the pollination bags are revisited at least three times, two or three days apart, and thoroughly shaken to ensure a good distribution of pollen. Two weeks after the last shake, when all danger of unwanted pollination is past, the bags are removed and replaced with nylon netting to catch the acorns. The harvested acorns are kept in cold storage for three months, then planted in separate containers, usually in December, and kept in a greenhouse until the seedlings are mature enough to be planted outside.

In his report in 1966 to the University of Utah Research Committee on the hybrid oak project, Dr. Cottam wrote: "When one considers that it takes 15 to 20 minutes to emasculate and to pollinate a single branchlet of oak and that approximately 600 of them have been pollinated this spring (counting the 120 lost by frost), and that it takes at least 10 minutes to plant an acorn properly in the greenhouse—when a thousand of them were planted by early February, it is safe to say that this project is challenging, interesting, scientifically rewarding, and I know that it is akin to labor. Time never drags, and I sometimes wonder how I ever had time to teach school."

When people told Cottam that only God could make a tree, he replied, "I'm God's little bumblebee."

But the tedious hybridizing was only one of the problems plaguing the project from the start. Time and again severe frosts or storms destroyed the developing hybrid acorns. In 1965 the team had to make four 600-mile round trips to the Pine Valley Mountains to repeat the cross-pollinations.

They planted some of their first seedlings on the university campus, some on the grounds of the Veterans Administration Hospital just south of the university, and some in the grove in Red Butte Canyon. This three-acre plot was given to the university for the hybrid oak project in 1964 and, after much of the Fort Douglas lands became surplus, the university received title to it in 1967. Cottam had planted about a hundred seedlings in the grove in the spring of 1964, but while university officials tried to decide what use to make of the newly acquired land, they allowed no further plantings after 1967. When the decision dragged on for two years, Cottam complained, "God made the earth in six days."

In a report to the research committee in 1969, he wrote: "We now have close to a thousand hybrids and parent oak seedlings planted in one-gallon or two-gallon cans. About half of these are more than two years old, and some are in great need of being transplanted because the bottoms of the cans have nearly rusted away. All of these seedlings will require greenhouse or well-protected nursery area housing this winter. Unless we get permission to utilize fully and permanently our nursery and planting area south of the fort swimming pool, our project will be in great jeopardy."

Plantings in the grove finally continued when the decision was made to make the area a part of the state arboretum. But problems with gophers and weeds and lack of a watering system added to the woes there. Other disasters occurred when most of the seedlings planted on the VA hospital grounds fell victim to a power mower operated by an undiscriminating groundsman. And Cottam constantly fought the use of the chemical 2-4-D on the university campus, where several times it caused hybrid acorns to abort. He also lost some young trees on campus—hoed out by an overzealous groundsman cleaning up a supposed weed patch.

But Cottam and Drobnick took these periodic setbacks in stride, so strong was their commitment to the project. In all the years he and Drobnick worked together, they received only $2,500 for the project. They paid all of their travel expenses out of pocket. The team had to go begging for greenhouses. Driving by the home of Salt Lake businessman Joseph Rosenblatt one day, Drobnick stopped the car. He had spotted an unused greenhouse in the yard. Drobnick went in, explained their oak project, and Rosenblatt generously gave them the greenhouse.

John Tucker, who had confirmed the first oak specimens found by Drobnick as hybrids, collaborated on the project over the years and, later, Frank S. Santamour Jr., research geneticist, U.S. National Arboretum, USDA-SEA, Washington, D.C., aided in confirming the hybrid crosses.

These two collaborators wrote of the team's efforts: "At the end of a successful season, to see Dr. Cottam and Rudy Drobnick harvesting their precious crop of acorns—like a pair of eager squirrels—was really to feel their enthusiasm. And with the germination of each season's crop of new hybrid seedlings—a sea of young green leaves poking out of innumerable milk cartons—their joy was something to behold!"

Even after writing his master's thesis in 1958, Drobnick continued to be deeply involved in all aspects of the project for several more years. But as time went on, his position with the Department of Wildlife Resources demanded more and more of his time, and Cottam was left to carry on alone.

Tucker and Santamour couldn't praise Cottam's efforts enough: "The lengths to which he went in order to get a job done and the long hours and hard work that were frequently necessary were probably an already familiar part of botanical research. But the dedication and gritty persistence with which he kept at the project for ten years and more, often in the face of severe difficulties (and even disasters)—these were indeed remarkable. And all this during his retirement years!"

One of the most exciting results of the project was a confirmed cross between a white and a black oak, something which does not occur in nature between the two subgenera. It is believed to be the first such cross made in America and possibly in the world. At first dubious about the cross, Tucker visited Utah to see the seedlings and check their characteristics. He told Cottam, "That's botanical history!"

The cross was made in the summer of 1965 with pollen from an evergreen black oak, *Quercus wislizenii,* sent to them by Tucker, being inserted on branchlets of *Q. turbinella,* the Dixie live oak, which is a white oak. The cross produced several hybrid acorns, and they produced seedlings, all but one of which later died. Planted in the oak grove, the remaining seedling thrived and grew to be more than six feet tall.

In their numerous cross-pollination efforts, Cottam and Drobnick found that *Q. turbinella,* whether used as a male or a female, was the most effective parent in all their hybrid experimentation. Cottam affectionately called *Q. turbinella* "the fast woman of the oak crowd."

Over the years, thousands of hybrid oaks have been planted in communities throughout Utah. Many others given to visitors have been planted in other states. And some have even found their way to Japan.

"Walter's pride in displaying his hybrids to appreciative visitors and the readiness with which he donated young seedlings to other institutions and plantsmen have served to make his project known in many parts of the country," Tucker and Santamour said. "His work in oak hybridizing will be remembered for years to come by a host of friends and professional acquaintances."

Working on his oak was therapy for Walter Cottam. He would come to the grove sometimes upset over something gone wrong with the project or with problems at home, and after spending a few hours "stroking" his oak, he would go home a tired, but happy man.

Often during midsummer, he would labor for hours in 90-degree heat, seeking relief at times in his "office"—a table and chair set up in the shade of a full-grown tree at the edge of the grove. His hybrids offered very little shade. They looked like oak, yet were different in several ways. Some closely resembled the native scrub, or Gambel, oak growing along Red Butte

Creek, which borders the grove. Others were very different, both in leaves and form: Some were slender trees, others more like shrubs. Some leaves were large, smooth and deeply lobed; others were small and leathery with sharp points.

One might wonder what the eminent ecologist Walter P. Cottam, much honored teacher and conservationist, was doing out in the hot sun toiling like a common laborer. But it was a labor of love for him. These trees were his children. He was the one with a gleam in his eye before they were conceived, their artificial inseminator, their midwife, and their nurturer.

Dr. Cottam resigned as head of the botany department in 1959 to devote more time to teaching and to the oak project. In 1962 he retired from the university at the age of 68. When he retired, someone asked him what he was going to do. "I don't know," he said. "I'm too old to teach and too young to be an apostle." The person who asked the question later visited Doc's brother Clarence in Texas and told him what Walter had said. "Well, you've talked to Walter, all right!" said Clarence.

But Walter Cottam wasn't one to sit back and relax in retirement. His oak project in particular kept him well occupied, along with lecturing and showing his slides to various civic groups, trips into the mountains and deserts, gardening and his family.

Chapter 10

Honors

Most of Dr. Cottam's honors and recognition came late in his career, totally unsolicited and generally as a complete surprise to him. He was a man who, for his own satisfaction, gave the best effort possible to any job he tackled. The thought of rewards never entered his mind. But when the honors came, he accepted them graciously, with no show of false modesty. The first honor was his selection to give the Reynolds Lecture in 1947. The lecture series had been designed to bring forth fresh ideas based on intellectual activity and scientific investigation and to be delivered by a distinguished member of the faculty.

The next came in 1957, when the Utah Forestry Club of Utah State University named him Man of the Year, its Forestry Award for outstanding contributions to conservation.

When the Ecological Society of America named Dr. Cottam Eminent Ecologist for 1960, his colleagues and friends in the Forest Service wrote him a flurry of letters of congratulations. His good friend Reed Bailey wrote: "This is news that will be received by your many friends with a feeling of complete approval. I want to speak as one of your friends and admirers of long standing and extend congratulations and say that it couldn't have happened to a grander fellow and a more deserving one."

Floyd Iverson, regional forester with the Forest Service in Ogden, wrote: "Personally I could think of no better nominee for that wonderful distinction, not the least of the reasons being that you have, through the years, made your knowledge and convictions known to all mankind. It is a pleasure to know and work with you".

From William D. Hurst, chief of the Division of Range Management with the Forest Service in Ogden, came this tribute: "This honor could not have been bestowed upon a more worthy individual. . . . We who are working in the field of conservation certainly appreciate your wise counsel and help on problems and conditions of mutual concern. We appreciate our close working relationship and want it to continue."

Raymond M. Turner, assistant professor of botany at the University of Arizona, wrote: "As one of your many former students devoted to you as a teacher, scientist and 'a man of quiet generosity,' I extend my sincere congratulations."

"This recognition is richly deserved," said Jack H. Berryman, wildlife specialist with the Extension Service at Utah State University, in his letter of congratulation. "I am sure that your many former students share with me a real sense of pride. I know of no one who has been more inspirational and more willing to speak out on behalf of sound resource management."

Then in 1962, American Motors presented Dr. Cottam its Conservation Award, citing him as "a fearless crusader for the preservation of the natural resources of the nation." It noted that during his 41 years as a teacher and educator, he had inspired thousands of students to pursue careers in ecology and conservation.

In a letter of congratulations to Dr. Cottam, Wallace F. Bennett, then a U.S. Senator from Utah, said: "Your name has come to stand for conservation in Utah, where your contributions have been frequent and significant. I'm particularly concerned with those wasteful aspects of our modern civilization which use up our water and other natural resources without making provision for their renewal or restoration. Your attempts to make us mindful of these dangers are most valuable."

Also in 1962, the National Council of State Garden Clubs presented him its Gold Seal Award for Conservation Teaching.

When the Board of Regents of the University of Utah selected Dr. Cottam to receive the honorary degree of Doctor of Science in 1963, a campus friend congratulated him, then added that it came as a great surprise to him that a mere teacher should be so honored. Cottam said later, "It was a profound shock to me as well and surely proves that the meek really can inherit the earth." President A. Ray Olpin wrote to Dr. Cottam from Japan on April 22, 1963, of his election by the regents to receive the honorary doctorate in June. "I had nominated you before leaving and left my ballot in your favor with the secretary. I knew of no one on the faculty more deserving of the recognition you are receiving, and I am looking forward to the pleasure of conferring the degree."

Daniel J. Dykstra, acting president of the university, also wrote to Cottam of his selection, saying: "I am certain that I speak for the entire faculty and for your many friends in the community when I again express my pleasure at your selection. It is good to know that our governing board takes account of academic attainments and contributions in selecting people for their highest award."

In his response to Dykstra, Dr. Cottam said the selection "carried an emotional shock from which I fear I shall not soon recover." He added: "The most wonderful thing about these surprise recognitions is the evidence of so many devoted friends that my associations over long years in the teaching profession seem to have garnered me. This is a bonus compensation, I find, that reaches far above any monetary consideration of success."

Following the awarding of the honorary degree at commencement exercises in June, Dr. Cottam wrote to President Olpin, in part: "It is impossible for me to express fully the gratitude I feel for the great honor bestowed upon me. . . . Dr. [Sterling M.] McMurrin's citation and your confirming response are so beautifully worded and so laudatory in spirit that it is still difficult for me to realize that it was of me you were speaking. The numerous congratulatory communications from friends, colleagues and especially from students far and near, some of whom I had almost forgotten, I must admit, are bonus products of this honorary degree that I can never forget and shall ever cherish."

Dr. Sherman Preece, assistant professor in the Department of Botany at Montana State University, said in his letter of congratulations: "No degree has given me more pleasure than the one you are receiving. The people of Utah could not honor a more deserving person. The people of Utah (and those of much of the entire country as well) will be the recipients of benefits for many, many years because of your outstanding studies, your devotion to teaching, your obsession with and protection of the resources of Utah, and last but by no means least, your fearless missionary spirit and activities in a land of many intellectual and political heathens. I personally will always be thankful for the privilege of working with you professionally and for the wonderful personal association I've enjoyed for so many years. In both respects I've gained much as an individual."

Ralph D. Thomson, University of Utah librarian and chairman of the commencement committee, was equally laudatory: "I think it is particularly fitting that you were given this honorary degree at this time. You have worked so hard to help preserve the natural resources of our land at a time when strenuous efforts are made at all sides to exploit the riches without always regarding the conservation necessary for intelligent use of our resources. It is good to have a voice such as yours, courageously calling our attention to the importance of conservation for now and for future generations."

Honors continued. In 1963 the Utah Academy of Sciences, Arts and Letters awarded him an Outstanding Achievement Award in the field of biological science. In 1971 the Utah Association of Nurserymen gave him a Certificate of Merit for his oak hybridization project and for his efforts in establishing the Utah State Arboretum. The Soil Conservation Society of America in 1972 cited him for "outstanding accomplishments through research, teaching, and writing in ecology and promotion of better use of soil and water."

With all his teaching, research, and lectures, Dr. Cottam still found time for membership in many organizations, including the American Association for the Advancement of Science; the Ecological Society of America; the Utah Academy of Science, Arts and Letters; the California Botanical Society; the American Association of University Professors; Sigma Xi; Phi Kappa Phi; the Utah State Historical Society; the Utah

Education Association; the BYU Alumni Association; the Timpanogas Club; and the Aztec Dinner Club. He was listed in *Who's Who in America; Who's Who in American Education*; and the *American Men of Science*.

Dr. Cottam was one of a group of dedicated ecologists and other scientists who gathered in upstate New York in 1951 to form a new conservation organization known as The Nature Conservancy. In August 1957, Dr. Cottam delivered a speech, "Our Social Responsibilities," at a Nature Conservancy Symposium at Stanford University in Palo Alto, California. In his speech he said that he would assume that the public responsibilities of the society will have been well served if the following provisions are met:

(1) If we continue to acquire or assist in the acquisition of private tracts of land throughout the Americas that may preserve for this and future generations at least small representations of all that remain of our once vast and varied primeval wilderness.
(2) If the Nature Conservancy will, through the competence and prestige of its membership, exert its great influence on government, both state and federal, to designate and to protect from all unnecessary impacts of civilization such public lands as could and should serve the social and scientific function of wilderness areas.
(3) If our society shall continue to recognize the urgent need for increasing its efforts in promoting a more complete biological inventory and ecological assessment of each natural area.
(4) If our organization assumes its fair share of public education on all conservation matters.

When the Great Basin Field Office of The Nature Conservancy was opened in the 1980s, the organization's newsletter included this comment:

> Dr. Cottam's dream was the establishment of an organization dedicated to the preservation of natural areas through non-confrontational means and well

> founded in land acquisition. While today The Nature Conservancy's achievements are perhaps best known in other parts of the country, it is exciting to think that the Conservancy's new Field Office in Salt Lake City—dedicated to both Utah and Nevada—represents a fulfillment of Dr. Cottam's original vision.
>
> As Dr. Cottam knew then, and other scientists have more recently acknowledged, the diverse ecology of the Great Basin makes this region unique. In fact, Conservancy scientists have determined that Utah and Nevada are tied for fifth among all states in a national ranking of ecological diversity.

In 1987, a $25,000 contribution from the Ezekiel R. Dumke and Edna Wattis Dumke Foundation and a land gift from George Melling expected to net $40,000 for the Great Basin Field Office were used to establish the Walter Cottam Land Preservation Fund. The fund is being used to purchase important wildlife areas in the Great Basin.

Chapter 11

A Renaissance Man

THE TEACHER

Dr. Cottam wasn't a ponderous, pontificating professor, but a fun-loving, enthusiastic, caring teacher who had the gift of igniting the joy of learning in his students and drawing the best out of them. "Teaching to me was the human relationship, the difference in students. Some of them were interested, and others were not. The challenge was to get those others interested. I developed a lot of gimmicks. I opened a lot of eyes," he said.

An anonymous student sent the following letter to the *University Chronicle* shortly before Dr. Cottam retired: "There is a biology professor on campus—I am sure former students know who I mean—who speaks with the voice of a child who has just seen a flower bloom for the first time. . . . Here is a man who tries awfully hard to be a 'tough' prof, but whose genuine interest in his students and total love of his subject give him a warmth and integrity that belie his wisecracks and tough exterior. . . . He demands more than any teacher I have known and he gets it, because his interest is contagious, his disappointment genuine if you fail your capabilities. . . . It is good to have curiosity again. Thanks, Prof."

Some students took Dr. Cottam's most popular class, Spring Flowers of the Wasatch, thinking it would be a snap course. Though they found out differently, most of them would declare later, "Best class I ever had!" Many students met their mates on Dr. Cottam's field trips. He always dismissed the class on the mountainside "and after that they were on their own."

Dr. Cottam often used a humorous anecdote to emphasize a point he was making. To illustrate the sharp line of demarcation that often occurs during sudden thunderstorms on the desert, he told this story: "A rabbit hunter found he had left his cigarettes in his car. Rather than tote his double-barreled shotgun back with him, he leaned it against a fence, the barrels pointing up, while he walked back to the car. He was gone about an hour, during which a desert shower occurred. When he checked the gun, he found one barrel full of water, the other one shiny and dry."

His humor was often contagious. On one of his field trips he pointed out a plant that the Indians used as a contraceptive. One of his students, a fellow named Spencer, had five children. The other students started calling the plant "Spencer's weed."

Asked what he felt had been his greatest contribution, Dr. Cottam, perhaps thinking of his outspoken criticism of the sheepmen and cattlemen who had caused widespread destruction of the land by overgrazing, answered, "I had the guts to stand up to the church." Many of the stockmen were also high officials in the LDS Church. But on second thought, he said his greatest contribution may have been his teaching. Twenty-six of his students earned advanced degrees, and many went on to become outstanding professionals in the fields of botany, taxonomy, and ecology. One of these was his son, Grant, who served as professor of botany and environmental studies at the University of Wisconsin until his own retirement in 1987.

When Walter Cottam was named Ecologist of the Year by the Ecological Society of America in 1960, the citation stated:

> As with most men eminent in any field, Dr. Cottam's personality has been the most obvious force in shaping his career. He is an intensely vital man, interested in all things and with the ability to accom-

> plish almost any task. Secondly, he has shown that he has the awareness and the temperament of a true artist in his field—being intensely aware of the beauties of the deserts and the mountains of his land and capable of capturing that beauty in photography and in his writing. Thirdly, he is a man who is forthright both in conviction and in action—one who has made an indelible impression on the students who have worked under him and with him.
>
> It is these characteristics which have made him a great teacher, for no one could participate in his classes without acquiring some of his enthusiasm about his subject or his feeling for the artistry of nature. In the intermountain area of the West where much of the land is in public ownership, the presence among the voting public of many of his former students in ecology is an important force in the battle for enlightened land use and management.

Dr. Cottam was always available to students who wanted to clarify a point or discuss a principle and would spend all the time necessary to put over a concept or an idea. He was interested not only in the course material but also in the individual student. If the classes had no laboratory or field work, he felt that he had missed an opportunity to get to know the students well. Field trips were a large part of his courses, and he often led classes out to the north end of the Oquirrh Mountains, where the smelter that processed ore from the Kennecott copper mine had spewed out pollution that had killed most of the trees and vegetation on the mountainside.

The great explorer and naturalist John Muir visited Utah in 1877 and wrote eloquently in his book *Steep Trails* of the beautiful flowers and vegetation he found on a hike up into the Oquirrhs in July of that year:

> I had not gone more than a mile from Lake Point ere I found the way profusely decked with flowers, mostly compositae and purple leguminosae, a hundred corollas or more to the square yard, with a corresponding abundance of winged blossoms above them,

> moths and butterflies, the leguminosae of the insect kingdom. This floweriness is maintained with delightful variety all the way up through rocks and bushes to the snow—violets, lilies, gilias, oenotheras, wallflowers, ivesias, saxifrages, smilax, and miles of blooming bushes, chiefly azalea, honeysuckle, brier rose, buckthorn, and eriogonum—all meeting and blending in divine accord. Two liliaceous plants in particular, *Erythronium grandiflorum* and *Fritillaria pudica*, are marvelously beautiful and abundant. Never before, in all my walks, have I met so glorious a throng of these fine showy liliaceous plants. The whole mountainside was aglow with them, from a height of fifty-five hundred feet to the very edge of the snow.

Higher on the mountainside he found the tracks of deer and the fresh trail of a flock of wild sheep. The trees he encountered were spruce and fir and quaking aspen.

The smelter was built about the turn of the century. Dr. Cottam believed that the trees and plants were all dead by 1920, killed by the fumes. Several times he took the same path Muir described, going up the west side of the Oquirrhs and coming down the north slope by Black Rock, but he came down gullies that had been washed out in intervening years. Ignoring "No Trespassing" signs posted by Kennecott, Dr. Cottam took many of his university students up on the mountainside to show them the destruction caused by the smelter fumes. Once a jeep drove up and two men, obviously Kennecott employees, got out and started walking toward the class. "The closer they came, the louder I talked about what bastards and sons of bitches they were," Cottam declared. "But the men didn't say anything, just got back in the jeep and drove off." The professor may have been slightly disappointed that they didn't haul him off to the "hoosegow," giving him an opportunity to lash out publicly at the perpetrators of the destruction.

The class had a profound effect on one of Cottam's students, Paul Rokich, who grew up in Magna, a small town at the north end of the Oquirrhs. As a small boy, he had noticed the sad condition of the mountain—no trees, no vegetation, no animals—and he knew that some day he was going to go up and replant the denuded slopes. Inspired by Cottam's words, he sneaked up one night in May 1958 onto Kennecott property, passed "No Trespassing" signs, and planted a Russian olive tree and two plots of wheat grass. Planting became an obsession with him. Using his own money, loans from relatives, and donations begged from seed companies, he kept on year after year, dodging Kennecott guards and single-handedly planting trees, shrubs, grasses and anything he thought might grow on the barren mountainsides.

He had many setbacks—trees killed by drought, by early frosts, by rock slides and by rabbits—but slowly the grass took hold, the shrubs became thickets, and the trees began providing shade for returning elk and deer. After years of looking the other way and allowing Rokich to pursue his dream at his own expense, Kennecott hired him in 1973 as their environmental engineer. He no longer had to smuggle in seedlings, but soon drove a company truck, planted trees by tractor and spread grass seed by the ton from a helicopter. Rokich, a strong, six-foot-one-inch, 200-pound man, estimates that he has personally planted at least 60,000 trees on 14,000 acres of the Oquirrhs since the project started. In recent years because of more environmental awareness, dozens of volunteer groups have helped with the planting.

In 1990, Rokich received the first Jean Giono Award of the American Forestry Association's Global ReLeaf campaign for his then 32 years of tree planting. In 1994 at age sixty-one, he was still going strong with no intention of retiring. "I'll probably be buried up there," he said. Rokich believes a letter Dr. Cottam wrote Kennecott officials in April 1960 played a great part in his being able to pursue his dream, with officials looking the other way during his early planting efforts and eventually hiring him. Dr. Cottam wrote:

> Gentlemen:
>
> The bearer of this note, Mr. Paul Rokich, for the past few years has been a student of mine at the University of Utah. Three years ago he took a class in ecology, which is the study of the relationships of organisms to their environment. He showed unusual

interest and aptitude in this class, particularly in regards to the possibility of revegetating areas denuded of plant life.

Paul was born and reared in Magna, Utah. He has a great interest in and affection for the Oquirrh Mountains, and he immediately began consideration of plans that might help him rehabilitate the north face of this range. I encouraged him in this project and suggested that he might spend a summer setting up some pilot studies, for which I would grant him special credit. He labored far beyond my expectations—planting several hundred trees and shrubs of various kinds and laying out several experimental grass plots, all at his own expense.

The success of these preliminary studies has kindled in him unbounded enthusiasm and an ambition to help rehabilitate this mountain. I have faith in this vigorous young man, and I hope sincerely that you will encourage him in the project and especially in completing his education.

America has great need for young men with the physical and mental stamina of Paul Rokich and especially with the unusual vision that he demonstrates. I believe that much if not most of the north face of the Oquirrhs does have the possibility of rehabilitation. Such an accomplishment is bound, I believe, to bring substantial economic returns in time. But what is more important even, a serious attempt by a great industrial institution such as yours to return life, beauty and security to a dead landscape is certain to receive the spiritual acclaim of many thousands of citizens in this vicinity and throughout the nation. It would be a most appropriate project to initiate during this season of Lent.

If after hearing Paul's story you may decide that something can be done to lift the great face of the north Oquirrhs, I wish you to know that I gladly pledge any professional help within my power to accomplish this.

Sincerely yours,
Walter P. Cottam, Professor of Botany

Some years later, Rokich planted a gully in the Oquirrhs with hundreds of Dr. Cottam's hybrid oak seedlings, a refuge now for elk and deer and other wildlife. He called it "Cottam's Gulch West."

As the honors and awards came Dr. Cottam's way in later years, so did the letters of congratulations from his former students.

Irving B. McNulty, who later became professor of biology and chairman of the botany department at the University of Utah, said of Dr. Cottam:

> His enthusiasm for the understanding of nature was so strong it made an indelible impression on students. I remember one student saying that he never took so few notes in a class nor learned as much as he did in a class from Dr. Cottam. . . .Rather than just telling students something, he would challenge them to explain something he had shown them. He would guide their thinking with questions until they found the right answer, which they never forgot. He taught them how to reason, and students couldn't help acquiring some of his enthusiasm for learning about nature and its beauty. I know, because he changed my whole life in the first course I took from him. From then on, I majored in botany and have been forever grateful to him.

A letter from Charles M. Woolf, associate professor of genetics, Arizona State University, said in part:

> As an undergraduate and graduate student at the University of Utah in your plant ecology and biogeography courses, I recognized quickly that I was in the presence of a teacher par excellence. I shall never forget those field trips and lectures when in your own unique way you made the principles of ecology come to life. Your love of biology was contagious, and I am numbered among the many who were guided into biology partly because of your stimulation as a teacher.
>
> The rewards you are now receiving locally and

> nationally, especially as ecologist of the year, are well deserved. The effect you have had on biology and conservation practices in the state of Utah will be everlasting.

Another former student, Bertrand F, Harrison, wrote, "It is gratifying that the university recognizes your great service and has taken this means of honoring you and of keeping ever fresh the memory of you." Recalling his introduction to St. George and Capitol Reef National Park, he added:

> As important as were these introductions, even more meaningful was the introduction you gave me to new ideas. I look back and recall what a naive kid I was and am ever grateful to you for giving me a sense of balance, an enthusiasm for the world of plants and some standards of excellence. My Dad gave me a love of the out-of-doors, but my high school biology class thoroughly killed any desire to follow that field as an occupation. You got me back on the track and made it possible for me to spend my life in the most interesting and challenging field there is. . . . I can never thank you enough for making it possible for me to teach at the BYU these forty-odd years. I am sure it was your recommendation that got me the job. I hope they have been productive years. Certainly I know of no more rewarding way to devote one's life than to help students build more rewarding lives and to share vicariously in their successes.

Fred Evans, on the faculty in the department of zoology and entomology at the U, wrote: "I would like you to know that you have had a greater influence on me at an important period in my life than any other person. You gave me both a challenge and an opportunity because you were a magnificent teacher. No one is more deserving than you of the numerous honors you have received during the past few years, and I wish to congratulate you."

Dr. William H. Behle, who later became a professor of

biology at the university and a highly respected authority on Utah birds, was a junior majoring in biology when Dr. Cottam transferred to the U of U from BYU. In a letter written in 1981 to his old friend and teacher, Dr. Behle said:

> I fondly recall taking your course in ecology and experiencing your many delightful field trips, especially the one to the Beaver Creek area on the western spur of the Uinta Mountains. Your course opened my eyes to an interpretation of nature. You had a visionary view of interrelationships that was shared by few others at the time. You were a truly great teacher, one whom I tried to emulate all through my teaching days. Particularly effective was your technique of illustrating your talks with slides and your fascinating commentary. I remember your hand coloring 3 1/4 x 4 1/4 transparencies in the days before Kodachrome film. I still have some on the colonial birds of Great Salt Lake that you colored for me, as well as some you did on Silver Reef for my uncle, Mark Pendleton. I also recall your printing black and white pictures for my Masters dissertation. This brings to mind another of your outstanding attributes, namely, the vast amount of help that you gave all your students whenever called upon.
>
> I could go on and on with such reminiscences. Let me just summarize by saying that I consider you the greatest in the history of the old Biology Department. You are renowned not only for your superb teaching, but also for your scholarly publications, the most outstanding of which, *"Is Utah Sahara Bound?"*, made a profound impact on a generation of students and conservationists the world over.
>
> Above all, I long ago came to appreciate your human qualities, such as your warmth and cordiality. I have cherished your friendship these many years. You are the most respected person I have ever had the privilege of knowing. You have been an inspiration to me through virtually all of my career.

THE ARTIST

Dr. Cottam was more than a scientist and educator: he was also an artist, a lover of beauty in all its forms. How could a man with his agile mind, working for days, weeks, and months on the desert methodically doing research on his scientific projects escape noticing the varying moods of the desert, its subtle colors, its wind and rain, its sunsets, its mystery?

Whatever Nature had to offer, he reveled in it, from the tiniest flower to the crashing thunderstorm. And the sheer joy of being part of this wonder he captured in everything he did, in his photography, in his lectures, in his teaching, and in his personal life. A vital, good-humored, keen-witted, dedicated man, he had just enough of the devil in him to make him a fascinating human being.

A scientific journal once rejected a paper he submitted about the desert because he included his feelings when the journal wanted only the scientific facts. "Scientists are human beings too," he said. "People think the desert is desolate and monotonous, but if you are alert to its changing moods, you come to love it."

That word "Love" may be the magic ingredient that set Dr. Cottam apart from many others. It's the thing conservationists Aldo Leopold and Joseph Wood Krutch believe is missing from many conservation efforts designed to preserve resources mainly for man's use.

Krutch wrote in an article titled *Conservation is Not Enough*, "To live healthily and successfully on the land, we must also live with it. We must be part not only of the human community, but of the whole community; we must acknowledge some sort of oneness not only with our neighbors, our countrymen, and our civilization, but also with the natural as well as the man-made community. . . . It is not a sentimental but a grimly literal fact that unless we share this terrestrial globe with creatures other than ourselves, we shall not be able to live on it for long."

He quoted Thoreau who once said, "This curious world which we inhabit is more wonderful than it is convenient; more beautiful than it is useful; it is more to be admired than it is to be used." Krutch added his thought, "Without realization that 'this curious world' is at least beautiful as well as useful, conservation is doomed. We must live for something besides making a living. If we do not permit the earth to produce beauty and joy, it will in the end not produce food either."

That Dr. Cottam subscribed to this philosophy wholeheartedly was apparent in all his endeavors—he had an unabashed love affair with Mother Nature. In his later years, he said, "I wouldn't mind dying; I just don't want to leave this earth."

Cottam's former BYU student Bertrand F. Harrison summed his professor up in a tribute at the Fifteenth Annual Arboretum Day in May 1979:

> I used to wonder how he came to know all the things he did. Later I came to understand, at least in part. He had an intense interest—akin to love—in the plants of his homeland, and this same interest and enthusiasm he transmitted to his students. He had a great curiosity about plants and was constantly looking, searching for answers, for relationships.
>
> Not content in finding answers only in books, he sought out the plants in their secluded niches to learn of their ways. When not in the schoolroom or laboratory, he was in the field—searching, observing and collecting.

Harrison and another student traveled with Dr. Cottam in his Model T Ford on a month-long field trip through southern Utah and the Arizona Strip in 1929. "From him I came to know the desert, its many moods, its harshness and its beauty," Harrison said. Of Dr. Cottam's teaching talents, he said, "His language was as colorful as the hills of his native Dixie. His figures of speech brought interest and meaning to his discussions. He was a sensitive artist and a superb photographer, and he used these talents to bring the outdoor world with all its intimacy, its beauty and its majesty into the classroom. . . . As a teacher his ultimate objective was to give to his students some of the wonder and the fascination of plants that he knew; to teach them to work and to think independently and speak up for that which they knew to be right." Speaking of Dr. Cottam's influence on a broader scale, he said: "Long before most people had ever heard the word 'ecology,' he was calling us to repentance for overgrazing our range lands, for over-harvesting our timber, and for recklessly denuding farmlands, roadsides and mining properties. . . . No one has been more effective in showing us the divine obligation of stewardship of our world; no one has given us greater appreciation of the beauty and fragility of our environment; no one has impressed us more with the urgency for its care."

Harrison said he once asked a friend who was raised in St. George how it was that so many notable people came from Utah's Dixie. The friend answered that the early Church Brethren sent all the outspoken, free-thinking Mormons to colonize Dixie. . . . "I don't know if there is any truth to that tale, but it could help to account for Dr. Cottam's insistence on thinking for himself, his complete intellectual honesty, and his courage and willingness to speak out against the abuse of the environment."

In a series of articles called "Latter-day Saint Artists" appearing in the *Young Woman's Journal*, a publication of the LDS Church in the August 1929 edition, Harrison R. Merrill wrote:

> I am placing Dr. Walter P. Cottam among the creative artists. Dr. Cottam does not use brushes or colors except in tinting his exquisite photographs and slides, but in my opinion he is a creative artist, nevertheless. He has an unusual eye for pictures—composition, lights and shadows and form. His photographs of scenes have guided the steps of many painters to unknown opportunities for sketching.
>
> Were Dr. Cottam merely a photographer who goes out and photographs a scene, I would not think of using him here. But he is much more than that. He is a poet in whose soul beauty creates an emotion. He beholds, he feels, and he has developed the power through his knowledge of lenses and chemistry to photograph not the scene, but his subjective interpretation of the scene. That is art.

Some of Dr. Cottam's best friends were artists, who often painted pictures from his color photographs. However, one friend, Orson Campbell, was obsessed with painting old barns. He did one showing a window high at the top of the barn and horse manure piled up in front of it almost to the window. Campbell asked Cottam what he thought of it, and Cottam replied, "Hell, Orson, I think you've got too much horse manure in it." The next time Cottam saw the picture, the manure had been cut down considerably.

After he retired, Dr. Cottam took an auto trip with prominent Utah artist Lynn Fausett and his wife. At one point during their conversation, the subject of ecology came up and Lynn was quoting some ideas of his nephew, who had been with the Bureau of Land Management. Dr. Cottam disputed what Fausett was saying. "You paint and I'll keep my mouth shut, but when you start talking ecology, I'm going to speak up," he said.

He was strolling through an art exhibit in the Union Building at the university one day and paused to admire the painting of a nude woman. Just at that time a student approached. "Dr Cottam, how are you?" "Fine," Cottam replied. "And how is Mrs. Cottam?" Nodding at the nude, Cottam replied, "Oh, about like that."

Once Dr. Cottam photographed a sepia etching of Alfred Lambourne, an early Utah artist, which had been done by another early artist, Mahonri Young. He printed the picture exactly the same size, then went over it with meticulous strokes in sepia color, producing an exact replica of the etching. He then attached a note to the back describing what he had done, framed the artwork and had it hanging in his home for several years. He eventually gave it to a niece, Grace Muir, who had a considerable collection of the works of Utah artists. Sometime later she called an appraiser to assess the collection, and he was immediately taken with the picture of Lambourne. He told Mrs. Muir that it was the finest thing she had. When she showed him the note on the back, he informed her that but for the note, he could have got $5,000 for it.

At one time, Dr. Cottam invited Henri Moser, another Utah artist, to live at the Cottam home while he painted—and he stayed for six weeks, much to Effie's chagrin. She was the one who managed the household and made it possible for her husband to be the free spirit that he was. He could pursue his fancies, get mad, forget his responsibilities and somehow she would be at the right place at the right time to make things work. In a way, the desire expressed in her Academy yearbook "to be a mother to Walter" had come true.

THE HUMORIST

Cottam's wry sense of humor surfaced continually throughout his long impressive career. Once he worked with two doctors for about a year studying pollen in the Salt Lake Valley. One of the doctors came to the university to see him while he was teaching a class. He made the man wait half an hour while he finished. When he came out, he told the doctor, "That was the best half hour I ever spent—knowing I was keeping a physician waiting!"

Dr. Henry Eyring, a brilliant, nationally known scientist and professor at the University of Utah, was Walter's cousin. Cottam had great respect for him as a scientist but couldn't see how Eyring, knowing as much as he did, could continue to embrace the Mormon religion. Once Walter had Eyring come to talk to one of his classes. Eyring's explanation of some chemical process was so explicit that Cottam declared, "I sat there tingling with excitement listening to him." Afterwards, he said to Eyring, "Henry, you made it so darned simple you made an atheist out of me," and walked out of the room. Ten minutes later his phone was ringing, with Eyring on the line asking if he was serious. Cottam told him he was. "Hell," he said, "I don't need a spirit to understand that."

Professor A. O. Garrett, a botany teacher at East High School and a good friend of Cottam's, over the years made a large collection of the area plants, which he later donated to the University of Utah. The herbarium there is now named the Garrett Herbarium. Cottam also contributed thousands of specimens to that herbarium throughout his career.

Garrett, a bachelor, lived alone in a house filled with cats. When Cottam went to visit him, he always took a couple of cigars, which the two men would smoke as they talked. Once a prominent botanist who came to Salt Lake was directed to Garrett as the man to talk to about the flora of the area. After the visitor had left town, Cottam stopped by Garrett's house. Garrett was fretting because the visiting botanist had complained that his house stunk. "Do you think it stinks?" he asked. "Why in hell do you think I bring cigars?" Cottam replied.

Walter Pace Cottam

Born March 3,1894
St. George, UT
Died December 22,1988
Gresham, OR

Marriages

Effie Frei
July 1,1915
Died August 28,1964

Doris Dollard Jump
September 8,1965
Died June 24, 1968

Georgina Wilson
July 6, 1970
Died May 22, 1983

WALTER'S PARENTS

Thomas P. Cottam

Born September 28,1857
Salt Lake City, UT
Married January 26,1882
Died March 16,1926
St. George, UT

Emmaline Jarvis

Born March 21,1863
St. George, UT
Died September 21, 1944
St. George, UT

WALTER'S GRANDPARENTS

Thomas Cottam

Born October 20,1820
West Bradford, Yorkshire, England
Married October 9,1847
Died November 10,1898
St. George, UT

Caroline Smith

Born October 11, 1820
Nottingham, Kent, England
Died February 19,1889
St. George, UT

George Jarvis

Born March 25,1823
Harlow, Essex, England
Married September 17,1846
Died January 6, 1913
St. George, UT

Ann Prior

Born December 29,1830
Middleson, London, England
Died January 10,1913
St. George, UT

Cottam family photo; Walter far right seated next to father.

Moroni, left, with his tormentor Walter.

Effie Frei became Mrs. Walter Cottam July 1, 1915.

Cottam receives his B.A. degree from BYU in 1916.

Ready for first teaching job at Jordan High.

Cottam children (back) Grant, Fae, Beatrice; (front) George, Richard.

Cottam earns Ph.D. from University of Chicago in 1926.

Dr. Cottam's Reynolds Lecture was an eye-opener.

Cottam's Gulch, still an oasis of beauty on U. campus.

Salt Lake Tribune photo of Cottam for feature story.

Dr. Cottam with just two of his numerous awards.

"A blazing campfire, a glass of wine, and thou..."

Dew-pearled evening primrose at Valley of Fire.

Doc and Judge Ellett with Bear Lake cisco.

Vard flirts with danger at the Wedge.

Eminent ecologist becomes a rock hound.

At Calf Creek Falls.

Doc uses aspen "bloom" as face powder.

Doc and Judge Ellett express environmental leanings.

Threesome pause for a photo session.

The Judge provides lunchtime entertainment.

Watermelon time - a Cottam tradition.

Wearing Georgina's hand-knit hats and scarves, the Cottams try snowshoeing.

Judge Ellett joins the Thursday Sabbath Club.

Doc's first arrowhead.

Doc goes to any length for a good photo.

John Riffey and Doc renew friendship at Toroweap.

Sinbad Overlook – a beautiful surprise.

Doc photographs pictographs at Head of Sinbad.

What is a Thursday trip without steaks?

Hikers cross snowfields on rugged Sheeprocks climb.

Doc and Vard enjoy solitude of the West Desert.

Artist Alvin Gittins and Dr. Cottam at unveiling of portrait.

Dr. Cottam with book on his hybrid oak project.

John Tucker and Doc speak at oak grove dedication.

Chapter 12

Life Changes

Dr. Cottam lost his boyhood sweetheart and wife of 49 years when she died August 28, 1964, as a result of injuries suffered in an automobile accident. Dick and his family had come from Pittsburgh for a visit and they were all going out to dinner, taking two cars. Dr. Cottam was driving his own car, Effie in the passenger seat beside him and Dick's wife and son in the back seat. Dick was following in the other car with his three other children. Cottam made a left turn and was struck on the passenger side by another car coming through the intersection. Effie, the only one injured, did fairly well for a brief time, then developed complications and died of gangrene of the small intestine and heart complications twelve days after the accident.

Dr. Cottam had learned to drive in the early days of the automobile and had never enjoyed the growing complexity of modern traffic. He liked to look at the passing scenery, to stop suddenly when he saw a flower by the side of the road. He was also having trouble with his vision. At the time of the accident, he had turned too slowly and was later cited as causing the accident, an assessment that appeared in the newspaper.

Letters of condolence poured in from a shocked community, recalling memories of Effie and her contributions to the university and the community.

Dr. Cottam asked Waldemer P. Read, professor of philosophy at the university, to speak at Effie's funeral, which turned out to be a huge event. Although Walter was not active in the LDS church, most members of his and Effie's families were, so he asked the bishop just to conduct the services. Though a Mormon, Read disagreed with the traditional beliefs of the Mormon Church. He said in part:

> I must tell you, my friends, that I happen to believe in death. Not in the way that I believe in exercise or proper diet or in truth telling or in chastity; not, that is, as an ideal. I believe in death as a fact—that it marks the end of a life. Whenever there is a death, a life is finished. The dying one will do no more, will fail no more, succeed no more, suffer no more, nor any more rejoice. That one has had it.
>
> Moreover, I think it would be well if all believed as I do. When the time comes that we face the fact of death honestly and recognize that whatever men and women are to enjoy, they must enjoy it here in this life, we will be less prone, in my opinion, to view with complacency the conditions of hardship and deprivation under which many live—a complacency made easy by the comforting rationalization that whatever they lack here on earth will be made up to them, according to their deserts, in the life beyond the grave. For "if in this life only we have hope" for achievement and joy, then we had better help each other now, doing what we can to soften the blows that come to the unfortunate.

He continued, stressing Effie's contributions and the influence she had on her family and in the community, saying hers was a life well-lived and the world was better for it. He concluded:

> Effie's life is now all in the past. She is finished; but she is not gone. She remains with us and is dear in

memory—to say nothing of her uncounted effects that carry on. And if there is a Cosmic Memory, Walter, if there is a Cosmic Memory, then her life will never perish, and all of the pathos and all of the sterling worth of it will forever be appreciated.

The bishop couldn't let the service conclude on that note, and he rose and delivered an impassioned speech proclaiming his belief in the hereafter. "The funeral developed into a debate," Cottam said. "It was the damnedest funeral ever held in Salt Lake City. Effie wouldn't have liked it at all. She wasn't the least bit argumentative." Walter recalled that the children had wanted a nice funeral for their mother, and they had selected an oak casket and arranged for the service, which cost $1500, "which I couldn't afford." Later when he took his check to the mortuary, Walter told the mortician that he was a damned parasite, living off people's grief and taking advantage of them. "I suppose you think I should be here with tears in my eyes," he said, "but I'll tell you how I feel. I feel like I'm paying for a dead horse. This is the last money you will ever get from me."

The funeral director told Walter that he had had people make comments before, but he had never heard an oration like that.

In memory of his wife, Dr. Cottam planted the Effie F. Cottam Pine Grove on the university campus, digging the deep holes for each of the 21 trees himself. Of her death, he said, "How I have loved that piece of flesh." That year he spent much time outside his house watering his yard. Doing so seemed to give him solace. By fall, his dahlias nearly reached the roof. And he hunted and found the letters he had written to Effie from England to see if he had ever told her he loved her.

On September 8, 1965, after a lonely year, Walter married Doris Dollard Jump, originally from Ohio and a former neighbor and English teacher. When the Cottams moved to Salt Lake City in 1931, they had bought a new home on property owned by the Jumps at 1114 McClelland Street. That modest one-story brick home was the base for the family throughout Dr. Cottam's years at the university and for most of his years in retirement.

Sometime after their marriage, Dr. Cottam, Doris and George signed papers donating their bodies to the University of

Utah medical school "in protest of the high cost of burial and the commercialization of this natural and highly private biological event."

After less than three years of marriage, Doris died suddenly of a heart attack on June 24, 1968. She had no heirs, but her sister came to the simple services held in the Unitarian Church in Salt Lake City. Though not an outdoors person, Doris had supported Walter's oak project, sewing the nylon bags used to catch the acorns. After her death, he planted an oak grove in her memory. And true to their agreement, he donated her body to the medical school.

When Effie died, Walter had studied her recipes, and with his usual enthusiasm for any experiment he tackled, he soon became a good cook. After Doris's death, he resumed his lonely bachelor's life, doing his own cooking, working on his oak project, taking care of George, tending his yard and garden—until a chance telephone call brought him two new friends and hundreds of trips into his beloved outdoors for the next twelve years.

❦

On July 9, 1970, the first anniversary of our first meeting with Doc, we drove to his house to pick him up for our regular Thursday outing. He was outside and we stopped to admire the purple clematis by the front door and the lilies in the yard. As we talked, a gray-haired lady in a flowered housecoat and some pink, feathery house slippers stepped out onto the porch and came down the steps and across the lawn toward us. "I'd like to introduce you," Doc said. "This is Vard and Maxine . . . and her name is Cottam." We were flabbergasted.

Vard's story "A Man and His Mountains" about Doc and his accomplishments had had a more profound effect than we dreamed. Doc had told us shortly after his return from California that a woman who had read the story in the *Salt Lake Tribune* had called him and said he sounded like the kind of man she would like to meet. But little more had been said, except now and then in recent weeks a casual mention of a lady friend. The romance had progressed without our knowledge. And they had driven to Ely, Nevada, on July 6 to be married.

She was Francis Georgina Wilson, widow of Joseph R.

Wilson, a pioneer Utah labor leader. After his death she had remarried briefly, then been widowed again.

Since Doc had married her with the understanding that she wouldn't interfere with his Thursday trips, he was ready for the day's outing. We invited her to go along, but being in charge of crafts for senior citizens at Fairmont Park, she had to go to a party there that afternoon. She said Doc could tell us all about the wedding. His expertise as a raconteur came into play as we drove along.

He said that they drove to Elko, but finding that Elko marriage licenses appeared in the paper almost as regularly as Salt Lake licenses did, they went on to Ely. They found the courthouse and went into the clerk's office, where Georgina asked the man if he knew which way was north. Cottam couldn't imagine what she had in mind, but the clerk replied, "Out that window." "Well then, why don't you hang your flag right, with the field of blue to the north?" she asked.

"I'm in charge of the flag for the American Legion, and I think I know how to display the flag," he replied. "I've been in charge of a statewide education campaign on the proper way to display the flag, and you don't know what you're talkin' about," she retorted.

By this time the four girls in the office were in hysterics, but one finally approached Cottam, standing on the sidelines, to ask if she could help him. "Well, I came here to get a wedding license," he said, "but it looks like I got sidetracked."

Eventually the license was issued, and the couple asked if there were any Mormon bishops in town to perform the ceremony. Two names were supplied, but then Cottam wondered if a justice of the peace might perform it instead. Georgina said that she had been married in the LDS Temple the first two times, and maybe she would like to try something different. They found a justice of the peace in the building and went to his office. He also acted as coroner and head of the juvenile division. He was smoking a cigarette when they went in, and Georgina said, "I hope you're going to put that out when you perform the ceremony."

She then proceeded to tell him that Dr. Cottam was the famous botanist from the University of Utah, perhaps the most famous botanist in the world, and that she would like to have the JP get the two handsomest highway patrolmen he could find to participate in the ceremony, one as the best man and one as the bridesmaid. The justice of the peace made three trips trying to find them, asking once if the couple would settle for two jailbirds in the nearby jail. But he finally returned with two highway patrolmen. "And the bridesmaid," Cottam said, "was smoking a big cigar." The bride-to-be promptly requested him to dispense with that, and he laid it in an ashtray on the table.

Finally ready for the ceremony, they lined up in a row in front of the JP, "the best man at my right and the bridesmaid at her left," Cottam said. After hearing Georgina's recital of Dr. Cottam's accomplishments, the JP was shaking like a leaf as he read the prepared written ceremony. When it came time for the best man to hand Cottam the ring, he couldn't get it out of the box. "Georgina reached over and took it from him, got it out of the box, and handed it back to him. Then he handed it to me," Cottam said.

After the ceremony, the groom gave her a peck, but the best man, the bridesmaid, and the justice of the peace each gave her a big kiss. Cottam then asked the going rate for the ceremony, and the judge told him $7. "I'm going to do better than that," Cottam said. "I'm going to give you $10, and I'm going to give the best man and the bridesmaid $5 each. That should be enough to get drunk on, shouldn't it?" "Well, it won't get us drunk, but it will give us a good start," the best man said. "It's not worth a damned bit more than that to me," Cottam said. About this time the bridesmaid asked if he could resume smoking his cigar.

Then Cottam asked the JP if the license had to be published, and the JP said that he thought he could arrange to keep it out of the papers. When he made his call, they heard only one side of the conversation, but the JP said it was the damnedest wedding he had ever performed. Both of the participants had "silver hair, not a golden thread in it."

Afterwards, Cottam asked his bride how the ceremony compared with her two previous ones, and she replied, "There's no comparison." At one point in the recitation, we kidded Doc that she apparently set her cap for him from the start. He said she told him once that she usually got what she went after.

He told of another incident when they bought groceries

and she protested when he picked up the sack to carry it to the car. She wanted him to let one of the boys carry it. He walked out carrying the sack. She said if everyone did that, they would lay off the boys who were hired for that job. Doc said he hadn't thought of that, then added, "I'm afraid I'm going to be continually embarrassed by that woman."

Georgina was two years older than Doc. During her marriage to Wilson, she had had seven children, six boys and one girl. She had been very active in the women's auxiliaries of the labor organization, as well as in the Mormon Church and in the USO.

Not a woman of great refinement, she was pushy, uninhibited, and tactless. But she was good-humored, never complained, a good sport, and just what Doc needed at this time in his life. She had a mindless, happy quality that helped shut out the approaching darkness. And he had always seemed to have a desperate need for female companionship. Although he had told her that there wasn't room for her in the car to join us on the Thursday trips, we felt obliged to invite her, and she soon was going most of the time. Hearing about their wedding from Doc had been hilarious, but having her along left much to be desired. Vard soon cursed the day he had written that article. After the first or second trip, she said to Doc, "Why you said there wasn't room for me in here. There's plenty of room!" Doc said, "Vard had to rearrange everything to do it."

Fate has a way of letting one know that things can't be perfect for very long. But for the pleasure of Doc's company, we would put up with anything.

Although Georgina had a house in Salt Lake, she moved in with Doc, adding even more clutter to a house already in disarray. A typical absent-minded professor, he had a long history of mislaying almost everything he touched, a habit which meant tearing the house apart in search of the mislaid article the next time he needed it. Though the degree of the clutter was new, this kind of search had been a family ritual throughout his life.

We took turns furnishing the food for dinner, and when it was the Cottams' turn, it was a shambles. They came to the car with boxes of food, thermoses, jackets, walking sticks, cameras, and, of course, her knitting or crocheting. On occasions when she didn't go along, she would stand by the car naming every article as Vard put it away, telling us what it was, how to prepare it, and almost when and how to eat it. Vard was so thankful that she wasn't going, he would grit his teeth and not say a word—except a few times when he'd heard all he could stand.

Sometimes on an outing she would announce that she couldn't go next week, then ask "Will you miss me?" When Vard and I remained silent, Doc would save us by answering, "Like a sore tooth." Often as we rode along, Georgina would be knitting and talking, usually about something asinine that met with little response. Then out of the blue, she would say, "Ain't we got fun!"

Often Doc and Georgina would be jawing at each other in the back seat. Doc used to threaten that if she died first, he would send her up to the "vat" at the university, where he had donated his body, and she used to threaten that if he died first, she would throw the biggest funeral in the history of Salt Lake for him.

Despite it all, we had some wonderful days—going on mountain drives, photographing Indian rock art in Nine-Mile Canyon, fishing on lakes in the Uinta Mountains, discovering new roads, new vistas, even snowshoeing.

Georgina even provided a little humor at times. She mentioned on one of our trips that she had told some friends that she and Doc took their harmonicas to bed one night and played until midnight. Doc said one of them remarked, "I always wondered what old people do when they go to bed."

At 76 Doc was still very much involved in his oak project, going up to the grove nearly every day, weeding and watering his diverse creations, fighting the gophers. He took us up to the grove early in our acquaintanceship, introduced us to the trees, and told us about the problems he had had with the university, trying to get greenhouse space, having groundskeepers use 2-4-D to kill dandelions, causing the trees he had planted on campus to die or the acorns to abort. His latest complaint was that the university wanted to charge him $7.50 to park—half price for emeritus professors—and he refused to pay. Instead, he parked his car off campus at a city meter and walked to his oak grove. Sometime after he married Georgina, he gave up driving and took the bus to the university. Occasionally he would miss the last bus in the evening and have to walk the three miles home.

I soon had enough information for a story about the oak hybridization project for the *Deseret News* and later about Cottam's Gulch. I asked if he and Rudy Drobnick were the only ones in the country crossing oak, and he said, "Nobody else would be such damned fools."

We usually stopped for coffee at Cottam's before heading out on our Thursday trips. There was always something going on in that household. Once Georgina asked if we'd like to see their louse. Doc had dispatched a number of gophers at his oak grove, and Georgina thought she could make something out of their skins. They took them home, but when they considered the skinning process, they noticed a little white spot at the end of every hair. The spots were lice that had departed the skin when the gophers died and had crawled out to the end of the hairs. Doc got one louse on a glass slide to look at under the microscope, but the gophers went into the garbage can. The louse was still alive when we looked at it and would wiggle its legs when we blew on it.

They had a duck once that thought Georgina was its mother. It would follow her all around the yard. Neighborhood children called the duck "Peep! Peep!" and the name stuck. Doc, Georgina and George all could be seen in the yard at times turning over dirt with a shovel to unearth worms for Peep Peep. Every night Georgina would give it a warm bath, then wrap it in a towel. I'm not sure where it spent the night. The story didn't have a happy ending. A dog got the duck once and ran down the street with it, injuring its leg. It recovered, but when the dog nearly got it again, the Cottams took Peep Peep to a relative's farm and left it in a pen with other ducks and geese and peacocks that promptly attacked him. They left to the sound of Peep Peep's crying for them to rescue him. They didn't sleep that night and vowed they would never get another pet.

Doc and Georgina went out to dinner with some friends one evening, went back to the house of the other couple afterward and surprised burglars, who ran out the front door as they entered the back door. The house was a shambles, every drawer ransacked, books pulled down, and cameras and jewelry on the beds. But the thieves had been packing up and had had time only to take a few items. Cottam said when he got home and went to his room downstairs, he looked around at all his stuff and thought if burglars ever broke in there, they would say, "By God, somebody got here before us!"

Chapter 13

Days of Discovery

Usually on our drive home from a Thursday outing, someone would say, "Where shall we go next week?" If no one had a suggestion or if we wanted to find a new place, we would refer to Ward J. Roylance's *Utah, The Incredible Land,* a guide book to the state published in 1965. Sometimes just a line or two would lead to the discovery of a wonderful new destination. It was that way with a paragraph in a section on the San Rafael Swell. "Among the most inspirational canyon overlooks in southern Utah are those from The Wedge along the northern rim of San Rafael River gorge west of Buckhorn Draw. From points a thousand feet above the river, the view encompasses a breathtaking panorama of mighty cliffs and canyons, and some of Utah's most majestic buttes."

So on a pleasant but cool and cloudy day in May 1971, we picked up the Cottams and headed south for The Wedge. We had been through Buckhorn Draw before and, as we neared that area, we saw a sign saying "Wedge—6 miles." We had been in flat, rather barren desert country, but soon we were winding up on the dirt road into juniper-covered hills. It's the kind of country we like, but we didn't see anything too striking until we came to a sign that said, "Danger—Dropoff 200 Feet."

We approached slowly. Suddenly the whole world opened up in front of us. We were on the rim of a great chasm with the San Rafael River a green ribbon far below. Across the chasm, stretching off into the distance ahead of us were colorful monoliths and buttes, and to the left, the gorge curved down toward Buckhorn Draw. The road we came in on ended abruptly—with no barriers at all to prevent a vehicle from plunging over the edge. But side roads to the left and right traversed the rim, offering spectacular views of the vista.

We spent some time there exploring, photographing, and exclaiming over the sight. When Vard said, "We're going to have dinner here!" no one objected. He set the table and chairs up on smooth slabs of stone near the edge of the gorge. After Doc sat down in the folding chair with his back to the gaping chasm, Georgina, sitting in the shade of a nearby juniper and knitting on a blue afghan, nearly had a fit. When Doc vacated the chair, Vard turned it around and sat with his legs crossed and feet sticking out in the air.

The dinner, the company, and the setting were ideal.

Sometime later Doc told us that he had described The Wedge to his good friend Utah Supreme Court Justice A. H. Ellett, who had impulsively driven down on his own. He took a wrong turn and got stuck in the sand by the river. It took him three hours to get out. We suggested to Doc that the Judge might like to go with us on a Thursday trip, and we could show him The Wedge. That trip didn't come about for a few months, but when it did, it was another day to remember—chiefly because the Judge replaced Georgina on most of our outings thereafter. Dr. Cottam had told us the Judge was a great guy and could talk about anything. He was right. From 8:00 a.m. when we picked him up on March 9, 1972, until 11:00 p.m. when we took him home, Ellett regaled us with stories and experiences about everything from the U.S. Supreme Court to the three Nephites. He told us he required 80 percent of the talking time, and he far exceeded his quota.

Judge Ellett had grown up on a farm in Texas and still carried a southern accent. He was converted to Mormonism when he was 17 years old and, although he found some of the teachings absurd and impossible to accept, he remained a good member of the church. He had been a school teacher, an accountant, a lawyer, a deputy Salt Lake County attorney, a city judge, a district court judge and was appointed to the Utah Supreme Court by Governor Calvin L. Rampton in 1967. He was 75 when we met him, completely bald, with blue eyes and a rather large mouth that wasn't often in repose.

The miles flew by as we drove south, listening to lawyer stories, tales of impoverished youth, arguments with a church authority about the age of the earth. We heard about cabins he had owned, about his love for dogs and hatred for cats, and about his overwhelming hatred for the U. S. Supreme Court and some of its decisions. "I hate that Supreme Court with such a vengeance," he said, "that if one of its members gets assassinated, I should be a prime suspect."

It wasn't the best time of day for photographing when we arrived at The Wedge but we took pictures from several viewpoints along the rim anyway. Ellett was very much impressed and said he wanted to come back to camp there and shoot scenes in the morning and evening light.

After lunch at the San Rafael Campground, we went exploring on a bumpy road that led us to the rim of the Black Box, where we looked down on a gorge hundreds of feet deep with very narrow, almost sheer, walls. Vard had been very careful driving along the way because of little gullies where water ran across the road when it rained. But one caught him unaware, and there was a terrific bounce then a great clatter of falling dishes in the back seat and exclamations from the two rear passengers. Both men had nearly gone through the roof. The Judge was rubbing his head and said he was glad he had his hat on. He said he used to have a stiff neck because of calcium in the vertebrae, but now his neck was "limber as a snake."

Despite this mishap and another incident when the Scout got hung up on a rock ledge, the Judge asked on the drive home, "How do you join this group?" "Just be available on Thursdays," Vard said.

Although he was still working full time on the court, Ellett started taking Thursdays off and then would work Saturdays to keep up with his cases. He would go back to work on Fridays with tales of his Thursday adventures, and soon the fellow justices, court clerks, and girls in the stenographic pool started asking him on Wednesday if he was going out on Thursday. To counter so many questions, he started wearing a red shirt on Wednesday to show he was going on Thursday. He tended to joke and kid with the stenographers, and it wasn't long before instead of saying T.G.I.F. for Thank God It's Friday, they were saying S.H.I.T—Sure Happy It's Thursday.

Having the Judge along added a new zest to the Thursday outings. He was a skilled photographer, as was Doc, and Vard and I were working on it. We photographed wildflowers in the spring and summer, Indian petroglyphs and pictographs, sunsets, Utah's spectacular fall colors, snow scenes in the winter, and shots of each other hiking, fishing, rock hounding, and sitting by campfires. Spirited but amiable conversations covered religion, capital punishment, the law, politics, geology, and the weather.

One intense discussion focused on the origin of life. The Judge couldn't believe it could have happened in a "sterile" world without a creator. Vard said his premise was wrong, that the world was not sterile. The Judge said he believed things have a "yen" to reproduce. Cottam said when man can't understand things, he creates a deity that requires even more explanation. Quoting John Burroughs, he said, "Show me your anthropomorphic God, and I'll ask him some very embarrassing questions."

Some of our mountain drives took us over areas that had been badly damaged by overgrazing years earlier but were now recovering. On the Sanpitch Plateau, Cottam pointed out one mountain slope that had been terraced to hold the new vegetation and prevent erosion. He swore at the Mormon sheepmen and cattlemen, who had caused so much damage to the land, and he praised the Forest Service for rehabilitating it. But he also pointed out that the work had been paid for by the taxpayers, not by the cattlemen who had become rich ruining the land.

On a drive up Farmington Canyon, he marveled at all the grass and vegetation, recalling the 1930s when that land had been denuded by overgrazing. He told us that his friend Reed Bailey, with the Forest Service, had pioneered contouring and terracing up there on the Farmington-Bountiful watershed. He felt that Bailey was an unsung hero for all the work he had done. Cottam also praised the Civilian Conservation Corps boys who had done a lot of the terracing and planting in the canyon.

Once the Judge told us about falling on the ice and hurting his shoulder when he came out of the Federal Reserve Bank "in a pretty stormy mood" because they wouldn't accept checks made out to him to pay for Treasury Bills but insisted the checks be made out to the bank. After we let Ellett out and were driving Doc home, Doc said he never could get much interested in money. He said he thought about his pay check only because he had to buy food once in awhile. "If someone would furnish me with food and a place to stay, I wouldn't care anything about money."

And yet there were some material things he thought worth having. In a letter to Bea he once wrote, "The older I get the more I am convinced that if one fails to enjoy life here, he runs great chances of never experiencing fun. We never did have a great amount of cash when we were rearing our kids, but I think back on our life then with great joy and considerable satisfaction. There are a few things I would do differently if I had the chance to relive my yesterdays even with the same financial difficulties. For example, I think that I would not compel you to wear shoes out of style, nor suffer the embarrassment of a rubber tree at Santa Claus time. Our motor vehicles from the Model T on were our chief luxuries, and I still think that we could never have made finer investments. They gave us the chance to enjoy a beautiful world, and I am convinced that they afforded us an atmosphere for family companionship that few people excel."

Another time when the Judge was complaining about being only five feet ten inches tall, Vard told him that was nearly six feet. Ellett said, "No, I have a lot of six footers breathing down my neck." "What do you suppose they do to me?" Doc asked, thinking of his five feet six and a half inches. "Doc," the Judge said, "they look up to you." As much as Doc liked trees, he didn't care much for bonsai. "I've been a bonsai all my life," he said.

For some time Dr. Cottam had been talking about a three-or-four-day trip to Toroweap at Grand Canyon National

Monument, about half way between Grand Canyon National Park and Lake Mead on the north rim. He had camped out there for six weeks in 1952 doing some transects and making a collection of all the plants in the area. So on June 29, 1972, the four of us loaded up the Scout and headed south to Kanab, on to Fredonia, Arizona, then over a dirt road to Toroweap. As we drove through Toroweap Valley, Cottam wondered if John Riffey, the superintendent, was still there. We didn't stop to check at his house, but continued on down to the rim and to a primitive campground. The view from the rim was awesome, three thousand feet straight down to the Colorado River, a tiny ribbon with little riffles in places that probably were in reality challenging rapids. We chose spots a comfortable distance back from the rim for our sleeping bags that night.

Doc thought we should go for a little hike before breakfast in the morning before it got too hot. We got up as the sun was turning the sky pink far across the canyon rim. We had some orange juice and sweet rolls and headed out.

Thinking a little hike meant only an hour or so, we traveled light, taking only our cameras and no water. Cottam led the way, his camera slung over his shoulder, sauntering along, not walking fast, but steadily covering the ground, observing everything in his path. We followed the canyon rim around for awhile, approaching the edge at times for vantage points for photographs, Doc pointing out various wonders along the way. We weren't sure if we could see Separation Rapids, but he said it was right near there that the Howland brothers and William Dunn left Major John Wesley Powell's first expedition down the Colorado River in 1869 and climbed out of the canyon to make their way back to civilization on land. They were ambushed and killed their first night out by Shivwit Indians. The rest of the Powell party continued on down the river and made it out safely.

Soon under the warming sun, thirst overtook us and, when we found a pool of water in the rocks, we brushed the pollywogs aside and had a good drink. About this time, the Judge decided he had seen enough wonders and returned to the campground. Cottam, Vard, and I pressed on. It appeared now that our goal was to reach the Devil's Bathtub, another of Doc's wonders.

We kept the canyon rim in sight most of the time, but went into little side canyons and finally sighted the Devil's Bathtub, looking from a distance like one of the little pollywog pools. It was situated on a rock ledge just below the upper rim of a little side canyon. Just above it on the upper rim was a deep worn chute in the rock, where flood waters would come pouring down with great force, crashing into the pool eight or ten feet below. The pool, when we reached it and tried it out, proved to be about eight feet deep and eight feet across, with steep, smooth sides. Cottam said he had jumped in there a few years ago and almost panicked when he couldn't find a handhold anywhere around the sides. However, we found a little ledge on one side where the water was only five or six inches deep. The temptation was too great. We took turns having a dip in the cool water before starting the hot, dry walk back. Our "little hike" had taken about four hours.

Periodically we had wondered how the Judge was faring since the car was locked and there was no water at the campground. But a couple camping there had given him a cup of water from their low supply, and when we arrived, they were about to give him something to eat. The Judge immediately announced that he thought we should not stop to eat there but should pack up and drive over to Nixon Springs, where we planned to camp that night. He was vehemently outvoted by three tired and hungry hikers.

Revived by some lunch, we packed up and were driving out when Cottam said he wouldn't dare leave without stopping to see if Riffey still lived there. As we drove up to the house near the entrance to the monument, a lean, gray-haired man came out to the car. He was smiling when he greeted Vard, but when he saw Cottam in the back seat, his face really lit up. He insisted that we come in and have some iced tea. He got his water from four 400-gallon cisterns up on the hill behind his house, and Cottam said it made wonderful tea. He was right. The Judge, being a good Mormon in some respects, didn't drink tea, coffee or liquor, so he had ice water. But Vard, Doc, and I downed our first glass of tea in a matter of minutes, and before we were through, Riffey had made a second pitcher full and we had about four glasses each.

Doc's collection of plants was still there in a den adjoining the living room where we sat and, while he went in to look up the names of some of the plants he had forgotten, we sat looking at the hummingbirds coming to a feeder just outside the window and at other birds coming to drink and splash in a little pool in the yard. Riffey had been there about thirty years as superintendent with no helper. He said the monument had had only about 1600 visitors in each of the two previous years. "People come here to see the canyon. They don't want to see people. They like the isolation," he said. We reluctantly left the iced tea and the air-conditioned home with Riffey urging Doc to come down again and spend some time with him.

Doc got us off on a wild goose chase that afternoon looking for Big Springs, but the rocky, bumpy road got so bad for even a four-wheel drive that we returned to a primitive camp ground near Nixon Springs to camp. During the night we heard coyotes howling far off in the distance, a wonderful sound to Cottam, who said he hadn't heard coyotes like that for years.

On the drive home, we took a five-mile detour off I-15 to the Kolob section of Zion Canyon, climbing 1300 feet through spectacular redrock formations to a viewpoint parking and picnic area. We shared a watermelon there while marveling at the view of sheer walled gorges and wild canyons. It was almost a trademark with Cottam to carry along a melon to celebrate reaching a goal on a mountain drive or hike.

Our last camp was at Panguitch Lake, where we fished a little, spent the night and let the Judge cook breakfast for us the next morning before heading home. For some reason, Halley's Comet came up in the conversation, and Cottam said he was 16 years old when it came around. It was then, he said, that he understood for the first time that he was really going to die some day. The comet was due to return in 75 years, but he knew he wouldn't be here to see it.

In July of 1972 we did a repeat of our Lake Blanche hike, this time with Judge Ellett and Arthur H. Holmgren and his wife, Doris. Art was another of Doc's students, now head of the botany department at Utah State University and curator of the Intermountain Herbarium. He was a taxonomist and the author of several handbooks, including *Mountain Plants of Northeastern Utah* and *Vascular Plants of the Northern Wasatch.* Holmgren was a big, hearty man with reddish hair and unbounded enthusiasm. Doris was small with short, curly gray hair, tan skin and no makeup. The day was cool and cloudy, perfect weather for hiking. We stopped often to talk and rest and admire the view and the flowers. Holmgren filled in the names of several flowers we weren't sure of and called our attention to some ferns. Doris laughed and told us about the time Art was teaching a class telling the students about the Maidenhair Fern. Only he kept calling it "maidenhead" fern and wondered why the students were snickering.

We stopped twice to have some snacks and drinks. Art said he liked the way our group hiked for awhile, then stopped to eat something and argue about things.

The hike up took five hours again, but this time we were successful in finding the Brownie Ladyslipper (*Cypripedium fasciculatum*). However, the flowers were past their prime, and this orchid is small and not very showy. We found dozens of them. Art was elated and, with our permission, he dug up one to plant at his home in Logan. He said he had several *Cypripediums* growing in his yard, one, the Yellow Ladyslipper, (*C. parviflorum*), once very common in Utah, but now nearly extinct.

We didn't stop as often going down the steep trail as we had going up, but we heard the Judge complaining about his 76-year-old knees. Doc, now 78, didn't complain, but even with the use of his walking stick, he was tottering a little. The Holmgrens went on ahead as they had to get home to pack for a trip to California the next day. Back at the cars, Vard and I thanked them for a wonderful day and bade them goodbye before our elderly companions hove into view.

It was a sorry sight. First came Doc, moving slowly and somewhat unsteadily down the path, bracing himself with his walking stick. At first we didn't see the Judge. Then I caught a glimpse of just his head and shoulders through the shrubs. His head hung down, his shoulders looked stiff and he was moving like a robot, mechanically and slowly, up and down. We couldn't see his feet and legs, but we could feel the agony in every step. They both had to use their hands to lift their legs up to get into the car. When we asked if they wanted to stop to cook dinner, the Judge said that if we wanted to eat, he would roll up in his poncho somewhere and wait for us. And Cottam said,

"Naw, let's take the Judge home." But he, too, was ready to call it a day. Commenting on the hike, he said, "This may be the last time I will do that."

Later that summer, we accepted an invitation to have breakfast with the Holmgrens at their home in Logan and then go hiking with them. It was another day to remember, eating Doris's delicious Swedish pancakes with syrup or sour cream and blueberries, Canadian bacon, and a cold fruit soup with raspberries and whipped cream—while listening to beautiful classical music on the sound system Art had installed throughout the house. Both Art and Doris were Swedish. Art told us about his Swedish mother, who complained, "I yust learn how to say yelly and they change it to yam." Doris said the Swedes who become Mormons think the rule about not drinking coffee applies to everyone but them.

We started our hike from Tony Grove, a lake and campground area about seven miles off the main Logan Canyon road. Art described some of the features of the area and he and Doc tested us on the wildflowers. After we had stopped for a while on the trail, Vard said, "Well, shall we push on?" Art replied, "Why not? Like the old fellow said, 'The farther in you go, the virginer it gets'."

When we stopped at a campground to have our steak dinner, Vard and Doc and I had some wine, but the Holmgrens declined. They said they had given up drinking because they felt it was getting a little out of hand. "Art is so enthusiastic about everything he does," Doris said. "He found he could buy a Brahms symphony for what he would spend for liquor."

Art earned his master's degree at Utah State University studying with Dr. Bassett Maguire, who had had a rare primrose, *Primula maguirei* named after him. Art said Maguire had been asked to teach a class in ecology, which was not his field, and he gave all the students in the class Bs. One student felt he should have had an A and told the professor so. Maguire declared, "I don't know enough about the subject for anyone to get an A."

At one point on the trip, we ended up talking about God and who believed in Him and who didn't. Doris said sometimes it was hard not to believe because if you were grateful for something, you felt as if you should thank someone.

We drove back to the Holmgren's for dessert—rhubarb cake and coffee—then reluctantly left with the promise to meet again.

The weather seldom interfered with our Thursday outings, but heavy snow the winter of 1972-73 curtailed our activities somewhat. Once on a Thursday when Ellett had to hear cases with the other supreme court justices, we took the Cottams and sat in on the hearings. (Georgina dropped her knitting needle only once.) The Judge took us to lunch at the Fort Douglas Country Club after the session.

We went snowshoeing a few times. Once we saw a dipper or water ouzel, flying up and down the mountain stream. We watched it land on rocks in the water, bob up and down, then wade into the cold rushing water to feed. Sometimes it swims under the water or walks on the bottom feeding on insects. It's a blackish-gray bird about seven or eight inches long. The reason it bobs up and down before going into the water is speculative. After watching and admiring this particular bird for a while, Cottam said that when he was growing up in St. George, they used to call it "teeter-ass."

Often we could drive far enough out of the Salt Lake area to get out of the snow and, one cold day in January 1973, we headed south to see if we could find a clear spot on the desert to hunt for something. We had introduced Doc to rock hounding and he loved to hunt for sunstones, topaz, white-banded agate and arrowheads. But on this day, we had driven clear to Nephi without seeing one spot of bare ground. On the road between Nephi and Leamington, Vard saw a little brown mouse in the middle of the road. We stopped and got out our cameras to take its picture. Deep snow covered both sides of the road. The mouse had nowhere to go. But moving slowly, it climbed up on a snowbank and huddled up in a little brown ball, with its tiny pink feet quivering against the snow. We wondered how it got lost. And we knew it was doomed. We commiserated with it, wondered what we could do to help it, but in the end all we did was take its picture. Later in the day, we decided we would each write a poem about the mouse to read on our next outing. When we picked up Dr. Cottam the next Thursday, he couldn't wait to read his poem. He said he had never written poetry. but when he saw the results of his effort, he couldn't understand why he had never tried it before:

To a Mouse—by Robert Burns the Fourth

The cutest mouse in all the nation
Left his bed last night for information.
Two things he thought he had to know:
Is it green outside, or is there snow?
What he certainly found to all his sorrow
Was a foot of snow and no tomorrow.
The moral of this story, not too hazy,
Is that mice, like men, are oft plumb crazy.

We had to agree that his poem was inspired, and after hearing the other poems—the Judge wrote two, in keeping with his demand for 80 percent of the talking time—we voted Doc's the best.

On another outing to take winter snow scene pictures in the Smith-Morehouse area, we noticed a gate across the road leading up a canyon to Holiday Park, an area of private homes and cabins. Cottam vehemently opposed the building of homes and cabins in the canyons and the closing of the canyons to the public. The mountains, he believed, should belong to all the people.

The subject of religion often came up in discussions on our Thursday outings. "Think of spending your whole damned lifetime thinking about nothing else," Cottam said. The topic this time was tithing, and the Judge told of his "dog-poor" days when he was paying $6 a month for a correspondence law course and needed some law books. A lawyer had died and left two sets of law books, but the price was $250. Having only about $120, the Judge decided to pay his tithing instead of buying the books, telling his wife that he was going to try the Lord out. The next day the lawyer's widow called to ask if Ellett would like the law books for $100. He bought both sets and immediately sold one set to someone else for $250. After he had used the other books as long as he wanted them, he sold them, too. "Paying that tithing set me on the right road," he said. "I was sure of that." "Well, why'd you stop?" Cottam asked. "I got better off, you see. I didn't have to depend on the Lord so much. It was just a priming device."

On another outing the Judge told about several young men who were going on church missions. Explaining why they were going, one said because his father and brothers had gone. Another said his brother had gone, and his mother wanted him to go too. The third one said, "I'm from Bingham and the people there always said I'd never go on a mission. I just did it to show the sons of bitches!" After hearing the Judge's story, Cottam said, "Maybe that's why I was the only one of ten children to question things."

One day in November, we decided that since it was too cold and snowy to do anything outside, we would go to the Springville Art Museum. We browsed around admiring both the special exhibit and the permanent collection. We also noticed some beautiful big plants around—ferns, begonia, and dieffenbachia. The ferns reminded Doc of a story.

A florist who had his shop near the railroad tracks suddenly watched his plants begin to die, and he couldn't figure out why. He asked Doc to come and see what he thought. Because Doc suspected gas, he tried an experiment. He took to the florist shop some young tomato plants, which are very susceptible to gas. He covered some with bell jars and left the others uncovered. All of the exposed tomatoes died. He suggested a check of the gas line out in the street. Sure enough, a leak was found. The railroad had apparently caused the leak during work on the tracks. An attorney advised the railroad to pay the florist what he asked since he had proof. "The florist got $10,000," Doc said "And do you know what he gave me?—A plant! A fern like that!"

But he accepted the gift and repotted the fern in a larger container each year until it had some fronds touching the ceiling and others draping down onto the floor. Everyone who saw it was amazed and asked, "How did you do that?" "Bat manure!" was the reply. He said some people didn't believe him, but that's what he used.

Thursday became the highlight of the week, not only for Doc but for all of us. One of our favorite places to go was No Name Road near the Little Sahara Sand Dunes, where we would drive up into the junipers and wander around looking for arrowheads. You could be alone with your thoughts yet comfortably aware of friends close by. And if you found an arrowhead, you could hold it in your hand, admire its perfection, and wonder who held it last. How did he live? Was he camped here or hunting here? Did he look out through the trees to the same desert country, the same mountains you are looking at now? Did he look up at the same blue sky? And did he have any sense of the beauty around him? Then a shout from Vard would signal a find, and we would interrupt our reveries to gather around and compare our treasures.

When it was time to start the fire to cook steaks, we'd gather dead juniper branches to add to the blaze in our makeshift firepit. Vard would set up the table and chairs and bring out the jug of wine. Settling in our chairs by the fire, we'd lift our glasses and drink a toast, quoting Omar Khayyam:

Come fill the Cup, and in the Fire of Spring
The Winter garment of Repentance fling:
The Bird of Time has but a little way
To fly—and Lo! the Bird is on the Wing.

Conversation around the campfire might range from such a mundane topic as Doc's recent visit to the dentist to a discussion about whether the sonic boom we heard was a one-time thing when the plane broke the sound barrier or if the boom continued along with the plane.

As we were eating our steaks after a particularly good day, Vard quoted someone as saying, "When you walk through life, there's nothing else; this is it, so stop and smell the flowers." "Well, I think that's what we've been doing," Doc said, "stopping to smell the flowers." "It goes into the rest of your life when you have days like these," Vard said. "You think about them and talk about them."

Looking at the starry night sky on the drive home, Cottam quoted Thomas Carlisle: "If those planets aren't inhabited, what a waste of space, and if they are, what a chance for misery."

On another outing after a day of rock-hounding in an area near Nephi, Doc stood with his hat full of rocks and said, "What a way for an old man to be spending his time." "But don't you enjoy it?" Vard asked. "More than you'll ever know," was Doc's reply.

Most of our Thursdays were like that—wonderful!

The Judge missed a few outings the summer of 1973 when he had a hernia operation. We took the Cottams to visit him in the hospital, and the poor man's suffering intensified when Georgina leaned over to give him a kiss and put her hand on his incision. But he recovered in time for a long-planned trip to the rain forest in the Olympic National Park in Washington in August. For this expedition, the Cottams rode with Georgina's son, Joe Wilson, in his truck. The Judge rode with Vard and me in a new Blazer bought especially for the occasion.

It was a memorable trip with many highlights and a few bad moments. The waterfalls along the Columbia River and the hikes in the rain forest were wonderful, but the campgrounds were too crowded, and keeping track of one another in separate vehicles without any radio communication got a little testy at times.

In the first campground, Doc got lost coming back from the john. He wandered around for half an hour at 3:00 a.m., clad only in his shoes, shorts and a sleeveless sweater. He was wearing his thick glasses but couldn't see well in the dark. He said he had plotted his return by the call of a hoot owl in a tree when he went to the john, but it had moved when he returned.

Joe, or Jody, as Georgina called him, was an artist and a house painter and carpenter, but a rather strange fellow. Sitting by the campfire with Vard and me one night, he told about discovering some hanky-panky going on in the City and County Building when he worked there. He said they were going to fire him and he "got the silent treatment from everyone but the deaf and dumb guy." Another of his classic remarks was "You haven't been poor till you own a goat." It became one of our favorite quotes.

Doc and Georgina stayed one night at the home of Doc's daughter and son-in-law, Fae and Charlie Olson, in Gresham, Oregon. In the morning, we stopped to visit briefly with the Olsons and to pick up the Cottams to continue our trip to the rain forest. There we found a nice camp spot, went to a campfire program in the evening, and hiked the next day. Walking through the dense vegetation with moss hanging from the huge trees, we noted the "nursing logs," fallen old trees that provide nourishment for young tree shoots and other vegetation. And we enjoyed the quiet.

The next day we drove down the Oregon coast, stopping to walk along the beach and look for agate and shells. But it was a cloudy and chilly day, so we turned inland to Eugene and then south on the freeway to Roseburg where we decided to get motel rooms for the night.

It became chaos on wheels! We lost the other car in traffic, found all the motel rooms taken and the campgrounds full when we got there. We wondered why Jody, who was supposed to be following us, was stopping every five minutes. We wandered around on back roads looking for another campground and never found one, assuaging our hunger pangs with apricot leather and other snacks. We finally got on a main highway leading to Crater Lake, our destination for the next day, and considered driving in the dark until we found a campground, tired and hungry as we were. But about that time we saw a motel sign, pulled in and found they had some rooms. The Cottams and the Judge were too tired to go across the street to a cafe, but Vard and Jody and I went. Jody said that both Doc and Georgina were telling him what to do during that hectic drive. "I've made a few mistakes," he said, "but according to them, I've been wrong two hundred times."

After breakfast at the cafe the next morning, we drove up the highway beside the Umpqua River, a beautiful stream open to fly fishing only and lined with fishermen. Our first glimpse of Crater Lake was quite spectacular, but because of the cloudy, overcast skies, it wasn't the beautiful shade of blue Doc had described. But we took pictures, hiked down a trail to the lake, had lunch at a cafe, and then started our trek home. It wasn't the best of trips, but it wasn't the worst of trips either.

Chapter 14

Signs of Change

Nineteen seventy-four was a year of change for the Cottam family. It began with the illness of Clarence, Doc's brother. Shortly before his death in March, Walter talked to him on the phone at his residence at the Welder Wildlife Refuge in Sinton, Texas, and also sent him a long letter, quoted here in part:

> Dear Brother Clarence:
>
> Your lovable and good son-in-law, Douglas, called me last evening to report your physical status, which, I am persuaded, is nothing to brag about. I was, of course, aware of this fact after our conversation over the phone a few days ago. Your feeble voice has haunted me ever since that hour, but the cheerfulness of your spirit and the firmness of your faith in the gospel of our beloved parents impressed me greatly.
>
> I want you to know, Clarence, that I admire you and love you for all the many virtues you have exhibited daily throughout your honorable, useful, and truly remarkable life. Indeed, you are what Thomas P. Cottam would have been had he been blessed with your educational opportunities. In my opinion, the two

of you are kindred spirits—both biologically and spiritually—and no finer compliment could possibly be paid to any human soul.

Clarence, you and I have enjoyed essentially a parallel existence, having been born of the same parents, subjected to much the same environments throughout our lives, nurtured under the same basic philosophies of living. We have followed the same profession, married wonderful women of similar backgrounds, and fathered families we feel are honorable and substantial people. Yet there are obvious differences between us. Why? I wish that I knew. It might be that one would need to go back to Genesis to find a parallel. Adam had his Cain and Abel; T.P.C., his Walter and Clarence. But I have no more regard for Cain's character than you do. So far as I know, I have never consciously wronged a living soul.

You have held firmly to the faith of our parents and have participated faithfully in its organizations and its philosophy. But I do believe you also accept the religion of the naturalist, which I strongly affirm. Long ago we shared the feelings of young naturalists along the creek south of the Dixie black-willow trees and on the Temple grounds in St. George, which played host to numerous species of birds. Those were the days when we had our own common names for both birds and flowers.

I presume that most people return to their old homesteads in thoughts as they grow older. Certainly I do. I am amazed how brilliant and accurate are the pictures in my mind of the familiar scenes and kind faces of my loved ones and of friends of childhood.

Clarence, our visit with you a year ago at your headquarters in Sinton was a joyous occasion, marred only by the absence from your marvelous castle of your dear wife, Margery. But the nice trip along the shoreline with her and you was priceless. Now we are in sorrow for both of you. All of us here in Zion love you dearly and are praying that God's blessings and mercy will be yours in these hours of pain and concern.

Yours with great affection,
Walter

Later that year the University of Utah renamed the Reynolds Lecture the Cottam Natural History Lecture in honor of the two brothers who had achieved national prominence as biologists and conservationists.

Sometime after Clarence died, Dr. Cottam's son Dick wrote a long letter to his father summing up his feelings about Walter's relationship with Clarence and what Dick saw as the differences between the two brothers.

Dear Dad,

I felt a real sense of loss when Uncle Clarence died. He had his share of vanity and even a trace of pomposity. But all in all he was a magnificent human being. He fought an important battle and fought it with great effectiveness. On many occasions he showed a courage that was clearly exceptional. His national reputation was a result of competence and integrity and a well-focused activism. I always sensed a rivalry between you two which I regretted. You were very different men in some critical ways. But you were overall much alike.

That which separated you was clearly too important to you for the kind of relationship that I would have liked to see exist. When we talked on the phone after Clarence's death, I heard you once again wonder about the differences between you. And I decided then to tell you how I see the difference. I hesitated to do so because I am as much the son of my mother as I am your son. She was not free, and she was not an original thinker. But she had an understanding of people that was as exceptional as you are. I envy both of you and think I have something from both of you. But with no false modesty, I must admit that I don't believe I measure up to either of you.

I am sure you have no real idea of how exceptional you are. You have been as free a man as our species produces. You and Clarence shared many values, but he was not at all free, and he was not a man of exceptional creativity. I think you judged him from the standard of a free man, but he had no wish for such freedom. You come as close to being self-actualized as anyone I know. He wasn't of that variety at all.

Most of all, Dad, in these days when you are feeling old and wondering about what it all meant, I wanted to be sure I told you of my affection and admiration for you. You were not an easy father. I was always proud of you, but I also feared you as a boy, and at times I thought you were cruel to the mother I worshiped. I saw you as a man of great vitality, color, intelligence, integrity and humane values. But I was apprehensive about the occasional temper flares and the sometimes prolonged periods of sulking. We didn't talk much as father and son, but that wasn't a real problem. I felt secure in your affection.

My judgment, quite simply, is that you have been the most exceptional human being I have known, and that is not a romantic judgment. I have seen creativity but none that impresses me more than yours. I have seen integrity but none greater than yours. Nor do I mean to say that that which caused me to fear you was a fault on your part. Marriage, I believe, is a most unnatural condition. Mom was a giving, loving, sensitive hausfrau. She offered great security. But she must have demanded much of your freedom.

Now you are in your eighties and still much the same. It does sound as if your body is older than your spirit. But you still have an esthetic sense that brings greater joy to you than many people are to know in their lifetimes. . . . You should have . . . the peace that comes from knowing that the people your life meant most to hold you in the deepest respect and affection.

Dick

In August of 1974, Doc's daughter Bea and her husband, Bill Fowler, moved to Denver after he left the University of Utah and joined the faculty at the University of Colorado at Denver. Their four oldest sons, all musicians, had left home; their youngest stayed in Salt Lake City to finish high school. Bea had been her father's typist and editor of most of his professional papers over the years, and she had noticed a change in the quality of an article he had written that spring. She asked Vard and me if we had noticed any deterioration in him, but we had not. He seemed as alert and interesting to us as ever, although forgetful at times.

Doc himself, however, now 80 years old, was beginning to feel the effects of aging. In a letter to Bea in October, he wrote of a trip he had made to Lake Powell with friends to see the big juniper tree he and Dean Brimhnall had discovered earlier.

> Going up Bowen canyon I managed to have my bad knee give way, and I rolled several feet down a steep incline, seriously bruising my left leg below the knee. I have had a bad time with it ever since I returned. My leg is still swollen, but much better now. I am always glad when Thursday rolls along and gives me an opportunity for a day's rest with it. I feel that I am fast deteriorating, both physically and mentally.
>
> I am certain that I have worked too hard this summer, especially cutting down ten-feet-high clover in the oak grove, and I am quite determined to quit this heavy work now that fall is here. Almost always I take the bus to the Fort and also to Georgina's place to attend to my garden and fifteen hundred or so oak seedlings that are growing in my nursery there.

In the same letter, he commented on the sad condition of his brother Arthur and of Arthur's wife. "I am old enough now to realize that this business of growing old is one hell of an experience."

Another sad event occurred that fall. Bea had given the Cottams a little black poodle named Yvette one Christmas. Yvette, a lively little dog, loved Doc. She would race up to the car when we came home from a Thursday outing and, as soon as the door opened, she would tear into the back seat, and Doc would say, "How's my baby? How's my little black baby?" And Yvette would race out of the car and back in again four or five times. When we got out of the car, she would dash around us, leaping three feet in the air, just bursting with joy. Then came the sad day when she was hit by a car and, after she had suffered for a week, the Cottams had to put her to sleep.

Informing Bea of the death, Doc wrote, "We are still in deep mourning over little Yvette. No day passes without conversation about her. She was not only smart but to us real human flesh and blood. I miss her most on Thursday nights when I come home from our trips. Often the hour of this homecoming approaches midnight, but never did she fail to be sitting on the front porch when I returned. The greetings I received from her surpassed any from the species *Homo sapiens.*"

On a happier note that year University President David Pierpont Gardner notified Dr. Cottam that he had been selected to have his portrait painted by Alvin Gittins, university professor and prominent portrait painter, "in consideration of the years of dedicated and loyal service you have rendered to the University of Utah."

In spite of the ups and downs of the year, the Thursday trips continued. Another outing with Art and Doris Holmgren came about in March of 1974, when we made an expedition out to see the pink *Sisyrinchium,* or Grass Widows, known to grow only on the Stockton Bar in Utah, although common in other Rocky Mountain states. Georgina replaced Judge Ellett on this trip, and the six of us crowded into the Blazer rather than take two cars. We found the *Sisyrinchium* growing in profusion on the bar, and Art dug up a few to plant in his yard in Logan. But it was a cold and rainy day and, after hunting awhile for white agate, we were forced to eat our dinner in the car. Vard was bustling outside heating up the stew and handing the bowls to us. Conditions were cramped, but better than eating outside.

On a one-day trip in April, Doc, the Judge, Vard, and I found a beautiful surprise at the end of a rocky mountain road not far from the trilobite beds 40 miles west of Delta. The road ended in a grove of junipers and we got out to explore. Almost as soon as we got through the trees, we found ourselves on the rim of a great crescent-shaped cliff, looking out across a vast expanse of shimmering desert floor. We learned later that this was the Sinbad Overlook. It was 3200 feet down to the hardpan in the valley. A vast panorama of whites and blues and grays spread out before us, seemingly empty except for a tiny ribbon of road and some miniature mountains poking up. Far in the distance to the northwest was the Fish Springs range of mountains and beyond that the Deep Creek range. At the time we didn't know what mountains we were seeing. Vard thought one prominent mountain to the left was Wheeler Peak and the range on the right the Deep Creeks. Doc thought he was wrong, and they argued most of the time we were there.

We explored around the rim and, from one rock ledge, we found we were looking down on the tops of a number of bristlecone pine trees. We also discovered paw prints of a mountain lion. Doc was so impressed with the area that he thought it should be made a state park.

In July Paul Rokich invited the group on an outing to see the work he had done in revegetating the Oquirrh Mountains. He enthusiastically showed us areas where grasses and trees were thriving not far from the Kennecott smelter stacks. We saw another place where he had directed a group of Boy Scouts in planting little Russian Olive trees. He showed us a meadow now filled with wildflowers and the tailings pond where grasses he had planted were making a good showing. A drive up one of the canyons took us to a clearing where we sat at tables on benches of bales of hay and had a delicious meal, Paul cooking elk steaks for us on the grill. Talking with Paul, Vard compared his little two-by-four garden with what Paul was doing. "How did you have the temerity to think you could revegetate a whole mountain?" Vard asked.

"Well," Paul said, "you just do one canyon at a time."

One of the most memorable outings of 1974 was a hike up Lamb's Canyon in August with just the four of us, Cottam, Ellett, Vard, and me. We photographed wild flowers, climbed to the summit of one of the mountains, admired the great views, had some snacks and talked. Doc really loved to climb mountains. He said to me, as we got up to start out again, "If I ever get so I can't hike, I don't want to live any more."

After spending some time on the mountain top, we started our descent and had just got off the bare ridge down into the trees when the sky clouded up and it started to rain. The storm picked up momentum, thunder banging all around us and the rain turning to a downpour. Vard and I sought shelter under a big tree, and Doc and the Judge huddled under another tree a little behind us. Doc was enjoying the storm. Once or twice when the thunder crashed around us, he laughed out, "Ha! Ha!"

The Judge wasn't taking it quite so calmly. "Don't you agnostics get too close to me!" he cried. "I don't want you diluting my prayers!"

The lightning was flashing all around us, and the rain, mixed with hail, was cold. We knew we weren't in the best position there in the trees, but we didn't have much choice. After one terrific crash, Vard said the lightning was not too far away. Minutes later, we looked through the trees to see the Judge slipping and sliding down the steep, slick slope. Doc called out to him, telling him the rain would stop soon, but the Judge said he couldn't get any wetter than he was, and kept on. We saw him fall three times.

Doc stayed in his "nest," and after awhile, we heard him whistling.

When the rain eased up, we got some walking sticks to brace ourselves and made our way down the mountain. On the way Doc told us that when that last bolt of lightning came so close, the Judge got scared. "I told him if you got hit by lightning, it would be all over, and you'd never know what happened." It was those words that set the Judge off. We found him wringing out his wet clothes when we reached the car.

"We saw you fall three times," I said. "Four," he corrected. Later we dried out around the campfire where we stopped for dinner.

Later in August the four of us made another outstanding trip to Calf Creek Falls and Hole-in-the-Rock in southern Utah. The first night we camped at the Calf Creek campground. The next morning we hiked two-and three-quarter miles to the falls. The dusty red trail serpentined along through the colorful canyon beside an unbelievably clear stream. Lush green vegetation contrasted sharply with the red and cream-colored Navajo sandstone formations.

In a cool oasis in the box canyon, the water appears as if by magic at the top of a rock ledge, dashes and splashes over several levels of colorful rock, then falls into a crystal pool 126 feet below. We ate our lunch in the shade of some trees and tried to soak up some of the coolness to last on the hike back. We had taken only one small canteen of water, planning to refill at the falls. When we learned that a man had drunk from the stream earlier in the summer and contracted hepatitis and died, we returned without water.

Vard was eagerly anticipating our next destination, the Hole-in-the-Rock, where Mormon colonists in 1879 had found their route blocked by the sheer walls of Glen Canyon. They spent six weeks blasting, chiseling, and picking out a narrow dugway through which they managed to drive their wagons down to the Colorado river. There they ferried across to even more formidable country beyond. Vard's grandfather, Kumen Jones, was in the party of colonists and he drove one of the first wagons down.

After resting from our hot, tiring hike to the falls, we headed for Escalante and then south on the Hole-in-the-Rock road to look for a campsite for the night. When we reached Dance Hall Rock, we knew we had found the perfect place. This huge sandstone formation provided a spacious amphitheater with a smooth floor where the pioneers had held dances and religious services during the wait for the roadway to be completed.

Since we couldn't drive quite over to the rock, which stood alone on a hill, we stopped in a flat area nearby, where others had camped. Doc said a number of rounded rocks that clung to the sloping hill by the Hall looked like the Saints in prayer. It was dark by the time we finished our dinner. The men took their sleeping bags over on the rock for the night and I slept in the Blazer. It was a beautiful, warm night. An almost full moon soon came up over the side of the rock and cast a spell over the whole scene. Toward morning we heard some faint, far-off yipping, possibly coyotes or kit foxes.

The scene was equally delightful the next morning as we prepared breakfast. Some large, white blossoms of jimson weed had come out during the night to add to the ambience. We explored the area some more, took pictures of one another dancing on Dance Hall Rock, and then continued on over the rough, up-and-down winding road to the Hole-in-the-Rock,

We had seemed to be all alone in this vast, empty land of

rocks, but there we saw three people standing near the notch, signing the Hole-in-the-Rock register. They were Californians who had climbed up the rocky trail to the top from Lake Powell below. Since they didn't know much about the history of the area, Vard was happy to enlighten them.

We took some pictures and talked about having a cold drink before starting down the trail, but Doc and the Judge went on ahead. Vard and I had a drink, put four oranges in a pack, got a canteen of water, and soon caught up with our two friends, who had stopped to photograph a little red *Mimulus* in a crevice of the rock ledge part way down the trail.

We went on ahead on what could hardly be considered a trail. It was more a matter of clambering down over rocks and boulders of various sizes. Vard had to help me down some of the worst spots. When we called to Doc and the Judge and got no answer, we knew they had decided not to continue on because both of them had bad knees. When we got out of the shadow of the rocks into the hot sun, we glimpsed a little inlet of the lake below. It acted like a magnet drawing us on. An end to the rocks and boulders finally came, and we made it down a steep, dusty path to Lake Powell, where we spent half an hour in the water getting revitalized.

With Vard's help, I made the climb back up. He went on ahead to look for Doc and the Judge and found them near where we had last seen them. Vard offered them a drink. And then they offered him one. They had found a little spot back under the rocks where water was dripping down, forming a little pool about the size of a small saucer. But it was difficult to get to. They had climbed back up the trail and gone looking for a flower stem they could use for a straw. They found a *Nolina*, a type of yucca; Doc hollowed the stem with his knife, and it worked perfectly. When Vard found them by their little water hole and they offered him the straw, he accepted the invitation. When I finished my climb up the rocks and joined them, I also flopped on my stomach, got my head up under the rocks, stuck the straw in the little pool and had a cool drink. Doc was really proud of his survival expertise, and it probably kept the Judge from wanting to kill us.

We stopped briefly to explore the picturesque rock formations in the Devil's Garden on the way back to Escalante, then drove back to the Calf Creek campground for the night. Doc complained some about his knee hurting after the Hole-in-the-Rock hike.

Vard, Doc, and I never thought of asking a blessing before we ate on our outings, but the Judge seemed compelled to say something, even though he tried to mask it by talking loud and making it humorous. At breakfast this morning, he intoned, "Lord, forgive these agnostics, who don't believe in You, but bless this food to nourish their bodies." Then he asked especially for the Lord to strengthen Doc's knee. At this point, Doc said quietly, "Tell Him it's the left knee."

Fall trips took us to Joy, where Doc found a perfect arrowhead; to the San Rafael Swell in search of petroglyphs at the Head of Sinbad; to the Delta area to look for sunstones; to Pahvant Butte, an extinct volcano near Fillmore, where we hunted for arrowheads. And always there were spirited conversations, delicious meals, the outdoors we loved, and the contentment that comes from being with kindred spirits.

On one trip, Doc brought along this poem a friend had written.

An Earth Lover's Prayer

Oh, God, let this be heaven—
I do not sigh for golden streets
Or long for jasper walls,
Nor do I seek for pearly shores
Where twilight never falls.
Just leave me here beside these peaks
In this rough western land,
I love this hard, old world of Thine.
Her ways I understand.

Oh, God, let this be heaven—
I do not seek for stainless robes,
I'll keep these marked by toil,
Instead of straight and narrow walks
I want trails soft with soil;
I have been healed by crystal streams—

But these from snow-crowned peaks
Where Dawn lights beacons of the day
And paints the sky in streaks.

Dear God, let this be heaven—
I do not ask for angel wings
Just leave that old peak there
And let me climb 'til comes the night—
I want no golden stair.
And when I say my last adieus
And all farewells are given,
Just leave my spirit here somewhere—
Dear God, let this be heaven.

When we finished reading the poem, Doc said, "That's how I feel about it too."

On one trip when Georgina was along, she said Doc couldn't wait to die. He protested, "That isn't what I said. Since I'm going to die, I wouldn't want to be deprived of the experience. I think it will be thrilling." He likened it to the time he had an operation and was given an anesthetic. He could hear the doctors talking, and one said, "I think he's gone." Then Doc said, "All of a sudden I went sailing off—I think death is going to be like that."

In a letter to Bea in January l975, he complained that his one good eye was deteriorating quite rapidly. He had prepared a short talk to give at BYU, "However, when I got up to read it, I discovered that I couldn't see a single word of it and was compelled to speak extemporaneously. This confused me greatly, and the only good thing about it was that it was damned brief." In the same letter he told of talking with Judge Ellett about the pitiful condition of the Judge's wife, who had diabetes and had had one leg amputated and faced the prospect of losing the other leg and an arm. "I told him that if the doctors withheld the insulin from her for twenty-four hours, she would be dead. To give it to her would obviously be playing God. I think that he agreed, but he could never bring himself even to ask others to do such a thing. Besides, he said that the doctor had told him that she was full of blood clots and that she could pass away any moment. One week later she did just that —last Sunday.

Funeral services were held Wednesday. And what a service! I thought back to your mother's funeral, and I was happy to remember that we had one speaker to challenge the nonsense of a Mormon funeral."

Later he wrote, "Tomorrow is Thursday, my sacred sabbath. We expected to go to the annual run of the endemic fish cisco but strange to say, they are not running yet. . . . Our last trip last Thursday took us to Delta, thence east fifteen miles to Oak City and the beautiful canyon east of town. About ten inches of new snow had fallen, and we hiked up the canyon in about fifteen inches of snow. We took our snowshoes along, but we didn't use them. Tomorrow we expect to go snowshoeing east of Heber City."

Religion entered into a letter he wrote in March. "Georgina's granddaughter, Donna Wilson, is to be married March 21 at the Idaho Falls Mormon Temple. Georgina, no doubt, will see her married, but poor old Joe, her father, and her heathenish adopted grandpa will surely miss this sacred and divine ceremony, which I characterized after my one and only experience with it as a truly divine comedy."

George played a part in another church-related incident. "The ward officials here felt always that poor George never could be trusted with the priesthood," Doc wrote. "I suppose they felt that George might perform unlawful baptisms or other functions improperly. But a few weeks ago, the Bishop told George that they now feel that he should be granted the priesthood, which, of course, pleased him no end. He was told that he was to be ordained a deacon on Sunday, March 16."

Doc wrote that he went to the church for the ceremony, held in the bishop's office with several of the brethren surrounding George, who was sitting on a stool. They told George of the honor and asked whom he would like to perform this holy task. George replied, "My father." "You can imagine my predicament. But there was no way out but to admit that I had no idea of the ceremony," Doc wrote. And they had to call on someone else to do it.

After a visit in May from Bea's husband and their sons, Doc wrote a nostalgic letter to Bea recalling an incident from the past. He wrote:

The boys came Sunday morning, They are great guys and seem more like my kids than my grandkids. I suppose this is natural considering our years together. I often think of the days at the university when it was difficult for me to go out for fresh lab materials without picking up Bruce and Steve.

Certainly I shall never forget the day when I took them out early one morning in the dead of winter down to the big pond on Thirty-Third South. . . . Bruce was unusually foxy that morning. Snow was on the ground, but the pond was warm and the large stream of water at the junction of Mill Creek west of the pond was completely green with a tiny fern that I had planted there when we first came from BYU.

This plant had covered the surface of the stream below the pond. I was collecting plants from the pond when I saw Bruce running down the bank. Upon reaching the stream, beautifully covered over with this coat of green, he took a grand leap and completely disappeared beneath the green just like a frog. You can bet that I wasted no time fishing him out of the stream. I am sure that he will never be more surprised over an unexpected turn of events if he should live to be a hundred years old. You can imagine that I wasted no time getting him home to you, scared though I was to encounter a wild mother. What pleases me most now in retrospect is to recall how this kid laughed all the way home after he quit shivering in the warmed car. So I suppose your kids recall when they were mere lads with some degree of pleasure, as I do. Those were truly great and exciting days in all our lives.

Chapter 15

More Thursday Trips

The year 1975 turned out to be a very good year for Thursday trips and for two or three extended outings. We went cisco fishing in January, caught fish, had a delicious stew by the campfire on the beach, talked about the ice age, varves in lakes, and argued on the drive home about whether Logan canyon had been glaciated. We each took a share of the little fish, and the Judge reported later that he didn't care much for cleaning them. "Oh, I enjoyed it," Doc said. "I looked at the sex of each fish!"

Late in January we headed for Delta, then on to old Fort Deseret, where we ate our lunch in the car. Then we had a little competition sketching some beautiful cottonwood trees across the road. Once again, we judged Doc's the best and Vard's next best. The Judge and I tied for worst. Being tired of pot dishes, Doc had brought steaks, which we cooked over a briquet fire at the Gunnison Massacre Monument after we had hunted for arrowheads for a while. As we started eating, a few flakes of snow began to fall. Suddenly our coffee cups filled with snow, and the picnic basket turned white. We were engulfed in a storm and hastily retreated to the car to finish dinner.

More than once on cold days, when it wasn't raining or snowing, we would first cook the steaks, then put the table right over the coals, pull up our chairs and eat there. The coals kept the feet warm and it was handy to just reach down and put a steak back on the grill if it wasn't done enough.

On a rare day in February, we climbed the steep slopes in Clear Creek Canyon to photograph marvelous panels of Indian rock art high on the cliff walls above the highway. The argument that day concerned which way the creek was running and whether we were going uphill or downhill in the canyon. Not to be outdone by Doc, I had brought steaks, which we cooked that evening over a charcoal fire on a side road near Kanosh.

On many of our drives we brought along slides of previous trips to look at in a little viewer we passed around. Once in a discussion of historic times, Vard asked, "What time would you have liked to live?" "From here on out!" said the Judge. "Just when I did," said Doc.

We took a spring break in April, traveling to St. George, the Valley of Fire in Nevada, on to Needles, then to Las Vegas, back to St. George and home. We photographed wildflowers, enjoyed the scenery and had some good meals. Georgina and Joe went along on this trip, but I avoided some of the mealtime shambles of the rain forest trip by keeping the food I brought separate from all of Georgina's dozens of boxes piled in Joe's truck.

The Valley of Fire campground the first night was a delight, with camp spots tucked back in among the beautiful red rocks and white evening primroses blooming in profusion in the red, sandy soil. One huge rock looming over us in the middle of the circle drive looked like a giant poodle sitting on its haunches.

In our travels, we stopped often to photograph the wildflowers. Once Doc said he wanted to show us an acacia bush. As Vard was approaching, his shirt caught on a little thorn, and he said, "Wait a minute." "That's what they call it," Doc said, "Wait-a-minute-bush!"

Doc and Georgina had broken their vow not to have any more pets, and their new dog, Buddy, came along on several of our trips that spring. Sometimes Buddy would climb up on the back seat behind Doc's head, then drape himself like a fur piece around Doc's neck. Once he fell off backwards, and Doc had to turn around and rescue him from the conglomeration of boxes. ice chests, picnic baskets, wood and tools.

On two very special days in May, the original foursome found Indian petroglyphs in the San Rafael area not far from the town of Ferron and discovered some outstanding pictographs from the Fremont culture at the Head of Sinbad, also in San Rafael Swell. These were in perfect condition and unlike any drawings we had seen before. We set up the table and chairs and had our dinner right there, feasting on food and on that remarkable artwork.

Doc had a goal he'd been talking about for some time—hiking up the highest mountain in the Sheeprock Range. The Judge had court that Thursday in June, but Doc, Vard, and I drove to Vernon, got directions to the closest road, followed it up into a little canyon as far as we could go, then started our hike from there.

Since there was no trail, we had to find our own way, and it was a steep, rough climb. We crossed several patches of snow, and once or twice we thought we had reached the peak, only to find it was still some distance away. The last time, we climbed to a little saddle, and there beyond us again was the main peak, very steep and covered with a lot of snow. By this time it was 4:30 p.m. Our better judgment made us abandon Doc's goal. When Vard suggested starting back down, Doc said, "I've got to say my prayers first." He sat there a minute or two, then got up to go. I told him I had expected some sort of outburst like those we always heard from the Judge, but Doc said his was a silent talk with the Lord.

Vard went on ahead to scout a different way back down the mountain. Doc had the dog Buddy along on the hike, and we followed, trying to keep Vard in sight, but losing track of him a few times. We kept on, carefully picking our way down the steep slope. We would see Vard out on a ridge; then he would disappear. When we reached the point where he had been, we could look down and see him. We followed this ritual for nearly two hours. Then, near the bottom of the mountain, we lost sight of Vard altogether. As I was going one way to get out to a point from which I could see down the slope, Doc and the dog chose a different route, and we became separated. When I realized Doc was no longer following me, I called and called, but got no answer. Finally, I reached a vantage point where I could see Vard below, waving. I made my way on down to the car, even though I knew I would hear about losing Doc.

While I had a drink and took a breather in the car, Vard started up the road calling for Doc. For a long time he got no answer. Then as I was about to join him in the search, Doc appeared on top of a ridge and made his way down to the car, Buddy trotting beside him. He had gone down the other side of the ridge, thinking the car was down there. He was thoroughly disgusted with himself. He had always prided himself on his sense of direction.

We had been eight hours on the mountain, and it was so late that we pulled off in sagebrush at the first wide spot in the road to have our dinner. When the steaks were ready, we moved the table over in front of Doc. We didn't want him even to have to stir from his chair. During dinner he mentioned again how disgusted he was with himself for getting confused about which canyon the car was in. We told him any 81-year-old man who could hike up and down that mountain the way he could didn't have to apologize for anything.

We agreed that the hike was the equal of that up to Lake Blanche, or maybe harder. Paintbrush all shades of red and orange had brightened our hike all the way. Pausing to rest, we could look out across a desert almost empty of human habitation, with a sense of serenity and contentment. At times like these, thinking how fortunate we were, Vard would say, "I wonder what the poor people are doing."

Doc had a hernia operation in July 1975 that kept him from several of his Thursday Sabbath outings, but he recovered nicely and began sitting for Alvin Gittins. Georgina thought the painting should be of Doc in his cap and gown. Everyone else, especially the artist, disagreed. Gittins took dozens of photographs of Doc in casual clothes at Cottam's Gulch and then had Doc come to his studio for sittings.

Doc was soon back at the Fort almost every day, weeding and watering his oak, and he had started working on his paper about the project. But he still found time for many Thursday outings the rest of the year. We went fishing, went on mountain drives, hunted pine nuts, sunstones, and arrowheads, and had a beautiful two-day trip to Cathedral Valley in a remote section of Capitol Reef National Park.

On a drive over the Alpine Loop in September with some of my visiting relatives, Doc had us stop and hike down among the trees to look for the huge, old white fir that had fallen several years earlier. He wanted to tell us its story: Many years before, when he was teaching at Aspen Grove and a road was being constructed through the area, Doc thought it a shame that people might drive along the road and not see that magnificent tree. So he personally cut down a number of aspens around the giant fir to clear the view. Some time later, a man showed up at Aspen Grove, asked if he was Cottam and if he had cut down all those trees. Doc admitted he had, but asked, "How did you find out I did it?" The fellow said he asked around and everyone knew who did it. He said he was with the Forest Service, and he ordered Doc to go up and cut up all those aspen trees he had cut down. "So I spent the summer going up there from Aspen Grove to cut up the trees." Not long after that, the Forest Service put up a sign on the road calling attention to the big white fir. "And they spelled the scientific name of the tree wrong, and I wrote a story about that," Doc said with some glee.

A few years later when the tree fell, a group went up from Aspen Grove to hold memorial services beside it. By counting the tree rings, they determined that it was about 350 years old. But the Forest Service had noted on the sign that it was nearly one thousand years old. "So I wrote another story about that," Doc said.

Vard commented later that standing there in a group listening to the recitation made him feel as if he was finally in one of Doc's classes.

For some time I had been gathering information and assembling slides about Dr. Cottam and his life and contributions and, after our last outing that year, we returned to the Judge's home for dinner and a viewing of the tribute with accompanying taped narration by Vard and me. On the way home, Doc said he'd like to have the tribute shown at his funeral.

On our trip to Bear Lake in January 1976 for the annual

running of the cisco fish, Doc mentioned that he had about seven hundred more oak to get out of the ground at the Fort and put in cartons in the greenhouse. Later in the summer he was going to offer them through the Arboretum Guild to cities and towns for planting.

At times he sounded as if he thought he should be working on his oak instead of taking Thursdays off. Then, sitting by the fire, he would say, "Ah, I like a day like this. What could be better?" And he was usually ready to go when the next Thursday rolled around.

The Cottams had acquired another little dog, Sissie, that just showed up at their home and they couldn't bear to turn her away. She and Buddy became inseparable. The two dogs lavished their affection not only on Doc, but on George, who cherished the attention and responded wholeheartedly. But tragedy struck again, and Bea received this mournful account from Doc in March.

> This family is deep in a genuine state of mourning. Last evening at about sundown, our doorbell rang. When I opened it, a tiny girl said, "Your puppy was run over." I looked out on McClelland at a large group who had assembled there, mostly youngsters, and one car. George was in the room, and he, of course, rushed over.
>
> In a few moments he returned with poor little Buddy draped over his arm like a disheveled fox stole. I shall never forget this funeral march. George's steps were slow and measured. At his side the inseparable friend, Sissie, walked backwards, punctuating each step by a leap upwards, caressing a paw or a leg or the dangling face of her beloved companion. Sissie, only a few months old, obviously demonstrated a total disbelief in death.
>
> This sad cortege, when it arrived home, was directed to the east side of the garage, where the deceased was tenderly placed on a cardboard to await immediate burial under the spreading branches of a beautiful forsythia shrub. I had the honor of digging the grave, while George stood silently and sorrowfully

> beside his lifeless dog. Sissie, still unconvinced that her Buddy could not be brought back to joyous playfulness, continued with her kisses and caresses until her love and our dear friend and companion was returned to mother earth.

Judge Ellett had married his secretary of many years, Miriam Parker—he called her Mirm—and hadn't been with us for some time, but they both joined the Cottams, Joe Wilson, Vard and me for a four-day trip in April to St. George and down through the Grand Wash to Lake Mead. Doc's brother-in-law Rex Frei put us up the first night, and in the evening I showed my slide tribute about Doc to a gathering of his St. George relatives. When we had talked earlier about showing the presentation, Doc had said, "All of my family are crazy now. We should have done it about ten years ago." But they seemed to enjoy the show and laughed in the right places, although the Mormon crowd fell silent when it came to the part about all the coffee and wine we had consumed on our trips over the years.

Rex accompanied us the next day to see his fields and irrigation system and then to the nearby town of Gunlock to see an old petrified tree in a friend's yard. Then it was on to Grand Wash, where we found a camp spot on the desert surrounded by beautiful red-rock formations and joshua trees backlighted by the evening sun. After exploring the Grand Wash area the next day, we continued on toward Lake Mead, retraced our tracks back to St. George and camped again in nearby Snow Canyon. It was an enjoyable trip with good meals, beautiful scenery, congenial companions—and not too many traumas.

Only a short time after our return home, the Cottams were summoned back to St. George for the funeral of an elderly relative who had been bedfast for a decade and had no memory of current events. Describing the horrible death in a letter to Bea in May 1976, Cottam said of the memory loss, "It is, I fear, a hereditary characteristic of our family. You perhaps recall my reaction to your account of the extremely pleasant death of your dear old dog. I told you at the time that I wished you could have sequestered a few drops of that stuff for me to use when I become as physiologically old and useless as he. It is wicked, I believe, that human beings seem to have no basic right to such a death." Bea recalled that she and Bill had to kill one of their three dogs in 1971. "When I told Dad how I had held Shadow and comforted him as he was receiving the fatal shot, Dad asked me to get him some. This was the first time I remember hearing him mention suicide."

Although 82, Doc's tenacity persisted, especially when it came to climbing mountains. On a pleasant day in May, he, Vard, and I were hiking up a trail in Oak City Canyon, photographing the wildflowers and admiring the groves of oak and aspens. The summit of the mountain we were on was still above us, but Vard said that since it was nearly four o'clock, we should probably turn back. Vard and I started down, but Doc stood there looking up at the mountain top, finally saying, "Don't you think we should see what's on the other side?" The judge had started on the hike but had turned back earlier, and Vard mentioned that he would be waiting. Doc hung there, leaning on his stick. "We could probably be up there in fifteen minutes," he said. "It'd be a shame not to go when we're this close."

Vard gave in reluctantly. Doc shot up the trail as if he wanted to get out of earshot before we changed our minds. He crossed a patch of snow across the stream bed and then went up the stream bed through the mud and through more patches of snow. Vard and I followed up the steep trail and saw Doc reach the summit and disappear from sight. When we caught up with him at the top, we expected to be looking out over the countryside. Instead we were looking down into a bowl completely encircled by other mountains. But, satisfied, Doc was ready to turn back.

We had noticed two rather long stretches of snow in the creek bed, and as Vard and I started hiking down on the trail, Doc said. "Oh, we've got to slide down on the snow." Vard blazed the trail, sliding down on his seat thirty or forty feet. I followed in his track, using my feet to slow down a little in this first-time venture for me. Doc came zipping down, holding his feet and his stick in the air to get all the momentum he could get. We did a repeat performance on the second chute, except we had Doc wait until we got our cameras ready to capture his descent on film. He told the Judge later how we ascended up the mountain and then ass-ended down on the snow. We found a few ticks crawling on us after the hike.

The day after our Oak City trip, Georgina fell at the Senior Center in Fairmont Park and broke her hip. Doctors operated and put a pin in her hip, but she was still in the hospital the next Thursday. There being little he could do for her, Doc went along on a trip to South Willow Canyon. He had mentioned that the house was getting back to its bachelor status. So on Sunday afternoon, I went over to offer my services. It wasn't a moment too soon. Dirty dishes covered the table in the breakfast nook, the kitchen cabinet, and some were on the floor for the dog. Doc helped do dishes up to a point; then I finished up. When George came home from the park, Doc said, "Come and meet your new mother." George started helping with the cleaning and, after Doc left the room, he started chuckling, "Dad's a character." I asked why he said that, and he answered, "Telling me to come and meet my new mother."

Georgina, a pack rat, had things sitting all over—sacks, cookies, plastic containers. In the hall outside the kitchen, a small cupboard stood open, everything imaginable spilling out of it. I put away a few things, but couldn't make a dent in the mess. After wiping off the table, cabinets, stove, and spills on the cupboard doors, I swept the floor, cleaned the basin in the bathroom and gave up. When I learned that Georgina was coming home, I went over the following Wednesday evening to see how I could help them get ready for her. Doc had walked from his oak grove at the Fort and didn't get home until 8:30 p.m., dead tired. When I walked in at 9:00 p.m., George said, "We haven't eaten." I fixed them some dinner, tidied up a little and left.

Bea drove from Denver to Salt Lake the next day and stayed about ten days, nursing Georgina and trying to get some order in the house. When Doc saw her, he said he had prayed that she would come. Georgina wept to see her but complained that their benefactor was not one of her family. Bea cleared out a lot of the clutter and got enough of Georgina's clothes put away to close the closet door. But more clothes were still hanging on two other doors. Bea had cut down the pile on top of the dresser by about half.

Later, Bea recalled the visit as the time of the "first great fight." The unhappy scene was a prelude of friction to come between Georgina and the Cottam family. Fae also had some complaints. "Dad is such a good story teller, and he can't even get started and she's interrupting him." She also resented Georgina's telling her there was nothing wrong with her, even though she had some health problems. After talking on the phone to Georgina at Easter, however, Fae wrote to Bea, "Speaking of our stepmother, I was impressed by her spirits when I talked to her on Easter. She was baking a leg of lamb and taking care of her invalids (George with his broken arm and Dad with his injured back) with real zest—rising to the occasion and loving it. She described how she shuffled around the house doing what she had to do. I can only say, 'long may she shuffle.'"

Alvin Gittins completed his portrait of Dr. Cottam in July 1976 and the unveiling occurred in special ceremonies at the University Museum of Natural History, where the painting was hung. More than a hundred faculty members, friends and relatives attended. Vard, Grant Cottam, and Bill McNulty spoke, extolling Doc's accomplishments as a conservationist, as a teacher, and as a father. Gittins spoke briefly about what he learned about people as he painted their portraits. He said he found in Dr. Cottam a "sweetness and straightforwardness" he hoped to convey in the painting. During the sittings, Doc had commented to his family, "That man Gittins can even paint your soul, and he's doing it."

In the afternoon before the unveiling, Doc's niece, Grace Muir, had a garden party at her beautiful home for about 50 Cottam family members. At Doc's and Georgina's request, I showed the slide presentation about Doc at the party, and everyone complimented us. Bea, who had come from Denver with her husband for the unveiling, called it "superb" and said she wanted a copy no matter what the cost. Grant and his wife, Diana, also came to Salt Lake for the unveiling, and we had a Thursday outing with them and Doc the next day, hiking to Cecret Lake in Albion Basin, drinking wine, eating steaks and talking about the environment and world food problems.

Dr. Cottam's last hike in July 1976 on Mt. Timpanogas, the mountain he had climbed more than one hundred times with the ease of a mountain goat, was nearly his undoing. But it was mostly his own fault. As we came over the Alpine Loop before dropping down to Aspen Grove and the start of the trail, he had us stop in a grove of alpine fir to look for a huge tree he had discovered there 50 years earlier. Of course, we didn't find it. But it delayed our start on the Timp trail until after 1:00 p.m. To go half way up the mountain to Emerald Lake or Hidden Lake and back takes nearly a full day at our pace. Considering our late start, Vard and I hadn't even considered going the three miles to the lakes. We took our time, stopping to photograph the wildflowers, drinking from the waterfalls, and admiring the view of the mountain, its snowfields and its terraces.

We kept pressing on until we came to a sign indicating we were only half way to the lakes. By this time, Doc was talking about getting up to Hidden Lake, where he had taken a picture many years before, from which B.F. Larson, a Utah artist and friend, had painted the big oil that still hung in Doc's dining room. We continued on up the steep trail, stopping to rest quite often. Once I asked Doc if he still intended to go on. Of course, he said he did. We kept thinking we didn't have much farther to go—until we met a backpacker who said Hidden Lake was still about three-quarters of a mile away. Discouraged, but by then committed, we pushed on and on and on, at last reaching our goal. Satisfied that we had met the challenge but concerned because it was 6:30 p.m., we allowed ourselves just half an hour to get to the proper spot to photograph the lake, relax for a minute and have some snacks. At 7:15 we started down the trail, setting a good pace in order to get as far as possible while it was still light. It had taken us five hours to get to the lake. Vard estimated it would take three hours to get down the mountain.

It was still fairly light when we got to the sign marking the halfway point, but as the light began to fade, I went ahead so Doc could see my light shirt and get an idea of the trail. With his contacts, he could still see a little, but had no depth perception. When total darkness engulfed us, he was virtually a blind man. Vard tried several methods of helping him, eventually walking behind him, clutching his belt to steady him when he slipped. Both of them were using heavy walking sticks to brace themselves. This slow, tortuous procession continued more than an hour in the black night until we finally collapsed in the car at 10:15 p.m.

"Well, it was a good experience," Vard said.

"I was terrified," was Doc's response.

We gave up any thought of having the dinner we had brought, just had some coffee and snacks in the car and drove one tired old man home.

The two men who were working with Doc on the oak project, Dr. Frank Santamour of the National Arboretum in Washington, D.C., and Dr. John Tucker of the University of California at Davis, came to Salt Lake in August to confer with Doc and coordinate the sections they were writing on the project.

During their visit, Dr. Obert C. Tanner, a prominent Salt Lake businessman and philanthropist, and his wife, Grace, hosted a garden party in their honor at their estate. Beautiful flowers and a fountain graced the rolling lawn set up with tables for 50 guests. Trees lined the outer edge of the grounds, blocking out the sight of any other houses and leaving only the mountains beyond as a backdrop. Guests strolled through the gardens admiring the flowers, climbed to a tower up the hill for a view of the city, and sipped drinks from the bar.

After dinner, Dr. Tanner introduced his wife, who was financing publication of the oak book. After she introduced Dr. Cottam, he said he had never expected to be honored at such an impressive gathering. He spoke briefly, then introduced Dr. Tucker and Dr. Santamour. In his remarks, Santamour said he had known Dr. Cottam only three days but felt as if he had known him all his life. He said that if he could choose a father, it would be someone like Dr. Cottam.

Vard had been on a backpacking trip and had missed everything. When he asked Doc what Tucker and Santamour had thought of the oak project, Doc replied, "We didn't have time to do much work with so many things going on."

On a beautiful day in September 1976, we found the Hondoo Arch we had long looked for in the San Rafael area. We were having dinner on a hill overlooking the cliffs and gorges of the Muddy River Loop. Vard and Doc were sitting on one side of the table, and I on the other, having some wine. The Judge was at the end, a little back from the table. Vard got up to go tend the fire; then Doc got up to get his camera and take a picture, leaving his half-full glass of wine on the table. When he came back, he picked up the wine and went to his chair. Reaching out his left hand for the arm of the chair, he started to sit down, but the chair slipped, and he went with it. It was a scene in slow motion as he and the chair and then the other chair tipped and went to the ground. He was on his knees with his left hand on the ground, but his right hand still holding the wine glass.

At this point, the Judge said, "Hold it there a minute, Doc, until I get my camera." Like a striking snake, Doc's right hand shot out, and the wine went flying on the Judge's shirt front and the top of his pants. The reaction was so quick it shocked us all, including Doc.

He muttered, "I knew you were going to say something." And the Judge countered with a few crude remarks about Doc down on his hands and knees with one leg up in the air.

Vard was in a paroxysm of laughter as we went over the details of the tableau. The Judge and I joined in and soon even Doc was laughing a little. Then he said under his breath, "Clumsy 82-year-old." Vard said he thought it wasn't clumsy at all to be down on his hands and knees like that and throw with such precision.

Later that month, Vard, Doc, and I went on a spectacular mountain drive on a narrow dirt road starting from Clear Creek Canyon, going up over the Tushar mountains and dropping down into the little town of Marysvale. About a mile up the canyon, we stopped for lunch at the Castle Rock campground, sitting in a grove of trees with the sun shining through and surrounded by rock formations similar to those in Bryce Canyon. The views were breathtaking as we climbed from 6,000 to 10,000 feet on the one-way road, with sharp dropoffs almost all the way. Glimpses almost straight down into the canyon weren't for the faint-hearted, but the brilliant fall colors invited us to stop at almost every wide spot in the road to take photographs. About eight miles up the road, we came to the abandoned mining town of Kimberly, where we stopped briefly to take pictures. At the summit we walked out to Winkler Point for spectacular panoramic views. Doc had been over the drive about 25 years earlier and remembered extensive stands of manzanita being there. Soon we found it growing all over the slopes and on both sides of the road along with almost a forest of mountain mahogany. Farther along, a grove of beautiful aspens backlighted by the sun demanded a stop for more photographs. We agreed it was one of the most beautiful mountain drives we had ever taken.

As we descended the mountain toward Marysvale, we began looking for a place to have our dinner but were near the bottom before pulling into a little clearing near a stream. We gathered wood for the fire, Vard set up the table and chairs, and Doc found a branch of squawbush as a centerpiece for the table. Vard and Doc each wandered off in different directions. Vard came back after awhile, and we were about to pour some wine when we heard Doc holler, a sound that indicated trouble. Because I had seen him going toward the stream, we headed through the trees in that direction. By the time we found him, he was up on his feet standing in the shallow water in the creek bed looking for his glasses. Two gouges on top of his head were bleeding and both of his elbows were skinned. He said his wrist and back hurt. We had him sit down on a rock to see if he was all right, and Vard found his glasses and picked up a coke can in the water. When Vard went to the car to get his first aid kit, Doc said, "I guess my hiking days are over." But soon he was able to climb up the creek bank and walk back to the car, where Vard bandaged his wounds.

Doc said he had gone down the steep bank to get some water in the coke can for the squawbush centerpiece. As he was climbing back up, he got hold of a rotting log that gave way, and he fell backwards down the bank. He muttered something then about fooling around with aesthetics and getting into trouble. He mentioned suicide and added, "Maybe if I had fallen 20 feet instead of three, it would have been all over."

He didn't want anything to eat but rested in the car while we ate a hasty dinner before starting the four-hour drive home. At Richfield, we asked if he wanted to stop to see a doctor, but by then he was feeling better. Later in the drive he sat up and talked, telling us more details of his oak project. Soon he seemed to forget about his fall. Vard helped him into the house when we arrived there about 10:00 p.m. When we checked with him a few days later, he said he had kept the heating pad on his back for a couple of days and was all right.

In a letter to Bea in October, he wrote, "Most of my waking hours outside of the sacred Thursday Sabbath have been spent with my oak project at Fort Douglas. It appears now that I can really begin to finish my part of three papers that we have agreed to write on this project." He said that he had a good start on his part, that John Tucker had nearly finished his paper on the taxonomic features of the hybrids, and that Dr. Santamour was working on the genetic aspects.

In the same letter he mentioned that he had been to St. George to attend the funeral of his sister Emma, who had died at the age of ninety-three. "Arthur and I occupied positions next to the deceased. We stood there for hours. The human lineup extended for two blocks. Near the end of this demonstration, I remarked to Arthur that of ten children, we represented the two remaining members, and 'Mark well, sir, the probable fact that you are next.' This almost brought on a riot and he loudly disdained such an assumption."

Doc had to miss some Thursday outings that fall and winter. Georgina had some health problems and was going to the doctor to have X-rays and other tests. But we took him along on trips to Topaz Mountain, Pahvant Butte, Antelope Island, and No Name Road. At No Name, sitting by the fire in a thoughtful mood, he said to Vard and me, "I wish I'd met you people ten years earlier. In all the years I went out with students, it wasn't like being with you. You saved my life."

I wasn't sure what he meant by the remark about the students, but Vard told me later that Cottam had said they were always taking from him, not giving to him. Advancing years may have clouded his memory of the great esteem they had for him. And his time with them had occurred when he was in his prime. He was their teacher and an independent spirit and probably would have disdained any offers of help. Even in his eighties, he often spurned Vard's offer of a helping hand over rocks and streams. Or perhaps he had a feeling of abandonment when his students learned all they could from him, then moved on with their lives. In a letter to Vard after the story "A Man and His Mountains" appeared in the *Salt Lake Tribune*, he had wondered if he might be abandoned now that Vard had his story.

As we were sitting around the campfire after dinner at Black Rock a couple of weeks later, Doc said, "I wish we could stop time when we get out here." Every now and then when we were out, he would say, "I don't know what would have happened to me if you two hadn't come along." Once he added, "Wherever I end up, I want to find the two of you there too."

Chapter 16
Declining Years

Doc had been having trouble with his eyes for some time. He had been using a magnifying glass for reading and thought that nothing else could be done for him. Then his doctor prescribed some new reading glasses, and he could see again. He said it was like a miracle.

In a letter to Bea in February 1977, he wrote, "There was very little good or bad throughout my years when you were not my chief friend and protector. I shall always love you for the help and comfort you brought into my life, especially in hours of trouble." Doc said the neighbors were kind to Georgina, taking her each week to shop for food. "So you see we are fast learning what it is like to be old. I have great difficulty remembering where I place things or what I read or hear. It's a hell of a stage of life. Amen."

This was the last letter Bea received from her father.

John Tucker and Frank Santamour were urging Dr. Cottam to get his paper on the oak project to them as soon as possible, and he had been trying to work on it, but was having trouble getting it organized. Vard took some of the material and made a tape of important parts he thought should be included. But when he pressed Doc for specific answers on unclear points,

Doc would get off the track, suggesting that he take Vard to see some beautiful specimens or wanting to get photographs of all the various leaf types. Pinning him down for definite answers was almost impossible. Vard had volunteered my services to type up the material he had taped, and he told Doc that once we got it down on paper, he could change it any way he wanted. Whenever we asked questions, he would digress and not return to the point.

When we stopped at his place for coffee before our Thursday outing April 7, Doc's old typewriter was sitting by the table with a sheet of paper in it. He said he was getting at his oak paper. It looked as if he was typing all over again what Vard had taped and what I was going to type for him.

I did type up the information we had, though, but had little luck getting any answers to my questions about the project. I called Rudy Drobnick, who had discovered the first hybrids and worked on the oak project in the early years. He clarified some points I inquired about and said he had given Doc some of his material a few days earlier, but intended to get with Doc again to help him sort things out. "He's going to need all the help he can get," Rudy said.

About two weeks later when I asked Doc how he was coming on the paper, he said, "Well, I've been thinking about it a lot." But the paper in his typewriter was still the same first page that had been there for two weeks.

Georgina went on the outing to the White Wash Sand Dunes with us on April 21 and, while Vard and Doc were off hunting agate, she said she had had a hard time talking Doc into going to the Emeritus Club dinner. He had insisted he had to work on his oak paper. But he did go and had a wonderful time talking to his old friends. She said she had asked him why he couldn't go a few hours to the dinner but could go out all day with us on Thursday. At that point, I told her that I thought she had agreed when they got married that she wouldn't interfere with his Thursday outings.

On some of our subsequent drives, I took the oak papers along and asked Doc questions. By May 5 I had finished about 15 pages of the oak paper, and Doc seemed to approve of what I had done. A few days later, John Tucker came to Salt Lake, picked up the paper and took it back to California to incorporate into his and Santamour's articles.

Later in May, Doc asked Vard and me to present a program at a dinner meeting of his Men's Garden Club. We picked the Cottams up for the drive to a downtown restaurant. Doc introduced us, saying we were the invited guests. Vard showed some flower slides and talked, and then we showed the tribute we had made earlier about Doc. The club members seemed to enjoy the program.

As everyone stood about visiting afterward, I went up and spoke to Doc. He seemed surprised to see me. "How did you get here?" he asked. Puzzled, I said, "Do you mean here to the meeting? I came with you and Vard." Then he said, referring to the tribute, "Have I seen this before?" "Two or three times," I answered.

This exchange indicated to us that Doc's problem was more than forgetfulness. But we still had many more wonderful days with him. He was better company in a declining state than most people are in their prime.

The Cottams joined us for two trips in June, the last one to photograph the wildflowers in the Uinta Mountains. Doc alone joined us on July 7 for a spectacular wildflower day at Joe's Valley and then for a drive along part of Skyline Drive, which winds for nearly one hundred miles along the Wasatch Plateau, offering magnificent views of the valleys below from its altitudes of nine thousand to eleven thousand feet. Georgina didn't go because her hip was aching. She believed she had hurt it when we hit a bump on our last trip. Vard, Doc, and I spent most of the day photographing the wildflowers. Blue *Polemonium* and beautiful mixtures of scarlet Gilia and purple *Penstemon* covered the hillsides on the drive from Joe's Valley up to Skyline Drive. A Sugarbowl plant stood out, one lone blossom still in flower in the center surrounded by others gone to seed and sporting wild feathery caps that looked like hippie hairdos. Later as we waited for our fire to burn down to cook dinner, we discovered hundreds of Parry Primroses growing in the granite rocks across the road from our camp. Doc said they were the most he had ever seen at one time. We took dozens of pictures.

It was still light as we finished our drive across the lofty mountains. From our vantage point, we could see one slope on the right that had almost no vegetation and that bore the scars of deep gullies going down its face. In sharp contrast the slopes on the other side were lush green on the Forest Service terraces formed by contour trenching some years ago. Most of those slopes converge on a canyon that goes down to Mt. Pleasant, a town badly damaged by some 20 raging floods in the early years when overgrazing almost denuded Skyline Drive. Doc didn't voice it, but he must have felt great satisfaction knowing the part he had played in bringing about the conservation efforts that were improving the face of the land.

An ailing hip kept Georgina in bed the following week and Doc missed his Thursday Sabbath, but he went along on another high mountain drive July 21. That trip was almost as tense and terrifying as the Skyline Drive had been beautiful. We drove south to Richfield, then took a narrow, winding road to the top of the Pahvant Plateau. This graded dirt road winds along at an elevation of about nine thousand feet with panoramic views in all directions. The road was dry, and all went well through lunch time. Then, as we came around a narrow dugway, the car began sliding around in a stretch of wet, sticky mud. Vard managed to keep the car on the road, but he had little control. We sighed in relief to get out of that mire, only to see moments later another wet stretch ahead. It seemed as if it went on like that for hours. We would no sooner get through one slick, treacherous stretch than we would come onto another. It was all Vard could do to keep the car on the road. Sometimes there were trees on the downward side of us, which would have kept us from overturning, at least, but not from getting hopelessly stuck if we had gone off the edge.

The experience had a strange effect on Doc. He started talking constantly. We saw some tan-colored cattle at the side of the road and he started talking about them. He had brought the dog Sissy along and he urged, "Get 'em! Get 'em!" trying to make her bark. Fortunately, the dog was quiet and well-behaved. Yvette had had a shrill, piercing bark and had yapped at everything, always with Doc's encouragement.

Once on a slick, uphill stretch, three cows were running just ahead of us with their big white rear ends just a few feet from the car and Vard praying that they wouldn't stop. If we lost momentum, we would be stuck. About this time Doc said very conversationally, "What kind of cows are those, Vard?" He didn't get much of an answer.

Sometimes I wondered how Vard had the courage just to plunge ahead when we came to a slick stretch that looked even worse than those we had come through, but he kept on, and we lucked out each time. We had seen only a few sprinkles of rain, but it must have come down in torrents earlier that day or sometime recently. After awhile, a very long while, we came onto dry road again and made it down off the mountain. Vard said there was no way he would have tried going down that steep, winding road with sharp dropoffs if it had been wet.

At one point on the slippery drive, Doc asked for water. He said he couldn't understand why his throat was so dry. Since Vard always got a dry mouth in a tense situation like that, I told Doc that I thought it was nervous tension. He claimed he wasn't nervous. But all of that talking must have been some tension and not all nonchalance.

Because Georgina found she had a fractured vertebra, Doc missed some trips in August, staying home to tend her. Vard and I usually stopped for coffee at their place anyway on Thursdays. Georgina was in bed when we got there one day, but as we were having coffee with Doc and showing some slides, she came hobbling out of the bedroom so as not to miss anything. She was wearing a floppy hat and said she had bought two hats for a quarter to wear on our trips, "And now I won't be able to go!" she lamented.

Doc did manage to get away for a fishing trip in the Uintas on August 18. We took a rough, rocky road up to Echo Lake, where we had been with Doc a few years earlier. It was a cloudy, cool day. We had lunch by the car, then struck out on an adventurous trek around the lake, catching a few fish, keeping Vard busy running between me and Doc to undo snags, to rebait hooks, and to try to find a few minutes to man his own fishing rod. At one point Doc asked Vard if he had ever been to that lake before. "Yes, and so have you," Vard replied, reminding him that it was two or three years ago and that they had gone out on a raft. Then Doc remembered—for the moment.

Doc hadn't done much fishing before he met us. He said

he always found too much going on on the bank to spend time fishing. He seemed to enjoy it now, but he was catastrophe in action with a fishing pole. He gave it little twitches that sent the line flying in a frenzy all around the pole, and then Vard would have to disentangle it. Near the end of our trek around the lake, he got a gigantic tangle in his line, and Vard had me help try to straighten it out. It was hopeless. He finally pushed the snarl into one mass and cut the line on either side. All the time we were trying to fix the tangle, Doc was sitting on a log, holding the pole, jiggling it, tapping it on the log, and generally being no help whatsoever.

The sun came out as we were having dinner, the usual steaks, corn and melon, with wild red raspberries we had gathered earlier for dessert. As we were driving out, Doc said. "Well, this is a new road for me." "No, it isn't," Vard said. "We were here before, you remember, and we fished from that raft." "Oh yes," Doc said. "I'll never forget that."

We hooted.

In an informal outdoor ceremony September 24, 1977, Dr. Cottam's hybrid oak grove was dedicated with more than 100 guests in attendance. A commemorative plaque on a large stone placed at the edge of the three-and-a-half-acre plot reads:

COTTAM HYBRID OAK GROVE

> The unique oak trees comprising this grove were hybridized, grown, and planted by Dr. Walter P. Cottam. This grove is dedicated in recognition of his ability as a distinguished teacher and researcher and for his accomplishments in fostering conservation as an eminent ecologist and as founder of the State Arboretum of Utah.
>
> State Arboretum of Utah
> September 24, 1977

Dr. David P. Gardner, University of Utah President, dedicated the grove; W. Richard Hildreth, Arboretum Director, told of plans for its future; Dr. Cottam explained the hybridization project; and Judge Ellett read a poem by Rufus Johnson. For several weeks Jody, at Georgina's direction, had been painting pictures to be presented to certain dignitaries at the end of the ceremonies. Dr. R.J. Snow, vice president of university relations, welcomed the guests and conducted the program. Of the 217 oak trees in the grove,137 were dedicated to specific friends, family members, colleagues and honored guests. In addition to the names of the honorees, a label attached to each tree listed the names of the two parent trees and the date of the cross.

Because Georgina was getting better, Doc was able to leave her and go with us on six more trips that year. She even went along on two outings.

Early in January 1978, Grant Cottam came for a visit and went with Vard, Judge Ellett, and me on a trip down to Pahvant Butte, a huge ancient volcanic crater west of Fillmore, and one of our favorite destinations. Doc didn't go because Georgina was ailing again. This time she had lost her voice. We were a little surprised that Grant wanted to go with us without Doc, but later in the day he asked what we thought about Doc's mental condition. He also expressed some concern about a new will that had been drawn up by Georgina's attorney, which Doc and Georgina wouldn't let Bea or Fae see. The family's main concern was that George should be provided for. All earlier wills, with the family's understanding, had left everything to George. Grant seemed to feel that under the new will, Georgina might get everything. When he suggested that Doc was getting senile, Vard said he thought that part of Doc's trouble was that Georgina always answered for him and didn't give him a chance to think. He told Grant that Doc talked all right when he was out alone with us but was forgetful at times.

It was a cold and windy day, but we had an interesting time. The Judge, in his usual form, told jokes and made lively conversation. He got into a friendly argument with Grant over what things in the environment might be exterminated. He didn't see much use for crabgrass and rattlesnakes. In response, Grant quoted Aldo Leopold: "An intelligent tinkerer keeps all the parts."

Vard and Grant braved a chill wind to explore a bit on the old volcano. Then we drove to a nearby sandy playa, where we found odd, convoluted rocks resembling human brains and hunted awhile for arrowheads. It had been a productive area for us on earlier occasions, and Grant found two good points this time.

At dinner time we built a campfire and heated a pot of stew. Because of the cold wind, we then initiated Grant into our ingenious way of setting the dining table over the fire. It was a fortuitous arrangement except that Grant's shoe caught fire. Vard smelled it and put the fire out before it burned past the sole.

We made two more trips to Pahvant Butte with Doc in February and March. On the first trip, he asked several times why he wasn't along when Grant went with us. We reminded him that, because Georgina was sick, he had to stay home to take care of her.

The outing in mid-March proved to be more eventful than we had anticipated. Because our favorite playa was a little damp, we parked the car near the end of it, then began our slow amble toward the west along the north slope. We kept a little distance apart as we scanned the ground, looking for sun glints on the obsidian, hoping for perfect arrowheads, but usually finding only chips. Everything is out in the open along there, and it was easy to keep Doc in sight. Sometimes he tended to go his own way, but Vard liked to keep an eye on him.

We made our way to the end of the playa without much luck; then I found a nearly perfect arrowhead, and we concentrated on hunting in that area for awhile before starting back toward the car. Since the sun was getting lower in the west, it was easy to see the glints on the obsidian, but you had to turn back to the west to see them and backtrack to check them out. Just as I said something to Doc about those glints seldom paying off, he reached down and picked up a perfect obsidian arrowhead. Vard and I strolled on ahead. When we reached the car, we looked back and saw Doc and the dog coming along in the right direction not far behind us.

While browsing around there waiting for Doc to reach the car, we went over a little hill and lost sight of him. After twenty minutes or so, we went up on the rise to see if he was at the car. He not only wasn't at the car; he was nowhere in sight. We could see up as far as we had been, all across the playa and up the south slope and part way along the north slope, although there were junipers and lava rocks there that could have hidden him. We started calling, but we got no answer.

Vard retraced our whole route up and down the playa, searching and calling, hunting among the junipers and rocks. We couldn't imagine what had happened to Doc. He was heading in the right direction when we last saw him. But our calls got no answer. We could see no trace of him, even when we used our binoculars. We got in the car and drove the length of the playa and back again, then out on the road for some distance until we felt we were getting away from where he might be. We returned to the playa, driving again to the west end and looking on foot for awhile, then driving back to the east end, parking the car and walking around there. Panic began to set in, and Vard wondered if we should go over to the Clear Lake headquarters and get some help in our hunt before it got dark. And I recalled Georgina's words as we left the house that morning, "Watch him. He's getting awfully forgetful."

As Vard and I continued searching, some distance apart, I called to him to see if he had found anything. He pointed across the playa—and there was Doc, coming down the south slope with the dog trotting along beside him. It was the best find of the day. We had spent more than an hour looking for him. When we asked him what had happened, he said he didn't see us and didn't see the car and couldn't remember where we were to meet, so he started walking toward the road.

He said that he heard us calling and he answered, but we didn't hear him. Vard said the wind was in the wrong direction for the sound to reach us. Doc said that when he realized he was lost, he checked to see if he had any matches, but he didn't have any. Vard and Doc went over and over the details of all the various routes taken during the search. I could only be thankful that we didn't have to go back and face Georgina without Doc. Vard and I later vowed never to let him out of our sight again.

Georgina was able to go on several trips with us that spring and summer, but she had to sit in the front seat, my seat, because she felt her broken back had resulted from the car's hitting a bump while she was riding in the back seat. She had suffered several broken bones since we had known her, including a fractured vertebra when she fell out of the Scout when we were on a trip in the Moab area in 1972. That time, while Vard and Doc and I were across the road photographing the Shafer Trail, she started to climb into the parked car and fell out backward. But she had remarkable recuperative powers and after each mishap was soon back on her feet.

Doc missed an outing in August when John Tucker came to town to confer with him on the oak project, and he canceled a planned trip with us one Thursday because he was despondent over being disoriented when he got up in the morning. He went on a three-day trip to Cedar City with Richard Hildreth of the State Arboretum of Utah in mid-September, and Hildreth told Vard later that Doc became disoriented once or twice on that trip.

Doc had some slides he wanted me to help identify. I went over on a Sunday afternoon, and we spent five hours going through the slides, taking time out for dinner. It was a slow process because Doc would start reminiscing about each slide. If it pictured a flower we couldn't identify, he would look it up in his key and read clues I couldn't understand. Then he would set the slide aside to look up the flower later at the herbarium, and soon the slide would be mixed up with all the others on the table. Looking at the jumble of slides, he asked me if I thought he could come back from heaven or hell, wherever he might go, and tell me what some of the flowers were that we couldn't identify.

A three-day trip with the Cottams in late September through the San Rafael Swell, along the Waterpocket Fold, over the Burr Trail and into the Circle Cliffs area became a strange combination of beautiful scenery and assorted traumas. The fall colors were reaching their peak on our route through Spanish Fork Canyon. In Buckhorn Draw, the cottonwood trees were just beginning to turn yellow. The colorful rock formations, buttes, and gorges all through the San Rafael Swell, past Temple Mountain, and on into Hanksville were spectacular.

We found the only motel in Hanksville and those in Capitol Reef National Park all full, but located two rooms at a motel in Torrey. I shared a room with Georgina, and Vard and

Doc took the other. After settling in, we drove to a camp spot and cooked our steak dinner. The next morning we packed up and headed out, looking for a place to cook breakfast. As we were driving along, Doc asked me, "Where is that guy I slept with last night?" I thought he was kidding and said, "He's up there driving the car." But Doc acted disturbed and said it was someone he didn't know who seemed to have disappeared.

It was a beautiful morning, and we found a pleasant spot for our morning meal, but Doc was quiet and a little despondent. He wandered around in the clearing while Vard and I prepared our bacon and egg breakfast.

We were soon on our way down the road along the Waterpocket Fold, where we met and talked with people on a photographic tour with professional photographer Phillip Hyde. He said that road was one of his favorites in Utah. Our goal was to continue on to the junction with the Burr Trail, which climbs in sharp switchbacks up the face of a cliff. Somewhere at the top of the cliff, we hoped to find the road leading into the Circle Cliffs area. I had read about some petrified wood there, and we planned to check it out. Vard had asked a service station attendant in Torrey about the area, and he said he had only been there five times, four of them with a wrecker to pull out stranded motorists.

After zigzagging up the Burr Trail, we stopped at the top to take pictures. A sign there indicated it was 17 miles to the Wolverine Petrified Wood area and 47 miles total to Boulder. We took off and found more beautiful scenery all the way. The dirt road wasn't bad, but it had little gullies across it in places. Vard had to slow down often to avoid any bad bounces. Georgina was still riding in the front passenger seat because of her fragile back. After awhile, we stopped and got out in the shade of a tree to have some lemonade. After we continued on, suddenly one of those gullies appeared before Vard could slow down, and there was a terrific bounce. I had my seat belt fastened, but I still felt my head hit the top of the car. In front of me I saw Georgina fly up in the air like a rag doll and then fall back down in the seat, crying, "Oh my back!"

We found that she hadn't fastened her seat belt when getting back into the car after the lemonade stop. Vard kept asking how she was feeling. She said, "All right." But her tone told us she wasn't. We went on. There was nothing else to do. About ten minutes later, Vard noticed that the car was acting funny and found a rear tire flat. When we hit the bump, we noticed that the tail pipe was bent, but there hadn't seemed to be any other damage.

We set up a chair in the shade of a tree for Georgina while Vard changed the tire. Doc stayed with her, and then they walked down the road a little way to see how she felt. She didn't get sick. When we were ready to go again, she was walking but not acting very frisky.

Soon we came to the petrified wood area, where we set up a chair again for Georgina. Vard, Doc, and I explored and photographed the wood area, then returned to the car for lunch. We continued on to Boulder, but Vard couldn't find anyone there to fix the flat. When we didn't see any motels, we went on to Escalante. The scenery was spectacular all the way, especially the final stretch, where the two-lane paved highway goes along the top of the mountain ridge for miles, with views on both sides of colorful, convoluted canyons and chasms. Down on our right was the Calf Creek Canyon gorge.

In Escalante we got motel rooms, walked to a nearby restaurant for dinner, then crept back up the hill to the motel with Georgina, who could barely walk by this time. She had been taking pain pills and soon was stretched out on her bed dead to the world. Vard took the flat tire to a service station for repairs and found it had a large nail in it. The tire damage wasn't related to the bump after all.

The next morning Georgina was barely moving. She took another pain pill as we headed out of town to look for a place to cook breakfast. Soon Georgina began drooping, her head hanging down on her chest, apparently knocked out by the pain pill. Doc was afraid that she couldn't breathe with her head hanging down that way, so he knelt down on the floor in back of her seat and reached around and held her head up. Occasionally he got his hand over her mouth, and we were afraid he might accidentally finish her off.

Since we felt that she should see a doctor, we returned to Escalante, only to find that the nearest doctor was in Panguitch. We headed that way, Doc kneeling behind Georgina's seat and holding her head up until the position began to hurt his knees.

After he sat back, he seemed to forget what was the matter with her and asked me several times why she was acting that way. I told him each time that it was probably because of the pain pills she had taken when she hurt her back.

Somewhere along the way, we stopped at a rest area with picnic tables, and Vard suggested we have breakfast there. Georgina was coming to a little, and she and Doc stayed in the car while Vard and I fixed breakfast. We all felt better after we had eaten. By this time Georgina was able to express her views, and she said she didn't want to see a doctor. So we drove directly back to Salt Lake. Georgina was barely able to make it into the house with help and collapsed on her bed. George, seeing the procession, said he had wondered about her going on that trip.

She ended up in the hospital with four fractured vertebrae. Once again Bea talked to Doc on the phone and learned of the latest misfortune. He told her that he couldn't find Georgina anywhere, but knew she was just playing hookey. When George reported that Doc got lost trying to find Cottonwood Hospital from the bus, Bea realized she was needed. Again she came to the rescue, flying in from Denver to care for Doc and George and later Georgina when she came home from the hospital.

During that visit, Bea was awakened at 4:00 a.m., October 18, 1978, by voices in the adjoining bedroom. Intrigued by what she overheard, she jotted down the sadly funny conversation.

Doc: Where are we?
Georgina: We're here in our beds where we oughta be.

Where will we get food?
We'll keep buying it.

How will we pay for it?
The money keeps coming in.

What relationship are you to me?
Your wife.

Who are you?
Francis Georgina Wilson.

Where are we?
Here on McClelland St.

But where is that? Locate it for hell sakes.
Salt Lake City.

What state?
Utah.

What relationship are you to me?
None.

Then why are you here? Did you sell yourself?
Yes. You paid a nickel for me. My father thought I wuz worth a million dollars. He'd be surprised to know I went so cheap.

Doc chuckles. Who was your father?
Georgina gives her whole genealogy back to the king and queen of France.

Where were you when all this was going on?
I'm giving you generation after generation.

Do you have children?
No.

Then who's Joe?
Jody? You know who Jody is. He's my son.

You said you didn't have any children.
I made myself famous having six sons. But I made myself more famous having seven great-grandsons in a row from one father.

Who's that?
Junior. You know Junior. But I don't know where he's

going to end, he's such a big spender.

Where does he get his money?
He earns it.

Do I have any children?
Yes. Don't you remember a son [Grant] who called you last night and a daughter who's here a waitin' on us—doing the work?

Who am I?
You're nothing—only a professor who raised all those trees.

More questions follow: Where are we? Are you well? Are you happy? How did we get here? What will we do for food? Have you ever heard of "Pippa Passes"? Doc starts to recite Robert Browning's poem:

The year's at the spring
And day's at the morn;
Morning's at seven;
The hill-side's dew-pearled;
The lark's on the wing;
The snail's on the thorn:
God's in his heaven—
All's right with the world!

Georgina interrupted: "Why are you asking all these crazy questions? Go to sleep so you'll know who you are and where you are."

During this visit Bea took her father to the Salt Lake Clinic for an examination, including a brain scan. She also observed that Georgina was making an effort to keep Doc from going on the Thursday outings, claiming he got lost or at least came home exhausted. Georgina also tried to enlist doctors on her side, asking them to say Doc shouldn't go on the trips any more.

Matters were soon smoothed over, but Doc's periodic dizzy spells and Georgina's condition kept him from going on any Thursday trips the rest of that year except for one outing in December to Utah Lake.

Chapter 17

Reality Fades Away

Dick Cottam came to Salt Lake from Pittsburgh in January 1979 to give lectures at the University of Utah. Jody drove Doc up to the university. Dick later wrote to Bea,

> Dad was lively and full of charm. My lecture went exceptionally well, and I commented on my father's presence. Dad seemed to understand every word I said and was glowing with pride. I don't think there was one person there, however, who knew what Dad had meant to the university.
>
> Soon I could see that his sense of reality was fading. A very nice woman anthropologist offered to take Dad home. As we left the dining room, I told Dad how pleased I was that he had been able to come for the first lecture, whereupon he shook my hand and said he was pleased to have met me. By then he had no idea what was going on. Lois told me he couldn't direct her to our house.
>
> When I got home, he was once again fully aware. But now he was nervous. He had purchased some huge steaks to feed me and was terribly anxious for the din-

> ner to go well. Georgina was no help. As usual she did all the talking, and Dad became frantic about the meal. It was black comedy. Dad finally did cook the steaks, but he didn't think of anything else to have with them until the steaks were almost ready. So we had a number of courses, with Dad running back and forth into the kitchen and with Georgina's mindless chatter for counterpoint.

It wasn't until after daughter Fae and her husband, Charlie, and son, Eric, came for a week's visit in March 1979 that Doc started going with us again. He had planned to go on a Thursday outing with them, but at the last minute, Georgina started to act up, and Doc told Vard that he couldn't "be a skunk and leave her." So we took the visitors out to the Little Sahara Sand Dunes and to No Name Road. Most of the day we spent airing our feelings about Georgina. We all contributed and got almost everything off our chests—but we only had ten hours.

Fae said she came for the visit determined to get along with Georgina and she tried, but she couldn't make it for a whole week. Georgina thought Fae should learn to cook and sew and tat. Fae told her that she would rather read a book and that Charlie did most of the cooking.

Fae reported one funny conversation, though. Georgina, a staunch member of the LDS faith, often talked about trying to bring Doc back into the fold. He had long ago made up his mind about the religion, of course, and her efforts had little effect. Now, during the Olsons' visit, she talked about how Doc felt dizzy when he got up in the morning and about how forgetful he was. Then she said, "When he loses all his sense, I'm going to make a high priest out of him."

Doc was able to go with us on several Thursday trips that spring, and he seemed fine most of the time. He said he was dizzy usually just when he got up in the morning, but would soon be all right. Once he did ask where we had gone on the trip with Fae and Charlie. "Did Eric go too? Did I go?" We answered his questions, but a few minutes later he asked the same questions again.

As we sat by our campfire at Cherry Creek one Thursday, he told some more stories of his youth in St. George. When he was about five years old, he and Joe Adkins, a playmate, were arguing about whose Pa was the biggest. The argument got pretty heated, and when Walter's older cousin came along, they asked him whose Pa was the biggest, and he said, "Why Joe's Pa is." Not to be outdone, Walter looked at a cow grazing in the field nearby and said, "Well, my Ma is bigger than Bentz's cow." He said it didn't take long for the story to spread all over St. George, and his mother didn't appreciate it much. When it came to stories from the past, Doc could remember every name and nuance.

He told another story, this one about an old rooster that fell into the swill barrel and drowned. They dressed it out to eat. A day or two later, when they had 15 or 16 people for dinner and the main dish was chicken, in front of everyone, Moroni piped up, "Is this the chicken that drowned in the swill barrel?" Their mortified mother disappeared into the pantry to cry.

After an adventurous day of exploring a new road through the Cricket Mountains and hunting arrowheads at Black Rock in April 1979, we got Doc home about 9:00 p.m. Georgina greeted him at the door with, "You must be tired after being out so long." But she no longer said anything about his not going, to us at least. We didn't know why he was suddenly going with us again after having made excuses all winter, unless he felt that Georgina was better and wouldn't die if he left her. Georgina seemed to have become his mother and all of his wives rolled into one. His motivation appeared to be to keep her alive so he wouldn't be abandoned again.

For the first time in months, the original foursome went together on a fishing trip to the Uintas in June. Because Doc didn't have a license, I went on a walk with him to look at wildflowers. He seemed a little subdued. His eyes were bothering him and he said that the doctor claimed there wasn't much more to be done for them. Judge Ellett, Vard, and I later caught our limit of fish, and Doc seemed all right the rest of the day.

But when Vard stopped at the Cottams the following Tuesday, as he usually did to see if Doc would be going Thursday, Georgina said he had had a little stroke the day after the fishing trip. She made it sound as if being out with us had caused the stroke. His face went numb and he couldn't talk for awhile, she said, but he stayed in bed two or three days and seemed to get over it. However, he said that he felt tired all the time. But he didn't see a doctor.

It wasn't until October, that Doc joined Vard, the Judge, and me again for trips to Locomotive Springs, Antelope Island, and Indian Canyon. On those trips he seemed all right, but somewhat subdued.

When we stopped to pick him up the morning of October 18 for a trip to Pahvant Butte, the Judge was already there. He and Georgina sat in the living room while Vard, Doc, and I had a cup of coffee in the dining room. Doc seemed depressed, saying, "I know I'm crazy. Why haven't you told me so?" We insisted we hadn't noticed anything except that he was forgetful at times. Then he said, "I'm not going with you. I've got to think this thing out."

We told him it would be better to get out than to sit home thinking about it all day. Even Georgina said she thought he should go. He finally agreed. At first there was some talk about Doc's thinking he was crazy, but after awhile he seemed to forget about it. We had a good day hunting sunstones and arrowheads. While ambling around, though, Doc tripped on something and fell. Vard helped him up. He didn't seem to be hurt much. Later we learned that he had spent the next day in bed because his hip ached. But he recovered and went on trips with us to Topaz Mountain, the trilobite beds near Delta and to Cedar Mountain, where we hunted red agate and had dinner. As we sat by the fire, Vard said, "This is a good way to round out a week." Doc replied, "This is a good way to round out a life."

Doc had been concerned about continuing to go with us because Dr. Eddie Hashimoto, his doctor and colleague at the university, had seen George at a ball game and had told him that Doc shouldn't go. "He's too old," Eddie had said.

Georgina also reported that Dr. Hashimoto had told her not to let Doc go. Georgina had pressed the doctor about the trips at the time of Doc's hernia surgery in 1975. We didn't think the diagnosis fair considering what the trips meant to Doc. I told Doc that if he felt like going, I thought he should go. Doc replied, "If I had to stay around here all the time, I'd die." Whether they got a second opinion from Dr. Hashimoto or Doc made the decision on his own, the trips continued into December.

Doc didn't feel well over the Christmas holidays and Dr. Hashimoto sent him to a heart specialist. Tests indicated that he had mild heart failure. He was given water pills and prescriptions for his heart and for depression. He tired easily and spent a lot of time in bed. On our Thursday outing with Judge Ellett on January 24, 1980, we stopped first at the Cottams and found Doc still ailing and lying down a lot. And he couldn't remember anything.

When Vard and I stopped on February 7, however, he was up and looking much better. He said he hoped to get out with us again soon. Georgina laughed when he made that remark, commenting on how much time he spent in bed. But on March 13 he said he would like to try going again, and Georgina didn't fight it. She even said it might do him good to get out. She said sometimes he would say he was going back to bed to die.

It was a beautiful day, sunny and quite warm. We drove to the Little Sahara Sand Dunes first, browsed around there and had lunch, then went over to our nearby "home away from home," No Name Road, where we hunted for arrowheads and had dinner. We kept a close eye on Doc to be sure he didn't wander off or fall. Georgina had told me that he had fallen in the house three times Saturday. But he didn't seem to have any problems. He was stooping to pick up rocks and examining them as always.

After awhile, we went back to the car, built a fire, and sat and talked. Since I knew he often got tired and went to bed at home, I asked, "Do you want to lie down?"

And he said, "Sure . . . if you do." That nearly broke Vard up, and I told Doc, "That wasn't exactly what I meant."

Later as we sat by the fire having dinner and some wine, he said, "Maybe being out with you is the therapy I need."

The following Thursday Doc fell at home and struck the wooden arm of the davenport, cutting a big gash on his head. Jody took him to Holy Cross Hospital near my home; I found them there in the emergency room. Doc was lying on a gurney with 20 stitches on the top of his head, waiting to have an electrocardiogram and X-rays. I sat in the waiting room with Joe while he had those procedures, then waited to learn what the doctor had to say. I wasn't sure how much attention Joe would pay to what the doctor said or what kind of garbled information he might tell Georgina, if anything. And I didn't think Doc would remember.

The doctor told me to have Doc stop taking all medication except the prescription he handed me for pain. We learned later that he had been taking a double dosage of water pills. Doc improved markedly after he stopped taking the pills and was ready for a trip to Stansbury Island with us on April 10.

We had an interesting day there seeing a few birds and spring flowers. On the drive back, Doc looked out at the water and asked, "Is that the Colorado River?"

Vard told him no, it was the Great Salt Lake. After awhile, Doc asked again if it was the Colorado River. Aside from that incident, he seemed fine. It was good to have him out with us again. And his head was healing nicely. Later that month he did a little work out in the yard, and one day he walked up to his oak grove at the Fort. He was nearly worn out when he got home though.

For some time Allan and Sally Randle, good neighbors of the Cottams, had been checking on them and reporting to Bea by letter and by phone how they were getting along. In a letter of May 1980, Sally wrote that she didn't see Doc every day, but saw him out in the yard between visits. "He always says that working in the yard is his best medicine." She added, "I know it's a big worry to be so far from your Dad. I know Georgina is good to him, and she's no dumbbell. She's a pretty sharp old lady. I just hope, as I am sure you do, that she doesn't give out before he does."

Georgina took him on a trip to St. George for a few days. And he was able to join us for several Thursday outings that summer. He seemed to enjoy going and had no problems.

Then in August, Georgina and her daughter-in-law, Beverly Wilson, took Doc on a trip to Idaho Falls, Idaho, where he fell again, was hospitalized and had another brain scan.

After two more Thursday trips with us in late October and early November, Doc went with Georgina and Beverly on a trip to Arizona, where he ran away once. He and Georgina both got sick, and they came home shortly before Thanksgiving. By early December, they were well enough to attend an Emeritus Club dinner at the University of Utah.

Bea kept in touch with the Cottams by frequent phone calls and, later in December, Georgina reported that she was having a bad time with Doc. She said he and George had had a fight and that she had not slept for several nights because Doc was so confused and threatening to go to St. George. "I just hope we can have a civilized Christmas," she said.

Near that same time Bea received a letter from Sally Randle saying that she and her husband had gone over to visit the Cottams and found them both in bed in the afternoon. When Georgina got up to answer the phone they started to leave. "Your Dad reared up and called us back," Sally wrote. "He looked really distraught, and he said he was getting goofy, losing his mind and wondered what he could do. I told him I didn't know, but he kept on asking questions, and I reminded him you had taken him to doctors, and he remembered that, but he kept saying he didn't want to live in that condition. I think he was having a bad day because I have been over several times since, and he has seemed alert and in a good mental state. I'm sure, however, that he is still forgetful. I really think you should be grateful for Georgina. She spends hours reading to him, and while she might not do things just like you would like them done, for her age she does pretty well. It's a terrible strain on her worrying for fear he'll wander away."

For some time Bea had been attending meetings on Alzheimer's disease at the University of Colorado Medical Center. Alzheimer's disease, a form of dementia just becoming widely publicized, appeared to Bea to be what her father might have. He was beginning to exhibit many of the symptoms—being disoriented, quarrelsome and self-destructive, and sometimes wandering. Her fears were compounded when she received a frantic phone call from Georgina at 2:15 a.m. on January 16, 1981, saying Doc had run away out in the cold without his coat after trying to go for two nights. He thought his home wasn't his home, Georgina wasn't his wife, and George wasn't his son. At Bea's suggestion, Georgina reluctantly called the police who found him nearly a mile from home running to keep warm.

Once again Bea flew to Salt Lake to help her father, staying thirteen days. During that time she questioned Georgina about using some of Doc's money to support her son Jody when it was apparent Doc might soon need that money himself. Bea learned later that Georgina had stated she would not be welcome in her father's house again.

But in less than two months she was forced to return again when Mr. Randle, the neighbor, called to say that the paramedics had just hauled Georgina away with a broken hip and someone should come immediately. On her arrival, Randle said, "Your father is gone. Can't you take him home to Denver with you?" Somewhat shocked at the suggestion, Bea said she would have to do some thinking, and noted that Georgina might have something to say about it.

During the visit Bea took her father to see Georgina each day in the hospital, but the only time Georgina spoke to her was to say, "That's why you came, to take him to Denver." And to Doc she said, "You was ready to fall right into their hands. I thought so highly of her. Then when she gets me down, she jumps on me."

Bea also told Joe that Georgina's family would have to hire someone to take care of her when she came home as Doc was incapable of that burden. She also became concerned about some changes being made in Doc's and George's accounts and, with the approval of her siblings, started an investigation into her father's money matters, hiring the neighbor's son Stephen R. Randle to act as their lawyer.

Before she returned to Denver on April 11, Bea sent her father to stay with Fae and Charlie in Oregon when attempts to find someone to help him at home failed. But he returned to Salt Lake in May, when Grant came for a hearing to determine if he could be appointed conservator of his father's estate. The judge deferred a decision, but later named First Security Bank conservator. During his two-week stay, Grant discovered that his father was bleeding. A biopsy revealed prostate cancer. But doctors said that he would not die from that condition and that surgery was not advised.

When Grant left, Eric Olson, Fae's son, came to stay with Dr. Cottam and George. Earlier Georgina had been moved from the hospital to a rest home for additional recovery. But shortly after Grant left, her family had her released from the rest home and she rejoined Doc and George at the Cottam home.

But their last week together was far from a happy reunion. Eric reported that she kept up such a stream of arguing that Doc finally grabbed her around the neck and Eric had to pull him off. The next day Georgina's family started to move her out of the house back into her own home. Doc had experienced some bleeding from the biopsy and was in the hospital when Georgina moved out on June 6.

Bea flew to Salt Lake on June 7 to take care of her father. While there, he called her into his bedroom, had her sit beside his bed, and told her, "You think I don't know what is happening to me. I've known every step of the process. I used to take my students to see the grounds around the mental hospital in Provo, and they would laugh at the inmates. And now I'm one of them."

Phone calls from Georgina so agitated Dr. Cottam that Bea made arrangements to take him to Denver with her. They left the Cottam family home on June 27, 1981.

Chapter 18

Last Years

The next fourteen months were a time-consuming, heart-breaking time for Bea and Bill, watching a brilliant mind slowly eroding in a still strong body, seeing a vigorous, loving father become despondent and even violent. At times he seemed almost his old self. At other times he became depressed, begging Bea to shoot him or give him cyanide.

He ran away from their home once shortly after their arrival in Denver and tried several times to walk away from the day-care centers where they placed him while Bea worked as a substitute teacher in Denver junior and senior high schools. He often talked about slipping away to live in the hills with the animals. He admired the Eskimo custom in which the old people just wandered away into the elements to die.

After a few weeks. Bea appealed to her brothers and sister for some help in caring for their father, possibly each taking him for a few months. She resisted their suggestions that it was time to place him in a nursing home.

Appealing to them again after ten months, she wrote:

> We are burned out. But we have not changed our minds about the necessity of Dad being cared for by

> loving family members in a family setting. . . . He is a feeling, lonely, frightened, confused old man who led a distinguished enough life to deserve a better end than being dumped in a nursing home before he is ready. Yes he has deteriorated, but slowly. He is still continent. He can still talk and walk and most of all enjoy. He can't remember, but the day is a treasure for him in itself. We took him to the Alzheimer meeting Saturday and then to the botanical gardens. He loved the day. And yesterday he worked in the yard all day. But he isn't feeling well tonight and has gone to bed in low spirits. How you cannot see some obligation to him, how you can dispose of him to avoid a three-month commitment is beyond my comprehension.

When Bea took Dr. Cottam to Denver, the family realized George would need close supervision the rest of his life. Son Dick Cottam and his wife Pat agreed to take him to live with them at their home in Pittsburgh. On their trip from Salt Lake back to Pittsburgh, they stopped in Denver to see their father. On learning what Dick was doing for George, he exclaimed, "That's the finest thing that's ever come into my life, the finest example of pure Christianity, real brotherhood. It's unheard of. Look at the difference in their I.Q.s!"

In later years Grant wrote a paper about George, noting that after eight months, Dick enrolled George in a program that provided him a home, counseling, and a make-work job that gave him a feeling of self-worth. "He has never been happier since mother died," Grant wrote.

> One of the things our mother tried to instill in George's mind was that sex was not for him. He firmly believed that message until he got a counselor who believed people in the program should live life to the fullest, including sex. So at the ripe old age of fifty-five, George had his first heterosexual experience. Since then he has had several girl friends, each of whom he wanted to marry. Dick asks him to wait a year or two before getting married. George is not very good about noting the passage of time, and he has another girl

before he realizes the time has come to marry the last one. But Don Juan he isn't.

The long-awaited report on Dr. Cottam's hybrid oak project was finally published in July 1982 by the State Arboretum of Utah under the title *Oak Hybridization at the University of Utah.*

Judge Ellett, his wife, and Vard and I attended a luncheon marking the occasion, but Grant was the only member of the immediate Cottam family able to attend. I was writing a column at the *Deseret News* at the time, so I wrote about the luncheon, the oak project, a brief summary of Doc's outstanding career, and a few of his humorous stories. I enclosed a clipping of the column in a letter to Doc, and Bea said that he asked her to read them both over and over again.

About this same time, daughter Fae and her husband Charlie Olson had agreed to take Dr. Cottam to live with them at their home in Gresham, Oregon. Bea agreed to the arrangement, but with the understanding that if they found they couldn't cope, she would have an opportunity to take him back.

So in early August the two sisters and their husbands returned to the family home in Salt Lake with Doc to start clearing out the house and getting it ready for sale. George also came from Pittsburgh to see his father and sisters again and to visit friends in the neighborhood.

Vard and I visited with them one evening, and it turned into quite a party with everyone in good spirits, talking and laughing. Doc looked very good and recognized us. We took pictures of him with his oak book. We took our copies along and he autographed them for us with no problem. In mine he wrote, "To Maxine" and his signature, all very legible. Bea's husband was surprised to see the signatures because at their home Doc apparently had almost lost his ability to write. The family had taken him to see his oak grove and his portrait at the Museum of Natural History earlier that day. After he had been in his home again for about three days, Doc said to Bea, "These rooms are beginning to seem familiar to me." But he didn't quite grasp the idea that they were going to sell the house. He mentioned Georgina a few times, but the family changed the subject and the visit ended with no potentially disrupting encounter with her.

When the Salt Lake visit ended, Fae and Charlie took Doc back to Oregon with them. During the first few weeks of his stay there Fae reported that he was doing very well. Charlie did the cooking and handled Doc's physical care, while Fae sat and visited with him or read to him. They took all medicines away from him, exercised him a lot and kept him busy. Fae told Bea that he seemed much smarter, was walking better, and was happy.

But the good news was short-lived. Doc had become increasingly agitated. In early November they found it necessary to put him in a retirement home a few blocks from their house. Fae and Charlie were very attentive, visiting him nearly every day, taking him for rides and to their home on holidays. Bea, however, felt betrayed that she hadn't been given the opportunity to take their father back, as promised. That and other disagreements with her brothers and sister about their father's care caused a rift between them that took some time to heal.

Georgina's move from the house they had shared for eleven years at 1114 McClelland Street and Dr. Cottam's move to Denver in 1981 marked the end of their days together and the beginning of the tragic decline of both their lives.

Georgina recuperated from her broken hip at a son's home for a time, then moved back into her own home with her sister Hannah caring for her. Then in the fall of 1981 she was found to have throat cancer. It was doubtful she would survive, but after a lengthy series of radiation treatments she was able to return to her home before Christmas, with Hannah still caring for her.

In March she sent a birthday card to Dr. Cottam with this plaintive message:

> Dear, dear Doctor: I am sending my love in Richard's care. I don't have Bea's address. I love you very much and always will. Why should this happen to us? I am living in my home. Spent eleven months in the hospital, came out in January, 1982, cannot walk yet, have to be taken care of, miss you so much, am in a wheel chair, have been very sick, was over eleven

months without eating, on a drinking diet, milk & etc. How I miss you, can't see hardly. We had such a good life, the 3 of us. I have spent what I had. I love you. . . Your loving Wife, Georgina.

On the back of the card, she had written, "Our wonderful life together."

She improved somewhat and was walking again, but in November 1982, the same month that Dr. Cottam was placed in a retirement home in Oregon, she fell against the stove in her home, suffering a bruised hip and cracked ribs. Again she recuperated at a son's home. Then in February 1983 she had a stroke, was hospitalized, then went to the home of a grandniece to recuperate. But on the morning of May 22, 1983, she suffered another stroke and died that evening in the hospital. She was 90 years old and had dwindled to 80 pounds.

When Dr. Cottam was told of the death of his wife, an aide at the retirement home said he didn't seem to care. He had become friendly with another resident named Irma and thought she was his wife. He continued on in much the same physical condition through his ninetieth birthday, March 3, 1984, befriended by the frail little Irma, who made life worth living for him. It had been his pattern to attach himself to a female resident wherever he stayed. At both day-cares in Denver, he had made similar liaisons.

Later in July 1984, however, Doc started having strange seizures, becoming comatose for as long as 20 minutes. Tests showed he had very slow brain waves and Fae and Charlie found it necessary to place him in a nursing home. His care there, however, proved to be far from satisfactory.

In a letter to me, Bea wrote, "About Dad, he's doing badly in the nursing home. He is still that independent spirit, a horrible candidate for a nursing home. He's now tied in a chair, walking little, drugged more." When Charlie went to the nursing home late in the afternoon one day and found Doc soaked and covered with food, he knew that he had been in that condition since lunch time. He immediately had him moved to a place closer to their home where the new staff was much more helpful.

During the summer of 1985, Vard and I went to Oregon to see Doc. We thought we saw a glint of recognition in his eyes when we visited him in the nursing home. The surroundings were pleasant, and he seemed to be well taken care of. Fae and Charlie went with us, and we took Doc out on the patio, where we sat and visited. But he seemed unaware of what was being said, and we didn't have an opportunity to try to draw him out more. It was good to see Doc again but sad to see the devastating effect of that humiliating disease on our cherished friend.

Fae once wrote of her father, "He always lived in his own private world of the mind and left the mundane matters to Mama." Now he was totally lost in the private world of his deteriorating mind with no way to escape back to reality.

In the fall of that year he underwent surgery for a life-threatening bowel obstruction, followed by pneumonia, but made an amazing recovery. Bea wrote, "His fighting spirit is making history in that hospital.They call him Old Hickory."

Doc lingered on for nearly three more years, his rugged constitution overcoming bouts of pneumonia, a urinary tract infection, and choking spells. Sometimes he was more alert than usual. When Bea visited him in the fall of 1988, she told him about a trip Vard and I had taken to Australia, then asked if he would like to have gone with us. A spark of his old self flickered in his reply, "Not if I had to pay for it."

His misery lasted only a short time longer. He had a problem clearing the phlegm from his throat, soon stopped eating, and died December 22, 1988, at the age of 94. An autopsy confirmed that he was the victim of Alzheimer's disease. But the autopsy ruled out donating the body to a medical school. He was cremated and the remains placed in a small pine box handmade by Gregg Olson, a grandson.

A celebration of the life of Walter P. Cottam was held in Salt Lake City on December 29, 1988, the chapel at Larkin Mortuary overflowing with friends, relatives, neighbors, former students, colleagues and others whose lives had been touched by Doc.

There were no hymns, prayers, or talk of the hereafter because Doc's religion was Nature. But his spirit was there in the words of the speakers and in the chorales from Bach's St. Matthew Passion, played by five Cottam grandsons.

Vard told of our meeting with Doc and the hundreds of wonderful Thursday Sabbath outings with him over the years. He noted that it seemed fitting that Doc left this earth for his last great journey on a Thursday and that this celebration of his life should also be on a Thursday.

Missing from the gathering was Judge Ellett, who had died Nov. 30, 1986, of a heart attack. He was 88.

Irving B. (Bill) McNulty, a former student who later became professor of biology and chairman of the botany department at the University of Utah, spoke of Doc's expertise as a teacher and how his enthusiasm had inspired McNulty to major in botany. Chuck Wullstein, a former student and colleague, read two of Doc's favorite poems.

Speaking for the family, Grant recalled the joys and sometimes the fears of growing up with the exciting, honest, forthright, brilliant man who was their father. "His versatility amazes me," he said. "Being a good scientist should have been enough. Most people would think that hard science is not compatible with the more romantic photography and writing that he did, but in him all these talents blended perfectly, and the family had the experience of living with this truly renaissance man."

Grant spoke of the slowly progressing tragedy of his father's last years, when he realized the loss of memory and fought against it. And he praised his sisters, Fae and Bea, and their husbands, who gave countless hours and endured the emotional stress of watching their father die by inches. Grant concluded by reading a letter his father wrote at the time he donated his body to the University of Utah Medical School to be used as a cadaver:

> Dear Medic:
>
> This nameless old body served me well for several decades. I never abused it, though I always strived to get the maximum use out of it. These feet wore out many a shoe and carried me over countless miles of desert expanse and to the summit of many a mountain. They enabled my eyes to see the sights, my ears to hear the sounds, and my nostrils to smell the odors of a beautiful and bountiful Nature that enriched my life far beyond the powers of expression.

> Now I bequeath this worn-out chassis to you as a final gesture of thanks for a wonderful life. I apologize for a couple of missing parts—an appendix and a gall bladder. But this is hearsay only, for I never saw them, nor did I miss them. Look over on the neighbor's cadaver for the structures of the missing organs in mine. Good Luck. Good carving. And may you glean from this old carcass much information that will serve mankind in future years.
>
> P.S. Please save the bits of dissection and plant them finally about a foot deep around the roots of some old campus tree so that some of me might soon flutter in its glossy green leaves or glow with beauty in its flowers. This might gladden the hearts of students passing by and, were I able to realize it, please me greatly.

Patches of snow lay on the ground in Mt. Olivet Cemetery as Cottam family members gathered around the small pine box and in quiet tones said their final goodbyes to their father and grandfather before the coffin was laid to rest in the ground beside Effie's grave.

AFTERWORD

In 1983, ground was broken for a new botanical garden at the University of Utah, east of Dr. Cottam's hybrid oak grove at the mouth of Red Butte Canyon. Gardens, trees, ponds, waterfalls, and an amphitheatre were completed from 1983-1991 and the area was dedicated as Red Butte Garden and Arboretum. In 1994 a new building named the Walter P. Cottam Visitor Center was completed to serve as a center for education and interpretation of horticulture and ecology in the Intermountain Region.

It was through Dr. Cottam's efforts that the Utah Legislature in l96l designated the entire University of Utah campus as the State Arboretum of Utah. The 150 acres at the mouth of Red Butte Canyon were preserved for the arboretum because of the efforts of Dr. Cottam and Dr. Bill McNulty when federal lands were transferred to the University of Utah in 1968. Sixty acres are designated for formal gardens and facilities and 90 acres as natural area for environmental education, research and recreation.

Dr. Cottam's portrait, painted by noted artist Alvin L. Gittins, now hangs in the visitor center. The plaque beside it reads:

Dr. Walter Pace Cottam devoted his entire life to

the study of the natural resources of the Intermountain West and to the preservation of those resources.

During his tenure as Distinguished Professor of Botany at the University of Utah, "Doc" taught thousands of students about the ecology and biology of Utah's flora, delivered the landmark paper, "Is Utah Sahara Bound?" conducted an extensive study of oak hybridization unequalled in the world, and was a founder of the nationwide organization, The Nature Conservancy.

Dr. Cottam is the founding father of the State Arboretum of Utah and Red Butte Garden. At his request, the State Legislature established the Arboretum on the University of Utah campus in 1961. Dr. Cottam's further efforts to establish a permanent, protected collection of plants in the Red Butte Garden area were successful in 1968 when the federal government donated lands to the University for academic expansion. He was instrumental in assuring that the land patent agreement specifically designated a portion of those lands, Research Park, as an arboretum. Today, that area is known as Red Butte Garden, a botanical garden protected in perpetuity as a result of Dr. Cottam's vision.

Red Butte Garden and Arboretum carries on Dr. Cottam's tradition by providing a living museum committed to fostering an understanding of regional horticulture and ecology through education, research, and public service. The Walter P. Cottam Visitor Center is dedicated to this man who touched so many with his love of plants, and as one biology student noted ". . . a biology teacher . . . who speaks with the voice of a child who has just seen a flower bloom for the first time. . ."

The George S. and Dore Eccles Foundation provided funds to build the center and it was dedicated in the anniversary year of Dr. Cottam's 100th birthday.

Acknowledgments

This biography could not have been written without the support and cooperation of Dr. Cottam's family, fortunately a family of savers. Most of the credit must go to daughter Beatrice Fowler, who, from her home in Denver, sent me package after package of copies of her father's personal letters, articles, speeches, accomplishments, honors, congratulatory letters, and remembrances of family life. She approved my approach to the biography and, with the help of her husband, William L. Fowler, put the entire typewritten manuscript on the computer, doing a bit of editing and adding more details of Dr. Cottam's final years as an Alzheimer's victim. The project was an absorbing diversion for Bea during a valiant struggle with cancer, which claimed her life June 8, 1996.

Son Grant Cottam sent copies of essays he had written on family life and taped conversations with his father for the biography. Son Dick Cottam permitted use of excerpts from a long personal letter to his father and an essay on the wildflower hunts. Daughter Fae Olson contributed memories and observations of her father.

Some of the early family history came from a book compiled by the Thomas Cottam Family Organization, *Thomas Cottam-Caroline Smith Descendants Vol. II.* Another valuable source of family background was a biography of Clarence

Cottam, *Clarence Cottam: Knight of the Wilderness,* written by his daughter Glenna Cottam Sanderson. A short biography, *The Life and Contributions of Dr. Walter P. Cottam, Educator - Scientist,* written by William Horsley Limb in 1962 and submitted as a master's thesis at the University of Utah, was also a helpful reference point.

Special thanks must go to Ruth Henson for her meticulous editing of the biography and most helpful suggestions for deletions, additions and rewriting, as well as to my niece, N. Marie Martz, for donating her time and computer expertise in helping me polish the final manuscript.

My deepest appreciation also to Bill McNulty for his encouragement and help in finding the right publisher, and to Carma Cannon for her devotion to the project and skillful guidance through the printing process.

Photographs for the biography were furnished by the Cottam family and by the author except where noted.